CW01659417

INNOVATIONS IN PARENT-INFANT PSYCHOTHERAPY

INNOVATIONS IN PARENT-INFANT PSYCHOTHERAPY

International Contributions

Edited by

Maria E. Pozzi-Monzo with Beverley Tydeman

KARNAC

First published in 2007 by
Karnac Books Ltd
118 Finchley Road
London NW3 5HT

British Library Cataloguing in Publication Data

A C.I.P for this book is available from the British Library

ISBN-13: 978–1–85575–458–4

Edited, designed, and produced by
Florence Production Ltd, Stoodleigh, Devon
www.florenceproduction.co.uk

www.karnacbooks.com

We dedicate this book to our ancestors and our current families; to the children and parents with whom we work: they are our source of inspiration and transformation.

CONTENTS

ACKNOWLEDGEMENTS

We would like to thank first of all, the many contributors who have been prepared to put in a lot of time, effort, and patience into writing their chapters for this book. They have generously shared their work and their skills in new ways of practising parent-infant psychotherapy.

Then we are indebted to all our inspirational teachers from the 1980s when the Under Five's Counselling Service was first set up at the Tavistock Clinic under the leadership of Lisa Miller and Alan Shuttleworth. The service and training nurtured in us a love for this work and made us aware of the privilege of being invited into the intimacy of the lives of those families with babies and young children who were referred to us.

Many thanks to Dilys Daws, Juliet Hopkins, and Angela Joyce for reading the manuscript and providing their thoughtful commentaries, which are rooted in their broad and deep experience in the field. Miranda Whyte put a lot of loving work into correcting the language of authors whose first language is not English. Chantal Bay stretched her creative artistic talent in producing the front cover design, which brings together the psychoanalytic couple of Klein and Freud with the parents, young children, and pets, which are all part of family life. The title of this book was conceived by Bob Monzo at the beginning of this project in Melbourne during a working lunch with Australian colleagues in the infant mental health team at the Children's Hospital in Melbourne.

Karnac's editing staff from Oliver Rathbone and Leena Hakkinen to Christelle Yeyet-Jacquot and Dr Dido Clark have been encouraging and supportive throughout the hard labour.

Many, many thanks again to all the above without whom the book could have not taken this shape.

Maria E. Pozzi-Monzo and Beverley Tydeman

FOREWORD

This welcome book should appeal to all who are fascinated by the development of babies and toddlers, whether as parents or as professionals concerned with mental health, preschool education or childcare. Its international character reflects the growth of psychoanalytic parent-infant psychotherapy and brings together contributions from all five continents. It also brings together several different psychoanalytic traditions – classical psychoanalysis as developed by Selma Fraiberg with its emphasis on intergenerational transmission, Kleinian psychoanalysis with its emphasis on infant observation and the significance of "here-and-now" experience, and family therapy with its emphasis on the influence of the cultural context in which the family lives. Several of the chapters show how the therapy connects with the culture of the family concerned or is inspired by the wider community and its perception of family needs.

Parent-infant psychotherapy recognises that the infant is not the patient, nor is the parent, though both make contributions to their mutual difficulties. Rather, the patient to be treated is the relationship between them. Increasingly there is awareness that attending to the relationship between the parents may also play a crucial part in a baby's recovery and some chapters illustrate this.

Parent-infant psychotherapy can inspire creativity. A baby represents a fresh start and therapists may respond with renewed energy and initiative to the need to find a way to help. The very wide range of approaches illustrated here may inspire both flexibility and innovation. The process of change for the patients is also a process of change for the therapist. The effect of working with the remarkable capacity for change that exists within the earliest relationships can be life-enhancing for the therapist. Being part of a process of repairing a relationship can be reparative.

The combined wisdom of the therapists and the rich details of the relationships of the babies and their parents makes absorbing reading for all who share a concern for secure development in earliest childhood.

ABOUT THE EDITORS AND CONTRIBUTORS

Astrid Berg, MB ChB, FFPsych, M.Phil was born and educated in South Africa. She is a child and adolescent psychiatrist as well as a Jungian analyst. She is an Associate Professor at the University of Cape Town and a senior consultant in the Division of Child & Adolescent Psychiatry at the Red Cross Children's Hospital in Cape Town where she heads the Infant Mental Health Unit. She is a founding member of the Western Cape Association of Infant Mental Health and its past Chair. She is also a founding member and past President of the Southern African Association of Jungian Analysts. She is currently Vice-President of the International Association of Analytical Psychology. She has published papers and chapters on transcultural clinical work and infant mental health. Amongst them: "Beyond the dyad: parent-infant psychotherapy in a multi-cultural society—reflections from a South African perspective", *Infant Mental Health Journal*, 24/3 (2003), and "Ancestor reverence in an urban community in South Africa—perspectives from analytical psychology", *Journal of Transcultural Psychiatry*, 40/2 (2003).

Carmen Bernasconi is a pediatric and psychiatric nurse who is specialized in home observation, both in hospital and community settings. She uses E. Bick's applied methodology, and offers support to parents with babies at risk of severe feeding and relational difficulties. She is a founding member of the Zero-Five's Centre (Association 0–5) in Ticino, Switzerland. She is married with two small children.

Lynne Cudmore originally qualified as a social worker. Between 1978 and 2006 she worked as a senior couples psychoanalytic psychotherapist at the Tavistock Centre for Couple Relationships, where she was the Organizing Tutor of the Professional Doctorate and Clinical Training in Couple Psychoanalytic Psychotherapy. Her research interests include the impact of infertility on couple relationships and the impact of a child's death on the parental partnership. She currently works as a child psychotherapist for the Under-Fives Service at the Tavistock Clinic and as a child psychotherapist in a Child and Adolescent Mental Health Team with fostered and adopted children in Westminster, London. She is the author of several papers.

Donatella Gilardoni is a speech and language therapist who specializes in working with children with cerebral palsy, severe language delays, and stuttering. She has a private practice and also works in public health services in Ticino, Switzerland. She applies her psychoanalytic understanding and the observational skills acquired from her infant observation training when treating children and their parents. She is a founding member of the Zero-Five's Centre (Association 0–5) in Ticino. She is the author of the forthcoming book *La Parola Liberata* (*The Word is Freed*). She is married and has three children.

Maggie Harris was, at the time of writing this book, a health visitor and team lead in Luton Bedfordshire. She has a Diploma in Counselling and an MA in Infant Mental Health from the Tavistock Centre. She is committed to raising awareness of the importance of the emotional development of children under five. Her current role, as a partnership development officer for under fives for the local authority, enables her to work in children's centres. She facilitates a multiethnic support group for depressed mothers and trains children centre, community, early years and school practitioners who work with families to use a therapeutic style of engagement based on the Solihull Approach.

Jessica James is a group analyst, trained at the Institute of Group Analysis. She specializes in working with parents and infants as a parent-infant psychotherapist at the Anna Freud Centre, where she conducts an analytic psychotherapy group for mothers and babies, and has developed the outreach group for homeless families described in this book. She runs therapy groups at the Women's Therapy Centre and works with non-clinical groups of parents preparing for birth and the transition to parenthood. Jessica also teaches, supervises, and publishes in this field. She has co-authored the book *The Practice of Psychoanalytic Parent-Infant Psychotherapy*, by Baradon, T. et al., published by Routledge in 2005.

Amanda Jones, Ph.D, is a family therapist and a parent-infant psychotherapist. Her doctoral research at the Tavistock is entitled "The Process of Change in Parent-Infant Psychotherapy". She is currently involved in further qualitative and quantitative research with Dr Howard Steele at University College London, where she continues to investigate the therapeutic process in parent-infant psychotherapy. She has spoken at national and international conferences on parent-infant treatment and is head of a Tier 3 National Health Service parent-infant mental health service based in north-east London.

Dora Knauer is a leading doctor in the Faculty of Medicine at Geneva University and is a member of the Swiss Psychoanalytic Society. She is the author and co-author with Palacio-Espasa and others of numerous publications that focus on parent-infant psychotherapy.

Maria Ludovica Terragni is a paediatrician and consultant infant and child neuropsychiatrist in St Anna's Hospital in Como, Italy. She specializes in parent-infant psychotherapy with babies at risk of severe psychophysical pathologies and their families. She is a founding member of the Zero-Five's Centre (Association 0–5) in Ticino, Switzerland.

Mariângela Mendes de Almeida is a clinical psychologist and psychotherapist in São Paulo, Brazil who has been working in the field of mental health and child development since 1982. Between 1988 and 1993, she was a Clinical Associate at the Child and Family Department, Tavistock Clinic, where she received her M.A. in Psychoanalytic Observational Studies (with the University of East London). She develops clinical teaching and supervising activities in psychotherapy, both in private practice and in the public sphere. She supervises infant observation groups. She is currently training as an analyst at the Institute of the Brazilian Society of Psychoanalysis of São Paulo. Her main interest is in clinical work with young children, infants, and parents. She specializes in early interventions on primitive states of mind in children with severe emotional disturbances. She has written chapters in *Exploring Feeding Difficulties in Children—The Generosity of Acceptance* (2004), (Ed. by Williams, G. et al.) and *Un Bisogno Vitale* (2002) (Ed. by Quagliata, E.).

Romana Negri is Associate Professor of Child Neuropsychiatry at Bergamo and Milan University. She has trained and worked with Donald Meltzer and Mattie Harris and undertaken observational research in foetal behaviour using ultrasound scans. A description of her long experience in intensive neonatal therapy can be found in *The Newborn in the Intensive Care Unit: a Neuropsychoanalytic Prevention Model*, published by Karnac in 1994.

Francisco Palacio-Espasa is Professor and Consultant Child and Adolescent Psychiatrist for the Psychiatric Service for Children and Adolescents at University Hospital, Geneva (Switzerland). He is a founder member of the Swiss Psycho-Analytical Society and the author and co-author of innumerable papers and books on the topic of parent-infant psychotherapy (with versions in French, Spanish, and Italian). His English publications include: "Parent-infant psychotherapy, the transition to parenthood and parental narcissism: implications for treatment", *Journal of Child Psychotherapy*, 30(2): 155–171 (2004), and "The narcissistic scenarios of parenthood", *International Journal of Psychoanalysis*, 80: 465–476 (1999).

Campbell Paul is a consultant child and adolescent psychiatrist, acting Clinical Director of the Mental Health Service and Associate Professor, at the Department of Paediatrics, University of Melbourne. He is also an Honorary Principal Fellow of the Infant Mental Health Program, based at the Department of Psychiatry, at the University of Melbourne. He has published papers on parent-infant psychology.

Marisa Pelella Mélega is a psychiatrist, a psychoanalyst in private practice, and a Training Analyst and Supervisor in the Brazilian Psycho-Analytical Society of São Paulo. She founded the Mother-Infant Relationship Study Centre in 1987 in São Paulo that received accreditation from the Centro Studi Martha Harris, Florence. She teaches at the Brazilian Institute as a child psychoanalyst, where she chaired the training in child analysis from 1990 to 1996. Her clinical and research interests include applications of the Esther Bick observation model, as "Therapeutic Interventions with Parents and Children and Assessments with Parents and Children". Her research project "A New Research Methodology to Study the Symbolic Activity in Infants" was undertaken during the Summer Research Programme in 1995 at University College London (supervised by Professor Peter Fonagy and funded by the Research Advisory Board of the IPA Trust). She has also completed a Ph.D in Literature at the University of São Paulo. She has published around fifty psychoanalytic papers and chapters in books. She wrote the following books: *Post-Autism. A Psychoanalytic Narrative* (1999), with Donald Meltzer's supervisions and *Eugenio Montale, Poetic Creativity and Psychoanalysis* (2001).

Maria E. Pozzi-Monzo was born in Italy, but moved to England to train as a child and adolescent psychotherapist at the Tavistock Clinic, and as an adult psychotherapist at the British Association of Psychotherapists. She has special interests in treating children with autism, Asperger's Syndrome, and mental handicap and in brief work with children under five and their families. She has been working in child and family clinics since 1984 and also privately. Presently she is a visiting tutor at the Tavistock Clinic, the B.A.P. and the London Centre for Psychotherapy. She also teaches and lectures in Italy and Switzerland on topics related to child and adolescent psychotherapy. She is at present involved in research that focuses on the process of change in brief work with families of children under five. Her publications include *Psychic Hooks and Bolts*, published by Karnac (2003), and *I Disagi dei Bambini*, published by Bruno Mondadori (2004), as well papers and book chapters on various topics. She was the winner of Frances Tustin Memorial Prize in 1999.

Pamela Sorensen, Ph.D, trained as a child psychotherapist at the Tavistock Clinic in the 1970s. She has been the Director of the Under Fives Study Center at the University of Virginia since 1994. She has published articles in the *Journal of Child Psychotherapy* and the *International Journal of Infant Observation* and has a special interest in bringing Kleinian concepts into non-psychoanalytic training contexts.

Frances Thomson Salo trained in the United Kingdom as an adult and child psychoanalyst. She is a Training Analyst and Deputy President of the Australian Psycho-analytical Society and currently in private practice in Melbourne. She is a Senior Lecturer for the University of Melbourne Graduate Diploma/Masters in Parent and Infant Mental Health, a senior clinician at the Royal Children's Hospital, and a Consultant Psychotherapist at Monash Medical Centre. She has taught over forty year-long infant observation seminars in the UK and Australia, and given keynote presentations, lectures, and workshops in Australia and overseas. She has published over twenty-five articles and chapters on infancy and child psychotherapy, including *You and your Baby* (Karnac), and co-edited *The Baby as Subject* with Campbell Paul. She is on the London Editorial Board of the *International Journal of Psychoanalysis*.

Beverley Tydeman is a consultant child and adolescent psychotherapist working in London at the Marlborough Family Service, where her clinical work is focused mainly on Infant Mental Health and on parenting assessments for court—this often involves being an expert witness in court. She is also a member of staff at the Tavistock Clinic, where she is involved in teaching those from varied disciplines the principles of therapeutic communication with children, thus contributing to the professional development of the generic mental health work force.

Hisako Watanabe is a child psychiatrist, and Assistant Professor and Director of the Mental Health Division in the Department of Pediatrics, School of Medicine, Keio University, Tokyo, Japan. She trained at the Tavistock Clinic in London from 1990 to 1992. Her clinical research includes: anorexia nervosa, childhood borderline personality, pervasive developmental disorders, abuse and postnatal depression, premature infant-mother interaction, mother-infant psychotherapy, perinatal bereavement, and the intergenerational transmission of psychopathology.

Annette Watillon-Naveau is a psychiatrist and a psychoanalyst, a training member of the Belgian Psychoanalytic Society and past President. She introduced baby-observation according to Esther Bick technique of infant observation to Belgium thirty years ago and she is still a trainer in that method. At present she works mainly with parents and young children. Amongst her many articles in French, which are mainly on parent-child psychotherapy are: "The dynamics of psychoanalytic therapies of the early parent-child", *International Journal of Psychoanalysis* , 74 (1993), and "The contribution of baby-observation to the technique of parent-infant psychotherapy", *International Journal of Infant Observation*, 3/1 (1999).

Judith Woodhead, MA, is an adult Jungian analyst trained by the Society of Analytical Psychology, in private practice in Bedford. She is also a parent-infant psychotherapist, supervises at the Anna Freud Centre and leads a Jungian infant observation seminar for the British Association of Psychotherapists. She has a special interest in making psychoanalytic practice widely available and has developed parent-infant psychotherapy in drop-in groups in National Health Service and community settings. Her doctoral research is on the development of self in early infancy. She has published papers on themes including Jung's constructive method, trauma, fathers, and group-work. She co-authored *The Practice of Psychoanalytic Parent-Infant Psychotherapy* by Baradon, T. et al. published by Routledge (2005).

SUMMARY

This book is about psychotherapeutic interventions for families with infants or young children. It brings together papers from around the world, including Australia, Brazil, Japan, Europe, South Africa and the United States. It is written by experienced clinicians, who have a psychodynamic framework and all of whom believe in the importance of early emotional experiences in the development of the personality within the context of family relationships. The vivid detail of the clinical vignettes brings to life intimate stories of the therapeutic process, either from the consulting room of those in private practice, or in the public sector, including projects in community settings where traditional psychoanalytic ideas are applied flexibly. The case histories span individual work with various combinations: mothers alone, mothers and babies with or without fathers, whole families, and mother-baby groups.

The book will be of interest to those working with or studying the early years from a variety of backgrounds: doctors, health visitors, teachers, psychologists, psychotherapists and psychoanalysts, neonatal nurses, nursery and community workers.

Introduction

This book has emerged from our excitement about the proliferation of parent-infant psychotherapy work around the world. Through Maria Pozzi's professional and personal relationships, various people were asked to contribute to this project.

Its final organization gradually emerged as the papers came in: threads and common aspects began to manifest. After reading and rereading the papers many times, discussing them at length, and letting thoughts come to us, the book took shape in its present form. Here are some of the threads, which woven together form the connective tissue of this book, which in its innovative way, develops the psychoanalytic model of working with parents, infants, and small children.

From a more traditional way of working psychotherapeutically either in private practice or in public service clinics across the globe, a new trend has surely developed. This model of parent-infant work has increasingly been taking place in community settings, adapting to the needs of emotionally deprived people, such as refugees and ethnically diverse groups. Skilled workers from a variety of disciplines have benefited from psychodynamic thinking and supervision without necessarily being formally trained psychoanalytically. We are referring here to talented clinicians—such as speech and language therapists, health visitors, specialist nurses, child psychiatrists and paediatricians, family therapists, and psychologists, etc—not just child and adult psychotherapists and psychoanalysts.

We have come full circle now when we think of Selma Fraiberg, in the States, who was one of the pioneers of this working model in parent-infant psychotherapy. In the 1970s she and her colleagues, who had backgrounds in social work, used to visit deprived and at-risk families in their homes and to practise what was then nicknamed "psychotherapy in the kitchen". This proved to be a very successful way of reaching previously unreachable families. Something very similar has now taken place again as a number of authors of this book testify. Many more people are working in community settings, not just in South Africa and Australia but also in Europe.

A similar phenomenon is occurring in the field of neuropsychology. There is an upsurge of interest in neuroscience that is reminiscent of Freud's interest, the "old neurologist". We are rediscovering some of the intricate connections between the development and functioning of the brain and the emergence of unconscious processes in relational and attachment systems.

Another common factor is the increasing presence of fathers or male partners and their involvement in these treatments. There is a wider acknowledgement that, when it is possible, treatment with the whole family contributes to a better understanding of the unconscious dynamics related to the child's difficulties. We can see this occurring in a number of case histories described by the authors.

This collection brings together papers from around the world including Australia, Brazil, Japan, Europe, South Africa, and the United States. It is written by experienced clinicians, who have a psychodynamic framework and all of whom believe in the importance of early emotional experiences in the development of the personality within the context of family relationships. The vivid detail of the clinical vignettes brings to life intimate stories of the therapeutic process, either from the consulting room of those in private practice, or in the public sector including projects in community settings where traditional psychoanalytic ideas are applied flexibly. The case histories span individual work with various combinations: mothers alone, mothers and babies with or without fathers, families, and mother and baby groups.

The use of the video camera to record parts of, or entire sessions is also widespread, and a number of authors have been adopting this as part of their common practice. This is proving to be an interesting and useful tool, which fosters the observation and understanding of minutiae in parent-child and therapist interactions. These would have otherwise been unnoticed. To watch the video material at a later time, in a different state of mind and usually at a safer distance seems to enhance both parental awareness and understanding of their relationship with their infant, as well as the therapist's thinking and transforming function, thus leading to therapeutic changes.

Chapter 1 is entitled "Looking at the symptoms as a starting point for understanding" and centres on work at the Under Fives Study Centre at the University of Virginia. Sorensen tells the story of Tony, a four-year-old boy referred because he was moody, argumentative, and jealous of his eighteen-month-old sister. He occasionally wet or soiled his pants. There were fourteen sessions in this treatment and we get to know this family through the vivid descriptions of the work undertaken, particularly from Tony's point of view. It is a story of understanding by the therapist that leads to integration within the child and with the family.

Chapter 2 is comprised of the joint paper by Mendes de Almeida and Pelella Mélega, who work in São Paulo, Brazil. They portray the value and contribution of training in infant observation according to Esther Bick and its application, in this case, to the treatment of two children aged two-and-a-half. Their work is inspired by Bion's understanding of group functioning, since families are seen as following similar unconscious modes of operating while rearing their children. The first child, called Pedro, presented common functional difficulties, i.e. sleep problems and rivalry towards his baby brother. He was helped by his parents who are able to withdraw their projections from him during treatment. The second child, Tony, presented a severe neuro-developmental disorder with autistic traits. The therapist's acute observation amplified the child's minute and seemingly banal communication, which was interpreted in the context of the family dynamics. This fostered awareness in the parents that their child needed a deeper therapeutic intervention than either speech therapy or even brief psychotherapy. This intervention is in line with Negri's therapeutic consultations with much younger infants at risk of severe psychopathology (Chapter 6).

Chapter 3 is entitled "Multidisciplinary early intervention with infants and young children presenting emotional, physical, and speech difficulties", by Bernasconi, Gilardoni, Pozzi, and Terragni from the Zero-Five Centre in Ticino, Switzerland. They describe two different case studies. The first examines the muscular hypotonia of newborn baby Andrea who was seen initially on a neonatal pathology ward. Through the intervention of the infant neuropsychiatrist and the paediatric community nurse, the psychological situation of the family was addressed. The first step entailed home visits by the nurse, followed by a series of family sessions at the local child psychiatric clinic, which attempted to tackle some deep-seated difficulties in relation to both mother's and father's families of origin. The work helped to free the infant of some burden, in that mother could begin to attend to her infant's needs, once she had recovered from the painfulness of the experience of childbirth and begun to separate her own difficulties from those of her infant. The second case study documents the work of a speech and language therapist with four-year-old Giacomo whose mother found it difficult to separate from him to the extent that his speech was delayed and he found it hard to let others in. The psychologically-minded intervention by the speech therapist gradually allowed mother and child to let go of each other and Giacomo's language blossomed.

In their brief treatments with both mothers and fathers, Palacio-Espasa and Knauer, from the Geneva Infant Psychiatric Clinic, put forward their thinking on various parental types of fantasies that usually underlie both the infant's symptoms and the relationship with both parents. Pre-oedipal fantasies, or anaclytic as the authors call them, as well as oedipal fantasies influence the therapeutic outcome. Clinical experience shows that pre-oedipal fantasies are easier to address in brief psychotherapy. Equally the positive pretransference fosters a high rate of success with brief interventions, while negative pretransference usually underlies either marital conflicts or severe psychopathology, most often in the mother, requiring longer and different psychotherapeutic interventions. Four clinical examples of brief interventions with different outcomes are described.

In Chapter 5, Watillon-Naveau, from Brussels, Belgium, presents a model of psychotherapy with children aged three to five, seen with their parents in a more traditional setting of her private consulting room. She, too, is indebted to the infant observation method introduced by Bick as a starting point to observe the parent-child relationship during sessions. She notices that the staging of the child's unconscious fantasies at specific moments during the parental narrative usually uncovers the parental projections on the child. Amongst the clinical vignettes, we read that five-year-old Lea, referred for encopresis, developed a nosebleed just at the point where her mother denied having been affected by an earlier abortion. Watillon-Naveau acts as a benevolent grandmother-type figure who plays with the child and offers a model that does not compete with the parents.

Chapter 6, by Negri, presents the infant from a neurodevelopmental and psychological perspective. She works in Bergamo, Italy and in her therapeutic consultations, which treat disorders in the parent-child relationship, she links the infant's neurological development with his or her emerging emotional life. Negri describes her way of observing infants and parents—inspired by Bick's method of infant observation—that focuses on infants who present autistic-like symptoms. She calls these "alarm symptoms"—they are present in children at risk, and may become a predominant part of their personality in that there is a loss of variability and a decrease in the ability to interact with the environment. Negri helps parents to draw their baby out of potential autistic encapsulations (Alvarez 1992; Tustin 1981). Her supportive affirming of parental strengths and non-interpretative guidance is rooted in her deep understanding of the unconscious relationship between parents and sick babies. We read that Daniel, a very troubled baby at risk of developing a serious psychopathology, is now a healthy seventeen-year-old young man, thanks to his parents' courage and trust in Negri's sensitive therapeutic input.

In Chapter 7, James and Woodhead, from the Anna Freud Centre in London, describe their innovative way of working with mothers and babies who are difficult to reach for many reasons, including dislocation and immigration. They bring the traditional model of parent-infant psychotherapy into the community, thus keeping alive the tradition of the War Nurseries established by Anna Freud in the 1940s. Drop-in groups are offered within existing structures. The first one described is part of a health centre next to a post-natal clinic where mothers come to have their babies weighed, checked, and to consult with their health visitors and general practitioners. The second drop-in group takes place in a hostel for homeless mothers. Both groups are co-run by a psychotherapist with a primary care worker. Responsiveness, flexibility, and adaptability of the professional are essential, together with clear time and place boundaries, which—together with a psychoanalytic frame of mind—define the setting. These groups, where mothers can drop in and out at any time during each session, allow parents to regulate their commitments, and to benefit from other mothers' support when professional staff may be experienced as too threatening.

Another innovative perspective is the group work with mothers and babies described in Chapter 8 by Paul and Thompson Salo, who work in the Children's Hospital in Melbourne, Australia. The babies in these groups are given a role as important as that given to their mothers. The babies are seen as "being of equal standing in the group", therefore the two therapists make comments to the babies and focus on the infants' activities as part of the group process. The babies' awareness of their peers, their social competences and exchanges with other babies, and their ability to be engaged in their own right in therapeutic work are very new discoveries and need further exploration. The authors analyse the therapeutic value as well as the preventative functions of these mother-baby groups, where mothers also bring their own issues into a safe environment.

"Parent-infant psychotherapy: when feelings of futility are prevalent" by Amanda Jones working for the Parent-Infant Mental Health Service in North East London, is a very moving chapter giving a detailed case study of work with Natalie and Nat (Chapter 9). The technique involves the use of video of mother and baby playing together for five minutes and then watching the clip during the following session. It links up with the theoretical ideas of Fairbairn on the traumatic consequences for an infant if the mother does not recognise her baby as existing in his own right. Such a situation can lead the infant to adapt with feelings of futility, as if object-seeking is somehow bad, but certainly unwanted. Such a state, if it becomes embedded in the infant, can lead to later schizoid pathology, such that it becomes futile to have dependency needs and to love. Through a very sensitive use of her countertransference and of the video camera, the author can achieve deep and lasting changes in the mother-baby relationship, setting the infant free on his or her developmental path.

Chapter 10 describes community-based work undertaken by Harris, a health visitor in south England, with two families who experienced different types of bereavements after the premature birth of their babies. The first family lost a baby twin soon after being born, while the second family had a baby with a profound global disability, which included being blind. The losses respectively of a live and of an ideal baby were gradually worked through by the parents and the siblings in the families, thanks to the sensitive and competent intervention by Harris. She accompanied them on their journey during her home visits, helping these two families to clarify their intergenerational "ghosts" (Fraiberg 1975) by offering them a secure base. She proposes an innovative model of health visiting, where painful feelings can be acknowledged and tolerated.

" 'It wasn't meant to happen like this': the complexity of mourning great expectations" comprises Chapter 11 by Cudmore that describes work in the innovative perinatal service, which is part of the Under-Five's Service at the Tavistock Child and Family Department. She explores the literature on trauma with particular reference to the loss of a belief in the predictability of the world and the protective function of one's good objects both internal and external. She discusses the aftermath of traumatic experiences of loss—the actual death of a foetus and the loss of an "inside" baby because of a very premature birth. Her sensitive therapeutic interventions, which focus on the parents' experience, is seen as being beneficial for the existing children or indeed for children yet to be born.

Chapter 12 is entitled "Ten years of parent-infant psychotherapy in a township in South Africa. What have we learnt?" by Astrid Berg. This focuses on work in the community in a township outside Cape Town. Failure to thrive in the infant is the symptom that brings the fifteen-year-old mother, Sihle, to the clinic with three-month-old Amanda. The failure to gain weight is examined from three angles: the collective and larger family dynamic, the conflict within the mind of the mother, and the effect of disrupted attachment on the child. On a theoretical level Stern's motherhood constellation (the mother-grandmother dyad), very much a western conceptualization, is discussed in the context of the customs and traditions in South Africa.

The contribution from Japan (Chapter 13) is striking in that not only cultural but also historical events of post-war modernized Japan form the backdrop of extreme difficulties in parent-infant relationships, as illustrated in Watanabe's account. "I don't want this baby!" is the first statement made by Megumi, Ken's mother, together with her suicidal and possibly infanticidal feelings and propensity. However, Watanabe manages—through parent-infant work, which includes father in this case—to unravel the intergenerational effects of the war-orphan maternal grandfather, who denigrated his wife and raised his daughter Megumi as if she were a boy. The author is able to reconnect Megumi with her own mother, who was also a victim of the war, and to help her discover motherhood as well as her place as a woman in modern Japan.

We are very pleased and grateful that all our contributors have put much work and patience into this project, which has resulted in the book in its present form. Its emergence coincides with a global consciousness about the necessity to take care of the early years in order to create good outcomes for all young children, to reduce inequalities, and provide more cohesive and accessible early childhood services.

References

Alvarez, A. (1992). *Live Company: Psychoanalytic Psychotherapy with Autistic, Borderline, Deprived, and Abused Children.* London & New York: Tavistock & Routledge.

Fraiberg, S., Adelson, E. & Shapiro, V. (1975). Ghosts in the nursery. *Journal of the American Academy of Child Psychiatry,* 14: 387–421.

Tustin, F. (1981). *Autistic States in Children.* London & New York: Tavistock & Routledge, 1992.

Maria E. Pozzi-Monzo and
Beverley Tydeman
London
July 2006

CHAPTER ONE

Looking at the symptoms as a starting point for understanding

Pamela B. Sorensen
Under Fives Study Center, University of Virginia

Introduction

Working with very young children and their families presents the clinician with special problems and special opportunities. The problems revolve around the fact that young children do what they cannot say. Therefore, we must be prepared, both through training and temperament, to regard behaviour as communication. If we are so prepared, then working with young children and their families allows for opportunities to understand problems at a deep level of psychological truth.

Because small children do what they cannot say, our work must be based on careful observation. For this reason we pay special attention to the sequence and detail of material as it unfolds in the session. It is especially important that we do not interfere with the unfolding of material by too many questions arising from our own preconceived notions about what may be important. Rather, we try to use our inquiries to clarify the issues brought spontaneously, either consciously or unconsciously, to our attention by young children and their parents.

Observation, however, is never entirely free from underlying basic assumptions about what is worthy of notice. The possible universe of material is infinite. Something must inform one's selection of data. And that something could be called a theory. A theory in our field is like a primitive map. One does not expect a map to be reality. Rather, one hopes that it will represent a sufficient approximation to reality to enable one to navigate with the reasonable hope of learning more about the [psychic] world.

In this paper, the theory providing the primitive map of basic assumptions about mental life and its development is British Object Relations Theory. I would like to identify a few of this theory's basic assumptions that influence the universe of observations included as data. First I would like to present the material itself and then come back, albeit briefly, to what shapes its selection and interpretation.

I chose this particular case for two reasons. The presenting symptoms are common; a four-year-old boy with aggressive behaviour, who occasionally soils his pants. Second, the work with this child and his family enabled several different perspectives on the symptoms to unfold. These perspectives eventually became integrated to the benefit of the entire family. And, as a by-product, the symptoms disappeared.

There were fourteen sessions in this treatment. I will use verbatim material from each session to illustrate how the relevant themes emerged.

The referral and initial interview

Tony is referred by his pediatrician because he has been moody, argumentative, and inordinately jealous of his eighteen-month-old sister Sophia. He occasionally wets or soils his pants for no apparent reason. Most worrying of all, he frequently hits his mother hard in the stomach and has foiled all her attempts at reasonable discipline.

When I first telephone mother to set up an appointment, I think I am talking to a child. In fact, I almost say, "May I speak with your mother, please?" but catch myself just in time. Mother's voice sounds not just young but breathy, languid, and helpless. I arrange to see her with Tony the following week.

When I greet them in the waiting room, mother is seated in a small chair at the play table with little Sophia snugly on her lap. They are playing together with a pop-up toy. Tony leans on the other side of the table, watching them.

Both children are beautiful, with dark hair and eyes, clear skin, and mischievous smiles. Mother wears shorts and sneakers, and has a soft but agitated look about her. She giggles as she rounds up the children to come downstairs to my office. Having learned that I have toys in my office, Tony wants to know if they are as good as those in the waiting room before he agrees to come down.

But once in the room, Tony does not touch anything. He leans on his mother while Sophia dives into everything. He looks on with a superior expression that conveys, "Well, what can you expect from a baby?" He listens as mother tells her story in her girlish voice, both of them reclining on my sofa as if they need to be supported by its firm cushions.

The family moved from Ohio just before Sophia's birth. Until that point, Tony had been cared for by his father and paternal grandmother while mother went to work. After the move, father worked while mother stayed home with the children. She suffered from both post-partum depression and a hernia after Sophia's arrival. She had been unable to pick Tony up since then and saw this mainly as an impediment to effective discipline.

Tony stays in contact with mother's body throughout her list of complaints. Among them is an account of how Tony had wet his pants while playing at his friend's house. When I asked Tony to tell me what had happened, he sprang to life, telling a rather gripping story of how he and his friend had been building a spaceship in the basement. He had to "go", but the toilet was all the way upstairs and he just knew that if he went up there, his friend would finish the project without him! Tony tells his story with dramatic hand gestures and colourful emotion. One can quite see that wet pants were by far the lesser evil to missing out on the completed spaceship.

I am struck in this initial interview by the contrast between Tony's articulate and vigorous speech and his lack of interest in the toys and other items in the room. I am also struck by the contrast between Tony and Sophia: he remains close to mother, she is the bold explorer. Mother and I agree it would be helpful to meet with father next time, and arrange to do so the following week.

The family of four fills my room to capacity. Mother and father sit next to each other on the small sofa, with Sophia confidently tucked in between, one hand flat on each parental thigh. She looks like a cherub sandwich. Tony leans on his mother, too big for the sandwich but too small, it seems, for his own chair.

Father is sad and disappointed. Under a thin bluster about a tidy house and an orderly routine, he expresses great disappointment that Tony only wants to be with his mother and is completely disinterested in the boyish games and outings father has planned to enjoy with his "big boy".

Gentle inquiry reveals that father was himself the oldest of two boys and that his father had been ill for many years while he was growing up. But father firmly makes it clear that he does not want to discuss this further. Tony listens to it all with big, solemn eyes, still clinging to his mother, and turned away from father.

The case takes shape

In the next family interview a week later, father comments that everyone has returned to the same places they had the previous week. It is as if a conversation were being continued. This time, however, Tony leaves his mother's side to concentrate with intensity on building a locomotive out of blocks, doing it skilfully inside the wooden box holding the blocks. As he builds, father continues with the theme of his disappointment that Tony will not relinquish his babyish behaviour for more grownup father-son activities.

Mother continues with her theme of helplessness in the face of Tony's aggression. Sophia investigates every nook and cranny of my room, pausing only to show mother and father some particularly choice treasure.

I remark on how compact and well-built Tony's locomotive is. Now the parents tell me that building, or "—struction", as Tony calls it, is his passion. He watches house-building programs on television, and tapes them for further study. He prefers these programs to cartoons, and mother uses them to calm Tony down when he becomes upset.

As he puts the finishing touches to the locomotive's smokestack, Sophia casually knocks off the top while Tony is looking in the other direction. He cries out, "Sophia, don't break my mama!"

My first thought is, "He didn't say that. I almost let it go. Perhaps I imagined it. Neither parent appears to have heard him. I ask them if they have heard what Tony has just said. Both say they have, although their expressions are utterly blank. I suggest that we take this seriously, although it appears to make no sense. Perhaps, I continue, Tony feels that something bad has happened to his mama and that it has something to do with her having a baby.

Then father describes mother's long crying spells and how he just couldn't understand it and how he wishes he could fix it but he can't. Tony, meanwhile, has repaired his locomotive.

The child's problems are now beginning to make some sense in the context of his family life. I feel that I would like to have a deeper look at things from the perspective of the couple, and from the perspective of Tony's fantasy about his parents and his role in relation to them. I invite the parents to come and see me without the children for two interviews, and then to bring Tony on his own for four more. Then, based on a more detailed understanding of these perspectives, we can decide how to proceed.

In the next interview, father haltingly and painfully describes how he watched his own father suffer successive amputations and eventually die from diabetes. As the eldest son, he functioned as "the man of the house", but felt helpless to relieve his mother's despair. Father easily made the link between his longing for a close relationship with his son and the close relationship he had missed with his own father. When Tony rejected him he was doubly hurt—hurt by his son and hurt again by his father. This realization brought considerable relief: perhaps he had expected too much from a four-year-old, he said. Maybe he needed to be more flexible. There was still a lot they could do together, even if it wasn't at the level of sustained camaraderie that father wanted.

The second parental interview was used by mother to talk about her family of origin. She was worried that Tony might turn out like her older brother, who had bullied her mercilessly ever since she could remember. Her own mother never stopped him. She was weak and could not say "no" to anyone. Her own brother had also bullied her. What if Tony became violent and irresponsible like her uncle and her brother? I suggested to mother that she was sometimes, perhaps often, in a state of confusion, mixing up her son and her brother. In the face of Tony's anger with her for having another baby, she felt not like a grown-up mother able to reassure him that he was valued and loved, but like a little girl helpless in the face of her big brother's jealous rage. Mother was very surprised at this, but willing to think about it.

Both parents could now see that Tony's aggressive, angry, and rejecting behavior had special and different meanings for each of them. To father, it underlined the loneliness he felt for his own father. To mother, it repeated her fear and impotence in relation to her own older brother. Each parent was inhibited from responding constructively to Tony's difficulties because each was caught in the private meaning that these difficulties had for them.

Tony's individual sessions

But what exactly did Tony's difficult behaviour mean to him? Tony is eager to come to his first individual session. He goes straight to the blocks and concentrates on making a series of vehicles-first, a locomotive, then a flatbed, then a tank, and finally a truck. Throughout, the emphasis is on *sturdiness*. As he works, he talks to me about his expertise in many areas. He explains that he gives classes to his friends in his room at home about sharing and doctoring. "Some people", he says condescendingly, "don't even know how to put on a Band-Aid." (a plaster).

This engaging, intelligent, and articulate four-year-old is deeply preoccupied with whether an object will hold together or fall apart, and if it does fall apart will he know how to fix it. I suggest to Tony that he may have this worry about people, too. Without missing a beat, Tony explains in the same breezy adult voice that his mother has a hernia, which means a crack in her tummy muscle. This means that she cannot lift him.

I tell Tony that his Big Boy self is trying to explain this to his Baby Self, but that I think his Baby Self feels quite upset that mama cannot pick him up. Tony blinks very dramatically and tells me that he is making a computer picture of me to keep in his mind until our next session.

In our next session, Tony returns to his building. He builds a box that can carry something "really heavy". The box has a hole on the top at one end. He experiments with putting cylinders in this hole. I ask what the really heavy thing is that the box must carry. Tony doesn't know, but says it is the heaviest thing in the world. I say that I think the heaviest thing in the world is a worry, a big worry, about whether the mama box is all right.

Just as I finish saying this, Tony swiftly moves a small block into position to cover the hole. I remark on how quickly he does this when I talk about the mama box being OK. Perhaps, I ask, he is worried that something bad might get in. "Yes!" he says, "like pavement. You know", he elaborates in response to my puzzled look, "that yucky, black, sticky stuff. Or gravel. Or smoke." I agree that would be bad, trying to stay with the mood. "Yes, very bad," says Tony, "because you couldn't get it out!"

I remark that the previous time Tony told me that mama had a crack in her tummy muscle, I thought he was worried about something inside leaking out. But I was wrong. Now I understand he is worried about something bad getting in.

"Oh", he hastily reassures me, "there is skin over it. Skin is tough." Nevertheless, I say, although his Big Boy self knows this, I think his Baby Self is scared that he hurt mama by pushing black, angry feelings into her when he was so jealous about Sophia and she could not pick him up.

Tony tells me that mama cried all the time. I tell him that he believed this was his fault and he did not know what to do. Tony replies that he watched videos about building. I explain that this made him feel better because he could see a daddy making the house strong. He needed his daddy to make mama better. Now Tony completes his boxcar. He puts a driver "with good hands" on a seat at the front and moves the diesel cylinder from the top to the bottom of the car, saying, "I'll put it underneath where it belongs."

Clearly, this session has helped to clarify the nature of Tony's anxieties and their relationship to his presenting symptoms. From Tony's point of view, his mama is broken: she has a hole in her tummy, she cries all the time, and she cannot pick him up. He believes he did it when he was angry, and now he cannot fix it.

So he keeps doing it to see if it might turn out differently this time. He punches her in the tummy. He pushes yucky, black, sticky stuff into his pants when he is angry. The idealized dream of the "—struction" daddy comes to the rescue in fantasy, but in reality he is still in a mess.

In his third individual session, Tony is able to explore his anxieties further through symbolic play. He experiments with things other than pavement going into the truck: grain, seeds, milk (*not* chocolate milk). When I suggest that he would feel better if the driver could put these good things into the truck, Tony tells me that he cannot because "his tube was taken away." He explains that his father had a vasectomy so he can't give any more seeds.

Following this quiet and matter-of-fact statement, Tony builds a tall tower out of cylindrical blocks and then knocks it down. I tell Tony that I think he's got another worry in addition to his first worry about the hole in mama's tummy. He also feels he might have hurt daddy's tube. Now Tony stages a fight between the king doll and the prince doll. The prince knocks the king off his block. The king boils him in hot water.

I tell Tony that I can see he is both excited and scared about a fight between the king and his son. Tony builds another tower and knocks it down, while pressing a cylindrical block against his penis. Then he tells me what he loves best is "—struction" programs. I say I can see why.

In Tony's final individual session, he constructs something different. For the first time, he builds *outside* the wooden box. There is a tower with working parts, including a ramp enabling trucks to move across to the box where they dig out dirt (*not* pavement) that they then get rid of through a hole in the road. There is a daddy driver and a brother to help with this work. The mama doll is barricaded in the doll's house, getting rid of pavement in the toilet. The daddy and many children protect the house from a bad guy. As we end the session, Tony tells me that he wants to build this at home. I agree that he has done important work here that he wants to continue.

My understanding of this sequence of sessions is that Tony has been able to use me to help him face fundamental anxieties about the state of repair of his parental objects. As is characteristic of infantile omnipotent thought, he has assumed that his angry and jealous feelings have *caused* his mother's hernia and depression and his father's vasectomy, which he interprets as a broken penis.

Using me as his partner to explore these fantasies, thoughts, and feelings, Tony has gone on to mobilize the reparative and helpful side of his personality to redress these problems. He has become more willing to permit a paternal figure a significant role in the reconstruction of the maternal object. He has also become more willing to include siblings in this project and feels less compelled to be the expert, more able to accept help.

This has important implications not only for his life at home, but also for his life at school, which he began in September as our individual sessions ended. Tony's parents are, of course, eager for him to succeed in this arena.

Integration

The next part of our work focuses on how we can help mother and father to put to use all that we have learned together. We arrange to have five final sessions in which mother and father will follow Tony's lead with my help. I might add that I do not believe these parents could have done this without first having been able to convey *their* experience of Tony's difficulties to me. Also, they wanted and got from me an account of my understanding of the precise nature of Tony's anxieties.

The parents find a babysitter for Sophia and come with Tony, willing to observe what he does and then think about it. At first, the material is a carry-over from Tony's individual sessions involving construction of an "Emily", his mother's first name. However, I notice that Tony consults his father about the engineering details of his building.

In the next session, father and Tony come alone because mother was unable to find a baby-sitter for Sophia. Tony uses most of the session to write large numbers. He is contemptuous of those kids who can only write 1, 2, 3, 4, 5. He can already do 100, 1,000, even a million. I am able to help father understand how humiliating it feels to Tony not to know something.

Father tells a wonderful story about how he could not learn to read from the nuns at school when he was a little boy. He had to wait for his kind Aunt Maria to teach him in her kitchen when he was eight. Tony, of course, loves this story. The idea that his big, smart daddy once couldn't read is *thrilling*. Father and son commiserate about how they both hate to feel small and not know something. Maybe they both act a bit know-it-all sometimes.

This theme of humiliation in the face of the grown-up world is continued in the next session. While Tony authoritatively draws numbers and letters he doesn't know, his parents describe how he effectively plays one off against the other, reducing one or both to impotent rage and humiliation. I point out that this is Tony's way of getting rid of his own feeling of smallness, faced with them as a grown-up couple who do things together that he cannot, such as make a baby. "*Yes!*" he yells, as he strikes furiously into the box of blocks.

Mother and father are surprised and moved by this expression of emotion. It leads them on to a careful and loving explanation of their aspirations for their family, including a thoughtful review of the vasectomy, which is enormously relieving to Tony. At the end of the session, Tony resumes his number work, but this time turning to his parents who each hold up both hands so Tony can count more modest numbers on their combined fingers.

Encouraged by Tony's growing ability to use the parental couple as a source of support for real learning, I am helped to see in the next interview how mother unwittingly undermines this step in development. Tony begins with bravado, which quickly changes to contrived babyish behaviour as father described mother feeling unwell at the weekend. Father is visibly annoyed by the manipulative quality of this, but mother responds dutifully as if Tony were a baby.

I explore this persistently, suggesting to mother that she can indeed discriminate between Tony's *faux* infant and his real neediness, but that for some reason she is *afraid* to get angry with him. Mother tells me that her own mother "collapses" if anyone expresses the slightest negative feelings toward her. I suggest to mother that she fears that her anger will crush Tony as it does her mother, and that is exacerbated by her guilt in relation to

Tony-she did not breastfeed him as she had so enjoyed doing with Sophia, and she was not there much during the first two years.

Now she feels that if she resists Tony when he tries to manipulate her, it is equivalent to her rejecting him when he was a baby. During this discussion, Tony has resumed his five-year-old voice and demeanor and is busy building a tower and undressing the dolls.

In our final session, mother's demeanor is subtly different. She seems more grown up. She and Tony have come without father because they could not find a baby-sitter. But I feel there is also unfinished business here which mother needs more time to work on. She sits on the floor next to Tony, not propped up on my couch, and hands him blocks in a comradely way while showing genuine interest in the details of his construction.

Mother reflects on how things have changed at home. She says she thinks about things in a different way now. "I guess sometimes there is conflict and it's just that way. Not the end of the world. Not so terrible. Not like it was with my mother." She goes on to say that she and father want to spend some time with Tony, maybe when Sophia is having her nap.

Tony, meanwhile, is undressing the dolls and announcing they are having a baby. Mother looks at me surprised and whispers, "I never told him about that." I say that this is what happened in their family and that it was a great shock and changed everything. Tony starts a siren sound and throws all of the people out of the doll's house. A fireman comes to save everyone and methodically puts the house back in order as mother and I review the many themes that have emerged from our visits.

When Tony has finished his work, he comes to sit on mother's lap. She smiles at me and says Tony likes to be held and she likes to hold him.

Summary and follow up

Six weeks later we had a follow-up visit, which I will describe in a moment. But first I want to summarize briefly what I think happened during this clinical intervention.

The parents came worried about symptoms they wished me to remove. From a psychoanalytic point of view a symptom is a starting point, because we see it as a failed attempt, or a distorted attempt, or an incomplete attempt, to address a problem that cannot be identified *because it arouses too much anxiety*. The objective, then, of the intervention is to create a working environment in which anxiety can be acknowledged and tolerated long enough for learning from experience to occur.

In other words, we are trying to liberate development, not eliminate life's problems. Parents often press us to tell them what to do. But sometimes what they suffer from is not a lack of information or common sense but an inability to use them. When we comply with the pressure by giving advice about management, we may be colluding with the family to avoid facing the anxieties that prevent them from figuring things out.

Figuring things out is the best any of us can do. There is no alternative to struggling with loss, disappointment, jealousy, and failure. It is resilience in the face of these inevitable problems that characterizes healthy development, not the absence of problems themselves.

When Tony and his family, including Sophia, enter my room for the follow-up visit, mother sits in a straight back chair, not on the sofa. Tony begins talking in a mock baby voice, and I remark that this had been the focus of attention the last time we were all together. Father says that this really has not been a problem lately. Mother firmly asks Tony to speak in his five-year-old voice, which he does.

As Tony builds a pirate ship, there is a family discussion about a book they had all read recently. Pirates work not just for themselves but for the king, to make their country rich. I comment that it seems that the pirates are a kind of family that works together. At this moment, Sophia knocks down Tony's ship. He mimes hitting her, but does not. Both parents sympathize with the loss of the ship and praise Tony for restraining himself. I recall our second session, when something similar happened. Tony looks resigned.

Mother describes some conflict Tony has experienced playing with two other boys, including a new boy in the neighbourhood. I suggest that it is hard to share an old friend with a new friend, as it was hard to share mama with Sophia. I add that three is a very hard number. Tony shrugs and says, "Two is easy." His parents laugh.

Tony retrieves the drawings I have saved from past sessions and hands them over to his father for safekeeping. Noticing the confident intimacy in this exchange, I ask father how he has been feeling about things at home. He replies that things are better, and that he feels he has changed more than Tony has. Father believes that he is more flexible now. Asked for an example, he describes how he will play what Tony wants, such as being knights together fighting a dragon. Though shy in detailing this romp on the lawn with props and effects, it is clear that this game was a triumph of cooperation and identification, not to mention displacement, giving enormous pleasure to both father and son. Pity the poor dragon!

Mother seems more resilient than she had been. She tells me she can be firmer with Tony now, and he is not hitting her anymore. She does not accept mock baby talk, but hugs him when he comes to her.

Now the parents bring a new problem. They encourage Tony to tell me about a bully on the school bus. But instead of turning to me for a solution to this problem, both parents discuss the options for action with Tony and work out a three-step plan. I am impressed by their collaboration, tenderness, and clarity.

Father does not think it necessary to arrange another follow-up visit since, although there are downs as well as ups, things are progressing. As they gather their things to leave, Tony mimes making a list of important things to do. Clearly, the work continues.

The role of theory

I would like to return to the role of theory in this brief intervention. Among the features of the psychoanalytic map that proved helpful in following Tony and his family are three easily identifiable basic assumptions influencing both what is observed and how it is understood. All three stem from British Object Relations Theory and particularly from the work of Melanie Klein.

First: Individuals' experiences of their worlds are not based simply on what happens to them, but also on the interaction between what happens and what they make of it, based on elements of their own personality and constitution. The internal world and the external world reciprocally influence one another. This can be seen in the material about the hernia and its particular meaning to Tony.

Second: The mother's body is the centre of the baby's world not only physically, but also mentally. Unconscious fantasies about the mother's body are of the utmost importance in shaping how relationships unfold. This can be seen in Tony's construction material, especially when he cries out, "Don't break my mama" and in his ideas about pavement.

Third: A crucial turning point in development is the capacity to feel concern for the object, with an increasingly realistic estimation of its relation to others and one's own powers relative to it. Melanie Klein's concept of the depressive position allows us to place moral development and the capacity for empathy in the context of the development of early object relationships. This can be seen in Tony's growing capacity for genuine learning rather than grandiose self-assertion about numbers. Having recognized that it is Daddy who must fix Mummy, the driver with good hands, he is free to accept what his collaborative parents have to offer him.

These are examples of how a theoretical map helps us find our way through the lively, colourful, and sometimes confusing activity of child and family psychotherapy. Perhaps, however, most helpful of all is our psychoanalytic conviction that behaviour is meaningful and that this meaning can bring relief when it is understood and integrated in the context of intimate relationships.

References

Bion, W. R. (1970). *Attention and Interpretation*. London: Tavistock.

Klein, M. (1969). *The Psychoanalysis of Children*. London: Hogarth Press and the Institute of Psycho-Analysis.

Klein, M. (1975). *Envy and Gratitude, and Other Works*. London: Hogarth Press and the Institute of Psycho-Analysis.

Klein, M. (1984). *Love, Guilt, and Reparation and Other Works*. New York: Free Press.

Miller, L., Rustin, M., Rustin, M., & Shuttleworth, J. (1989). *Closely Observed Infants*. London: Duckworth.

CHAPTER TWO

Echoes from overseas: Brazilian experiences in psychoanalytic observation, its developments, and therapeutic interventions with parents and small children

Marisa Pelella Mélega and
Mariângela Mendes de Almeida
São Paulo, Brazil

Introduction: spreading the seeds of psychoanalytic observation and the history of a training centre

The development of psychoanalytic observation in Brazil was greatly stimulated by the foundation of the Mother-Infant Relationship Study Centre in São Paulo in 1987 by Dr Marisa Pelella Mélega, a psychiatrist and psychoanalyst, always concerned with the promotion of individual and family mental health.

The Centre adapted the Psychoanalytic Observational Studies course model developed by the Tavistock Clinic and gained accreditation from the Centro Studi Martha Harris (Italy), through its chair Gianna Williams, a consultant child and adolescent psychotherapist at the Tavistock Clinic.

Initially, the main aim of the Centre was the training of professionals working in the field of mental health and education. Infant observation was introduced as an innovative tool to deepen the professionals' contact with the mental life within themselves and others. This complemented their work with patients and pupils, whether privately or in institutions. Later, Dr Mélega used the psychoanalytic observation to improve the professionals' psychotherapeutic skills. This technique and its applications became the central pillars of a training in child psychotherapy.

The provision of National Health services in Brazil is paltry in comparison to the population's great need. Government organizations provide little for child mental health. The emphasis remains on assessment, which is not always psychodynamic. Psychotherapy is rare for those who cannot afford fees.

Dr Mélega believed it possible to contribute to the wider community by brief "Therapeutic Interventions" focused on child-family relationship and related problems. From 1990 to 1995, the Centre developed research projects to apply the Bick method to non-clinical settings such as paediatric units, nurseries, crèches, and schools. Thus, the staff had the opportunity to build up services in the community, predominantly through supervision groups.

By working with families below the poverty line, the professionals became aware of peculiar "beliefs" among parents concerning the way they brought up their children. A high degree of starvation, for example, could be due not only to the shortage of food but also to the way mothers were feeding their babies. Connections were also found between sleep disturbances and premature separation.

Much thought was given to the development of courses for professionals within the primary health and education areas. However, attendance at these courses was poor, perhaps because of poorly paid public posts, extremely long working hours, or even lack of motivation to invest in professional development.

Dr Mélega and her team came to the conclusion that the best action would be to invest in the training of clinical psychologists, who were already community oriented. In Brazil, clinical psychologists are the main professionals trained to undertake psychotherapy, and who therefore seek professional development in this field. Enabling them to use psychoanalytic observation as a working tool allowed the development of effective work in crèches, nurseries, schools, and paediatric units. This work generated several papers, all of them illustrative of the preventive mental health project developed by the team, which were published in the 1991 journal of the Centre, *Publicações Científicas* (Volume 3, 1991). This includes English translations, and is available at the Tavistock Library, London.

From infant observation to therapeutic interventions with parents and small children

In 1996, Dr Mélega started a study group to test clinical interventions inspired by psychoanalytic observation. Patients were assessed and treated by members of the team, using a low-fee scheme. A new clinical approach was based on this study, known as "Therapeutic Interventions with Parents and Small Children".

Years of practice and discussion of infant observation in supervision have certainly contributed to the maturation of this approach. The presence of a "psychoanalytic observer" may promote a field of attention and observation within the visited family. Mothers seem to use the experience of being visited by an observer as a model of functioning, which can be noticed in the development of maternal attitudes towards the baby (Mélega 1990).

Therapeutic Interventions with Parents and Small Children constitutes an application of Bick's model of infant observation. To be in a state of mind which facilitates observation, the therapist has to be:

- receptive,
- sensitive to the emotional atmosphere which involves the object of observation, and
- able to deal with the emotions awakened by the function of observing, and not actively intervening in the object of observation.

Obviously, in applying this model to a clinical context, we are introducing a variable that may take us from the function of observing within the classical mode, to that of "actively promoting communication and thought", which is regarded as a Therapeutic Intervention. Professionals using this approach are expected to have had a consistent training in infant observation and clinical experience with children and adolescents.

In this approach, the focus is on the interactions, especially the adults' parental functions towards their children. We learn from their ways of relating as a family, as we follow their communication through verbal or pre-verbal language, play or enactment.

In this paper we discuss the theoretical foundations, technical issues and applications of the Therapeutic Interventions with Parents and Small Children. Two clinical illustrations are given as examples of how this approach can be useful for a wide range of families in dealing with the child's upsets, psychosomatic symptoms, emotional, or relational difficulties. In the first case, a detailed account is given of the interactions with the corresponding interventions during joint sessions. In the second case, we emphasize how psychoanalytic observation has informed our work with more severely disturbed young children and their families, and how Therapeutic Interventions with Parents and Small Children can be useful in preparing the ground for further analytical treatment for the child.

Therapeutic Interventions with Parents and Small Children

Theoretical foundations

We consider now some theoretical issues that are relevant to the understanding of group processes, and therefore to the development of our approach of parents and children within the family.

W. Bion's contribution to the work in groups (Bion 1961), acts as the basis for applying the analytical method to the family group. When asked to assist task groups experiencing internal tensions, Bion used the analytical perspective of observation, taking into account the observer's intuition and emotional reactions to the group's functioning. He could then understand phenomena that occurred in the group context. He realized that the participants' behaviours, their attitudes, and their choice of methods to attain proposed aims were poor, not rational, and did not correspond to their intelligence and ability shown outside the group situation. The group was not using a reality-based approach to solve problems.

Bion observed and described to the group the situations that appeared to oppose the proposed task, thus helping the group to overcome the impediments. In Therapeutic Interventions with Parents and Small Children, we see how important it is to observe and describe for the family the situations created by the group that may either be hampering the task, or facilitating and solving the presenting problem.

In considering the family group, one of the tasks is the exercise of parental functions which, in an ordinary family, would be to generate love, sustain hope, and contain depressive suffering and thought (Meltzer & Harris 1986). Meltzer and Harris deduced some general principles that drive relationships in a family group and that tend to favour, in the members, one of these modes of learning:

- learning from experience.
- learning by projective identification.
- learning by selecting, and/or obsessively collecting inanimate objects, facts, and memories.
- learning by submission to a persecutor.
- learning by stealing.
- learning by adhesive identification.

These, therefore, were a source of inspiration in setting up our work, particularly in reflecting on the impediments that a group might have in learning from experience.

Bion's concept of containment and his understanding of the development of thinking and symbolic functioning within the context of both mother-infant relationships and therapist-family relationships are also essential pillars in this clinical work.

Technical issues

On seeing a family for the first time, the therapist will inform them of the purpose of the first meeting, which is to assess, with their help, the presenting problem. Toys and drawing materials are made available, so that the children may express themselves according to their age.

At the outset, the therapist will try, as far as possible, to maintain an attitude of observation and listening, and to pay close attention to the participants' interaction, while attempting to foster an atmosphere that allows communication to take place. At this stage, interventions by the therapist will be necessary when:

- Misunderstanding in communication between members occurs, which makes continuity of dialogue difficult.
- Communication between members is based on anti-thinking, and lying, and nobody is intervening to stop it.
- The children's play communication during the session is not understandable to the parents.

- The transference relation with the therapist is being acted out.
- Anxieties appear to be disruptive or are hindering the continuity of a session.

Listening, observing detail, and emotional containment by the therapist are crucial to facilitate an understanding of psychic reality and to promote an atmosphere in which thinking may occur. As this mode of work lends importance to establishing an atmosphere that will be favourable to dream-thought during the sessions, the demand for a constant internal examination by the therapist is intense. Transference and countertransference movements, though not interpreted directly, are attentively followed by the therapist.

This framework, plus the therapist's interventions when opportune, provide examples of mental functioning for the group members. Something similar takes place within mother-infant relationships when the mother intervenes to make sense of the baby's confusion and anxiety.

The function of intervening during a session is not exclusively performed by the therapist. Parents and children may also make valuable contributions, which are received and integrated by the therapist, who, as coordinator of the group, aims to promote autonomy and independence. Interventions by the therapist will stem from the observation of the participants' interactions and will serve to clarify and motivate thoughts, as well as to offer containment and meaning to the material that gradually arises in the group. A search for new understandings may occur, clarified by the therapist as hypotheses or "modes of viewing", which may be accepted or rejected by the participants.

This approach allows a redistribution of authorship and responsibility among members, and promotes awareness that the presenting problem or the index patient are often emerging signs of conflicts or of misfit within the family group.

Considering Kleinian psychoanalytic contributions regarding the analysis of small children, and the importance of both verbal and non-verbal communication, the technique used in these Interventions considers playing and drawing as communicating the children's states of mind, including their unconscious fantasies. The translation of this language by the therapist broadens the communication and understanding among members of the group. We could also say that the actual parent-child interaction taking place in these sessions corresponds to free association in adult analytic sessions and to play in child analysis, being equivalent, therefore, to the language of dream-thought.

Clinical illustration 1

We will describe some scenes extracted from sessions of a Therapeutic Intervention with Parents and Small Children carried out by Maria da Graça Palmigiani, a clinical psychologist and psychotherapist from the Mother-Infant Relationship Study Centre, who was supervised by Marisa Mélega.

The baby in this family was being observed by a student taking part in an infant observation seminar. The observer often presented scenes in which the baby's brother, Pedro, who was two years old, cried during lunch, and refused food. He was reported as not sleeping well, and showed frustration and unhappiness. The mother was anxious and had difficulties dealing with Pedro's distress.

One day, the mother asked for help and the observer suggested that a professional from the Mother-Infant Relationship Study Centre assessed Pedro's situation. The whole family was invited to come.

Scene I in the first meeting: father, mother, Pedro (aged two years and ten months old) and the baby (aged one), are present.

Mother, with baby on her lap, informs the therapist about Pedro: crying, not eating properly, and waking several times a night. Meanwhile, Pedro approaches father to play, as if repairing objects and plant leaves. Mother comments that Pedro imitates his father "who repairs everything at home". The therapist says that Pedro might be showing a need to repair what is not working properly between the family members. Mother is astonished with this formulation.

We can see here how, while the mother talks about a "wrong, broken" boy, Pedro makes an effort to show he is able to repair things, to preserve life. A field of work is established through the therapist's intervention, indicating an understanding of the child's play in a non-ordinary way, providing an emotional meaning for the parents to the child's behaviour.

Scene II in the second meeting: father, mother, baby and Pedro are present.

The situation of Pedro "repairing everything" is resumed as he plays in the session and while mother mentions it. At a certain moment, mother, baby, and Pedro get closer to the therapist, sitting on the couch. Mother says she had six abortions and that she had had a baby, but that it died soon after birth. Meanwhile, Pedro starts undressing until he is wearing just his underpants.

Father comments that when mother was pregnant with Pedro, her pregnancy "came to an end" (went to full-term) only because mother was busy with the maternal grandmother's illness.

Here, the mother is able to address one of the main aspects of Pedro's conflicts: his need to repair everything. Repair what? Did damage occur in the mother's mind because of her history? Would Pedro have to take upon himself the mother's projective identification? Does Pedro fear loosing other siblings? And what about his own possible death? Pedro understands there is a place where he can get undressed, get rid of the burden of mother's projective identifications, and be himself.

Scene III in the third meeting: father, mother, and Pedro are present while the baby was left at home.

Here we see a succession of "dream images":

Pedro enters asking the therapist: "Where is the yellow one?" He searches in the box, continuously and urgently, for a yellow piece of lego, throwing away each thing that is in his way. He had left it out of the box in the previous session. His parents insist on him greeting the therapist and, finally, he asks, "How are you?" The therapist answers and asks him the same question. He replies: "I'm fine, I hit the baby, I cuddled the baby . . ." and getting closer to the therapist, he asks: "Why didn't the baby come?" The therapist makes it clear that she needed to be with just the three of them. Father gets closer to Pedro and offers help to look for the yellow piece. Pedro and father find it and entertain themselves assembling lego.

The therapist and mother sit, looking at them. Pedro approaches the therapist asking what is "that bed" for? The therapist describes the use of the couch in the sessions. Pedro climbs on the couch and undresses completely. Mother comments that he is going to repeat everything, as he did in the previous session. The therapist reminds her that this happened when mother talked about the abortions and the death of her baby. Pedro asks the therapist to protect the small plant that he had overturned in the first session. He was worried that he had killed it. The therapist accedes to the request. Pedro invites his mother to play hide-and-seek and hides under the bedspread that covers the couch. His mother explains that he can't do that. Pedro insists on removing the bedspread, but gives in to mother's request. He asks the therapist where he can hide. His parents try to dissuade him from the idea. Pedro insists. The therapist indicates a place behind the couch and beside her armchair. Pedro asks mother to close her eyes, and hides himself. Mother finds him. Pedro continues playing hide-and-seek. From this moment onwards, when mother delays finding him, he makes noises and gives clues as to where he is. Pedro then leaves his hiding-place before being discovered. He goes to the couch, lies down and says something the therapist doesn't understand. Mother translates: he is talking about death. She adds that a few days ago, he asked father why he had killed his mother (the paternal grandmother). Father explained to him that people die of illnesses and accidents. The therapist asks the parents if Pedro's play makes them think about something. Their answer is negative. The therapist wonders whether Pedro wanted to know about the babies' deaths. Who or what had killed them? The parents retort that they have never talked to him about this and seem astonished with the therapist's formulation. Standing beside father, Pedro says that he is going to make a gun (with lego). Then, he shoots the therapist and instructs her to die. The therapist says that should she die, she wouldn't be able to talk to them about "these things" anymore. Pedro answers: "That's right." Pedro doesn't want to leave when the session ends, and asks the therapist if baby can come next time.

This meeting begins with Pedro's expression of anxiety. He doubts that the therapist is going to maintain the promised place.

Will she go on containing and understanding his fantasies, or does she expel children, interrupt experiences, like his mother did with the babies, and why? This is shown through the amazing play image Pedro is able to convey through the search for the yellow piece, which had been thrown out of the box by him in the previous session. The piece of lego could be seen as a representative of his baby brother. He makes inquiries, testing his fantasies, and expecting a meaning.

It is interesting to follow Pedro's elaboration process of his brother's absence from the meeting. Pedro feels the urgency of finding the yellow piece of lego as soon as he enters the room. He asks the therapist about it and then his father, who, at last, helps to look for it, after the therapist's answer about why the baby has not come. Helped by his father, Pedro makes constructions with the lego pieces. Being contained in his curiosity about the couch, i.e. "the bed", by the therapist, he climbs on it and starts to get undressed. The therapist adds more understanding about Pedro's play, saying that he may want to know more about the babies.

At this moment, the configuration that emerges is not about the past to be uncovered, but it concerns Pedro's attempts to think about his emotional experiences with his mother. He is having difficulty in internalizing good aspects of her, due to the amount of non-transformed terror or death that comes with nourishment or life. Now, making use of the therapist as a container that observes him, understands him, and offers him meaning, he starts being the boy he cannot be in his mother's eyes.

Pedro asks the therapist to protect the small plant, which represents a baby who is developing session after session. He wants to make sure there is a more creative relationship, less invaded by anxiety and death. By assuring himself of the existence of a container that preserves life, he can then turn to his mother.

For the first time in the sessions, he invites his mother to play hide-and-seek. By hiding under the bedspread in order to be discovered, he produces an interesting representation of birth. When this is not allowed, he finds another solution.

This child shows a striking capacity for overcoming frustrations, and a persistent impulse for knowledge. These two elements that had not been previously recognized or understood, are now finding a way of being expressed within the therapeutic setting. In Pedro's proposed play with his mother, he wants her to find him, to recognize him, to see him, but he still fears not being found. Then, he co-operates with her, making sounds to give his mother clues. Should he not be found, should he not be born to his mother's look, he may die metaphorically by not developing a thinking mind.

Pedro's symptoms—crying too much, not accepting nourishment, and not sleeping—seem to convey his state of mind, as if he were in a constant nightmare, facing intense indigestible experiences. This lack of a barrier between consciousness and unconsciousness seems to relate to his difficulty in transforming the emotional experiences into alpha elements, in symbolic visual forms available for dream-thought.

Pedro starts "dreaming" during the session, and gradual improvement is through an experience of being understood and contained. We can follow the evolution of Pedro's symbolic route. When, after the hide-and-seek game, he says something, which the therapist doesn't understand, his mother translates for the therapist that Pedro is talking about death. He now wants to know about death as he feels safer and not under threat.

The therapist evokes a strong reaction from the parents, when she tells them that Pedro may want to know who killed the babies. When constructing a weapon and playing at killing the therapist, Pedro seems to be showing his desire to be rid of the death threat, leaving it with the therapist. This enables him to leave the session feeling that his brother can be alive with him. "Can baby come next time?" is his last question. This seems to imply a better integration between his loving and hating feelings towards his baby brother.

Therapeutic interventions with parents and small children with severe emotional disturbances

Here we discuss the contribution of the training in infant observation and its developments as Therapeutic Interventions with Parents and Small Children, with regard to children with severe emotional difficulties, mainly within the wide spectrum of autistic disorders.

According to Bick, training in infant observation should "increase the student's understanding of the child's non-verbal behaviour and his play, as well as the behaviour of the child who neither speaks nor plays" (1963: 240).

Besides furthering our understanding of ordinary development, Bick's infant observation model has widened our contact with infantile fragmented states and primitive levels of emotional development. It has brought important contributions to the field of early interventions with parents and infants, in clinical and research developments. It has also contributed to important developments in the psychoanalytic technique itself, when working with children within the autistic spectrum. Susan Reid states that "insights gained from infant observation have informed changes in technique, making it possible to work more effectively with patients who are hard to reach or who would previously have been considered unsuitable for psychoanalytical psychotherapy" (Reid 1997).

It has been increasingly shown, both in literature and clinical experiences, how interventions at a very early age are significant in promoting possible contact with areas of health within parent-infant/child relationships, even when atypical development is taking shape. If it is clear to professionals that the young child will be needing individual long-term psychotherapy, this referral may have a better chance of being taken forward and supported by parents if, during the initial phase of work, they can be involved and their anxieties contained. This may take place in prolonged assessments before treatment, or sometimes in parallel work with the couple while the child is already being seen. We stress the possibility of fostering containment and awareness of the child's difficulties through Therapeutic Interventions with Parents and Small Children, before and to the benefit of further referral to individual psychotherapy. This may facilitate integration of parental perceptions about the child in the context of their relationship, and acknowledge the quality of their child's ways of being, which may be very painful for the parents.

Working with children on the autistic spectrum challenges us in our containing function, which is essential in the analytic relationship, in the development of thinking processes (Bion 1962b) and, together with the parental input, is essential for the infant's development and psychic growth. When thinking about how this containing function expresses itself and what technical nuances contribute to enhance its impact with such uncontained states, some elements have been noticed in our clinical experience. When working with these children, we amplify features of the containing function that the maternal figure develops with her infant.

Some of the features of this function are:

- attention to the slightest signals and attempts at communication expressed by the child by sharing the child's rudimentary interests in mental and emotional features of those present in the room.
- attribution of possible intentionality and mental quality to the child's communications, even when they are faint and incipient.
- demonstration of mental functioning with a developing sense of internal spaces that can process sensorial and perceptive experience of the external and internal world and therefore harbour emotional experience.
- integration of different levels and registers of experience, when we associate, for example, verbal and symbolic elements to the child's pre-verbal and sensorial experience.
- regulation of distances by allowing space for the child's rhythms to unfold without overloading or invading the child with needs, projections, and expectations of one's own.

These features of the containing function, present in healthy parents, may require strengthening by the therapist, so that the parents of disturbed children (often deeply injured in their expectations by their child's disturbance and lack of response), can resume a cycle of investment in health and life.

The contact with primitive states of mind is enhanced by the training in infant observation. Coupled with contributions from child development studies, the enhancement of parent-infant relational functions by the therapist within a Therapeutic Intervention contributes to the understanding and integration of fragmented aspects of the internal worlds of children and parents within the context of their relationship. The formation of a "containing field" is made possible within the family, allowing emotional content to be tolerated and metabolized.

Clinical illustration 2

Tony is two years and eight months old. His young parents are very concerned about his lack of speech. They are referred by a sensitive paediatrician, who is doubtful about the level of Tony's disturbances and type of treatment needed. She thinks there may be something autistic in his development, but also interactional aspects that the parents and the child may be helped with. The family is seen initially for four meetings, in a Therapeutic Intervention with Parents and Small Children setting. The therapists in this case are Mariângela Mendes de Almeida and Magaly Miranda Marconato, clinical psychologists and psychotherapists in São Paulo, both trained in Psychoanalytical Observation at the Tavistock Clinic and former members of the Mother-Infant Relationship Study Centre staff.

As in infant observation, subtle and tiny details illuminate our understanding of crucial emotional dynamics within the family:

Tony impresses us from the beginning with his big, alert eyes and determined look. He is well built, agile in his movements, though silent and apparently self-sufficient. At the same time, he shows an intense need for physical closeness with his mother. When not next to her, he needs to have her always in his visual field. He seems not to notice us during our first contacts, ignoring our attempts to capture his attention with our comments or engage him with our looks. The parents' main concern is Tony's inability to speak, and they desperately try to stimulate speech, teaching him words for colours, shapes, numbers, and letters.

During the first session, sitting at the little table in a very serious and neat posture, with mother next to him, Tony silently entertains himself with the coloured pencils, carefully taking them out of the box and placing them back again. He repeats the scene, ritualistically. Father is in another part of the room. Mother is the only one allowed to take part in the activity and she seems proud of it. When a pencil falls on the floor, I pick it up. When I offer it back to him, he stares at the pencil and starts to reach for it, but suddenly, his movement stops, suspended in the air, and he withdraws his hand quickly, avoiding the interchange. While he does this, he shows no change in his facial expression, no sign of shyness, joy, fear, or cheekiness . . . I ask mother whether she has noticed what has happened. "What might be going on in his mind?" we wonder. Mother says: "He only takes it from me!" She demonstrates this by giving him one of the pencils. He takes the pencil from her, but mechanically, and again, he looks impassive. A real interchange seems once more avoided.

Following the child's movement suspended in the air, the therapist also introduces "in the air" a query for them to think about together: "What might be going on in his mind?" We can see here how therapists in a Therapeutic Intervention with Parents and Small Children use psychoanalytic observational resources as amplifying lenses, inviting the parents to think about the child's internal movements expressed through subtle interactions in the room.

Although Tony's autistic features were evident from the first meeting, our task during these four sessions was to help the parents to acknowledge the pervasiveness of their child's problems and to facilitate contact with their avoided and painful perceptions that his need for help might be greater than the acquisition of skills. Could he be helped to learn from experience rather than by adhesive identification or by collecting words of names, colours, shapes, and numbers?

Tony arrives at the second session with his mother, while father comes later. When his father enters the room, Tony, who is wandering and playing briefly with the pencils beside his mother, looks at him and smiles discreetly. His father asks for a kiss, and prepares to receive Tony in his arms. Tony moves quickly towards his father, but stops suddenly, rigidly turns round towards his mother and rushes to kiss her first. He makes his way back to his father and only then can Tony let himself be kissed and hugged by him as well.

The scene surprised us all, triggering an empathic laugh among the parents and therapists. It is not possible to ignore Tony's hesitation and deliberate change of track. Spontaneous comments by the therapists, still in the atmosphere of humour evoked by the scene, stress this moment and invite them to see beyond the movement, to consider it as a window that allows access to possibly important configurations in that family: "Daddy cannot be kissed if Mummy is not kissed first!" It looked as if Tony wanted to go to Daddy but he worried that he would be leaving Mummy alone.

This sequence seems to refer to the same emotional dynamics in the first session; the therapist represents the third element and intruder within the fused mother-child relationship, and in the second session, the same configuration is enacted with the father. As paradoxically concrete metaphors, these "clusters of meaning" (Mendes de Almeida, Marconato, & Pereira da Silva 2004) suggest a symbolic image. The little boy symbiotically fused with his mother, does not exist as a separate identity, and fears allowing space for a third element, i.e. the father, the therapist, or any other presence. These scenes are also manifested in their daily life. Without the amplification provided by the setting and the therapists, they could be easily overlooked. Providing the "slow motion" look (something that is trained for in psychoanalytic observation), allows us to retain details like this as significant "clinical windows" through which we can view and feel what it is like to be with Tony and his parents. To a non-trained observer, these details may not deserve any special attention—indeed they may be ordinary and may not bring about any "deep" psychoanalytical revelations. However, the fact that they are probably an enactment of a family dynamic observable in the session allows all participants to become intrigued, and to reflect together, thus leading to possible pathways to change.

As the sessions progress, background data and observations of their relationship cluster around issues of maternal states of depression and loneliness. This includes periods of mother feeling very much on her own during Tony's early years, when he was already showing relational difficulties. Acknowledgement and wider emotional contact with Tony's actual deficits and the parents' feelings towards them are essential before the family can look for and accept intensive individual psychotherapy for the child.

For this family, the spur to seek help was their panic over Tony's lack of speech: "Tony can't speak. Something must be done for him to speak." During our sessions, we attempt to rephrase the initial formulation. "Tony can't relate, therefore he can't speak. Something is going on that needs to be understood, so that something can be done to help him." Or "At this particular moment in this family, Tony can't show who he is, he has no voice. He is seen as needing training to speak, while in fact he has wider difficulties that need noticing. This is Tony."

The family returns for the fourth session after holidays during which both parents were very close to Tony. They comment, in a sad but much more articulated way, how they noticed that Tony is different from other children, how he isolates himself and does not make requests of other people as their little niece does, how he does not play or look at other people as they see other children doing. Mother then, with tears in her eyes, allows herself to mention that she has noticed this since he was a little baby and she has been worried about it all this time. We are moved by their observations and stress how they seem to be much closer to the actual Tony and to their possibility of helping him when they allow themselves to notice his serious difficulties, however painful and sad that may be. We also comment that they seem much more together as a couple, noticing his basic difficulties, without accusing each other of not stimulating Tony properly, or blaming each other for having too high expectations of resolving his problems.

With the parents' emerging awareness of Tony's problems, we find a space to discuss our suggestions regarding the child's pervasive difficulties, and ideas for continuity of psychoanalytic treatment. This can then be accepted by them.

In the fourth session, Tony spends some time looking attentively at himself in the mirror. He shows a growing awareness of us as a presence he can acknowledge and does not need to avoid us. He tolerates eye contact with us better. He can accept physical closeness and can exchange toys with us. He is also requesting father's involvement much more than before and walks from mother to father in a much more natural way.

At the end of this intervention, we may have helped Tony and his family to consider his actual needs. Tony's interest in his image in the mirror may be indicating his incipient sense of an emerging self.

> Before going out of the room, Tony holds his parents' hands and leaves with them. He does not need to clutch at his mother excluding his father. His mother, accordingly, allows this without rushing to be the only protector of her son. The parents seem to feel supported by each other. Though concerned, they seem less anxious, being part of a couple who jointly look after the great needs of their child.
>
> The parents seem to be more in contact with their function of generating love, sustaining hope, and containing depressive suffering and thought. In this last scene, Tony seems able to link with both parents as a couple while at the same time there is a sense that he may eventually experience separateness.

Conclusions

We hope to have shown how Psychoanalytic Observation and its developments, especially the Therapeutic Interventions with Parents and Small Children, have contributed to the promotion of child and family mental health within the context of some Brazilian experiences, in the setting up of relevant training, and in the development of clinical work with a wide range of therapeutic needs.

This approach allows us to expand the parents' understanding of pre-verbal and play language in the context of their relationship and to enlarge parental perceptions of the actual, observed child and of themselves as parents. This may, within a few sessions, foster attunement between parents and children with possible remission of behaviour disorders. In these meetings, emergent issues may be dealt with sufficiently and not require further individual psychotherapy as in the first case presented.

However, with severely disturbed young children and their families, as we have seen in the second case, the Therapeutic Interventions with Parents and Small Children may be an alternative to premature referrals to intensive treatment, which parents may find difficult to take up unless some work can be done with them and the child together. In this setting, through containment by the therapist who facilitates contact within the family, split-off parts of the parents' minds may be reintegrated with their perception of the child. While it does not always stop severe symptoms, the Therapeutic Interventions with Parents and Small Children can, in cases of more pronounced disturbances, foster healthier developments and allow more sustainable treatments to take place.

We hope to have shown here the connection between the observation of behaviours and their meaning as expressions of unconscious content, as a mode of communication, claiming for integration, and representation. We have emphasized the relevance of understanding transference and countertransference as resources to inform our interventions, even when we do not interpret directly.

With Pedro, Tony, and their respective parents, we hope to have made clear how the therapeutic tools (inspired and developed within the tradition of psychoanalytic observation, and their clinical applications), can be useful for children and families with various degrees of needs and individual searches for psychic integration.

We would like to thank Mariza Leita Da Costa for her careful review of this paper. We are also grateful to her and to Maria Pozzi for their useful suggestions.

References and Further Bibliography

Alvarez, A. (1992). *Live Company: Psychoanalytic Psychotherapy with Autistic, Borderline, Deprived, and Abused Children*. London & New York: Tavistock & Routledge.

Alvarez, A, & Reid, S. (1999). *Autism and Personality—Findings from the Tavistock Autism Workshop*. London: Routledge.

Bick, E. (1963). Notes on infant observation in psychoanalytic training. In: M. H. Williams (Ed.), *Collected Papers of Martha Harris and Esther Bick*. Perthshire: Clunie Press. Rolland Harris Education Trust, 1987.

Bion, W. R. (1961). *Experiences in Groups, Volumes 1–4, Human Relations, 1948–51*. London: Tavistock Publications.

Bion, W. R. (1962a). *Learning from Experience*. London: Karnac Books.

Bion, W. R. (1962b). A theory of thinking. *International Journal of Psychoanalysis*, 43(4/5). [*Second Thoughts: Selected Papers on Psycho-Analysis*. London: Heinemann, 1967.]

Lebovici, S., & Stoleru, S. (1983). *La Mère, le Nourisson et le Psychanalyste, Les Interactions Prècoces*. Paris: Le Centurion.

Mélega, M. P. (1987). Observação da relação mãe-bebê-instrumento de ensino em. .psicanálise. *Revista Brasileira de Psicanálise*, 21: 309.

Mélega, M. P. (1990). *L'osservatore Psicoanalítica come Contenitore della Funzione Maternal-Movimenti del Transfert e del Controtransfert*. Naples: Interazioni Terapeutiche Contesti, Instituto Italiano per gli Studi Filosofici.

Mélega, M. P. (1992). Application of psychoanalytical concepts to work in nonclinical contexts. *Publicações Científicas do CEPSI-MBF*, 3: 77–81.

Mélega, M. P. (1998). Intervenções terapêuticas conjuntas pais-filhos. *Alter: Jornal de Estudos Psicodinâmicos, Brasília*, 17/2.

Mélega, M. P. (2002). Generating meanings in the parent-children work. *Revista Brasileira de Psicanálise*, 36/3: 531–540.

Mélega, M. P., & Palmigiani, M, G. (1992). The psychoanalytic observer in the paediatric assessment. *Publicações Científicas do CEPSI-MBF*, 3: 109–121.

Meltzer, D., & Harris, M. (1986). Chapter XIV. In: D. Meltzer (Ed.), *Studies in Extended Metapsychology. Clinical Applications of Bion's Ideas*. Perthshire: Clunie Press.

Mendes de Almeida Pinheiro, M. (1993). *A Clinical Study of Early Feeding Difficulties: Risk and Resilience in Early Mismatches Within Parent-Infant Relationships*. M. A. Thesis in Psychoanalytical Observational Studies. Tavistock Clinic Paper.

Mendes de Almeida, M. (2002). Infant observation and its developments: repercussions within the work with severely disturbed children, paper presented at the 6th International Congress on Infant Observation, Krakow, Poland.

Mendes de Almeida, M., Marconato, M. M., & Pereira da Silva, M. C. (2004). Clusters of meaning: live evidence within clinical interventions with young children and their families. *Revista Brasileira de Psicanálise*, 38/3: 637–648.

Pozzi, M. (2003). *Psychic Hooks and Bolts. Psychoanalytic Work with Children under Five and their Families*. Karnac: London and New York.

Reid, S. (1997). Introduction: psychoanalytic infant observation. In: S. Reid (Ed.), *Developments in Infant Observation—The Tavistock Model*. London: Routledge.

Tuckett, D. (1994). Developing a grounded hypothesis to understand a clinical process: the role of conceptualisation in validation. *International Journal of Psychoanalysis*, 75: 1159–1180.

CHAPTER THREE

Multidisciplinary early intervention with infants and young children presenting emotional, physical, and speech difficulties

C. Bernasconi, D. Gilardoni, M.E. Pozzi, and M.L. Terragni
Associazione Zero-Cinque (Zero-Five's Centre), Vacallo, Italy-Switzerland

Introduction

This chapter owes its existence to some of the members of the workshop entitled "Zero to Five". This is part of the Italian-Swiss Association "Zero-Cinque". A small group of Swiss and Italian professionals from various disciplines, working with infants, small children, and their families, gathered together several years ago to address their growing concern regarding the age group neonate to five years old. Psychopathology among infants and young children was increasing in an alarming way; families and professionals were respectively, needing help, and needing to know more about this age group and what to offer these families in trouble. A monthly multidisciplinary workshop "Zero to Five" was then set up, led by Pagliarani and Pozzi, a child and adult psychoanalyst and psychotherapist respectively. They met to discuss worrying situations encountered by the multi-professional members, and to read about and to deepen their understanding of early infancy and parenthood. Amongst the participants there were child psychiatrists and paediatricians, child psychologists and psychotherapists, occupational, speech and language therapists, nursery teachers, and paediatric nurses. All the participants, as well as having years of experience in their respective professional fields with children, had undertaken infant observation based on Esther Bick's methodology, as well as individual psychotherapy or psychoanalysis. In October 2004 the Associazione Insubrica Zerocinque (the Zero-Five's Centre for Insubria) was legally founded in Vacallo, in the Canton Ticino, where the workshop had been taking place. This offered a more formalized structure for training professionals in counselling infants, small children, and their families. (Insubria is an Italian-Swiss region that includes the Italian cities of Como, Varese, Lugano, and the Swiss Canton Ticino.)

The Centre trains counsellors and psychotherapists, who then offer, in their respective work places, brief psychoanalytically informed psychotherapy to parents, infants, and young children. The training offered is rooted in the Tavistock Under-Five's counselling model, which originated in the early 1980s in London. It has broadened out to include not only psychoanalytic, classical Freudian and object relations theory, but also attachment theory, as well as ideas from family therapy, child development, and neuropsychology. As well as training and research, the Centre also undertakes translations of psychoanalytic literature. Recently, a collection of papers was translated from English and French into Italian by some of the workshop members. This will enable the public to benefit from reading some psychoanalytic literature that is not yet published in Italian. As a result of the expansion of the Centre and of its training programme, an exciting liaison has been forged with the maternity ward of a local hospital in Canton Ticino, and a new protocol has been agreed and set in place. Accordingly, there will be only one main key-worker for each mother and baby and no longer a turnover of many, nameless workers. This has fostered a close monitoring and tracking of severe pre-birth states of anxiety and post-natal depression. The project includes auditing this new protocol.

This chapter is the product of a joint collaboration consisting of two interesting pieces of work, which appear innovative since both of them approach severe problems in early infancy via a community-based psychotherapeutic input. This goes beyond the traditional model of parent-infant psychotherapy as it is often practised in child, adolescent, and family psychiatric clinics or hospital departments. The first case describes an infant presenting with severe pre-autistic floppiness, refusal to feed, and absence of response to stimulation soon after birth. This was treated by close liaison between the hospital perinatal paediatrician and the community child neuropsychiatrist and her home-visiting team. The second child, aged four, was treated by the community speech and language therapist in joint mother-child sessions. It is unusual for a speech therapist to work jointly with mother and child and to have specialist supervision with a child psychotherapist, which fosters an understanding of the parent-child relationship and projections. These sessions allowed this child to separate safely from his mother and to resolve his early difficulties with eating solids and speaking.

Baby Andrea's story

BACKGROUND

In this work we want to show the importance and the meaning of multidisciplinary and early intervention in the case of a child presenting with serious physical symptoms at birth.

It was possible to realize all this through the close cooperation developed between the neonatal pathology ward of a city hospital in a northern Italian town, and the community infant psychiatry team. The team offers specialized advice required particularly for infants in the intensive therapy unit, and it carries out supportive interventions with parents regarding the neurological and psychomotor development of their babies. The infant neuropsychiatrist is concerned with the prevention programme, and, in close cooperation with neonatologists, plans a series of controls coinciding with the most crucial phases of the child's development.

The hospital neuropsychiatrist and her colleagues on this case have completed the training in both infant observation according to E. Bick's method and in parent-infant and the Under-Five's psychotherapy inspired by the Tavistock model.

In the case we are presenting, we have been able to identify a situation of serious psychopathological risk dating from the first days of the infant's life. We carried out a prompt intervention programme with home support from a paediatric nurse, who worked with this infant from the first to the eighth month of his life. She visited weekly or twice weekly when the situation seemed particularly serious. The infant neuropsychiatrist proposed family psychotherapy when problems in the parental couple emerged during the home visits, at a time when the infant was six months old. It lasted until he was over thirteen months old. A significant improvement took place after only a few sessions of family work and, although the latter had been indispensable for the resolution of the symptoms, it only represented the last step of a treatment, which, without the previous home interventions, would not have been possible.

Early history and family issues

Andrea was the only and much-wanted child of parents Anna and Luca, both thirty years old and married for about two years. One year into her marriage, Andrea's mother suffered from depression and was treated pharmacologically. The depression had been triggered by tension between her husband and her family. Both parents come from southern Italy and had suffered from intergenerational, unresolved bereavements and losses due to family dislocation and migration to the north of Italy.

Andrea was born by natural delivery two weeks late, after a threatened miscarriage at six week's gestation. Mother stopped working and rested until the end of the pregnancy, despite her gynaecologist's advice to lead an ordinary life. This extended bed rest may be evidence that the mother wanted to counteract an unconscious wish to expel her foetus. This is in line with both Soulè's theory on the psychosomatic origin of abortions during the first weeks of pregnancy as well as the theories by Giannotti, Lanza, and Del Pidio (1994) and Piontelli (1992) whereby the foetus is believed to be strongly influenced by the pathobiology of the parental couple and of mother in particular.

Soon after Andrea's birth a condition of diffused hypotonicity associated with hyporeactivity was noticed. The child was hospitalized in the neonatal pathology ward, where he was immediately seen by the infant neuropsychiatrist. She did not find any sign of damage to the central nervous system, but suggested a series of medical and neurological tests in order to exclude possible congenital or genetic pathologies.

During the sixth session of family psychotherapy, when Andrea was thirteen months old, his parents remembered his first days of life: "At the hospital they told us, and we could see for ourselves, that the child was totally apathetic. He took any position he was put in, passively, without reacting. Even his limbs never moved and he looked as if he had no perception of any kind of pain. He slept and slept and did not eat."

All the tests being negative, the hypothesis of an organic pathology was excluded. However, mother's extreme anxiety and feeling of physical exhaustion were such that she experienced episodes of loss of consciousness and she declared that she got into panic attacks just at the thought of being alone with her child. The child's condition improved a little by the ninth day and he was discharged from the hospital, even though his hypotonicity had not gone completely. Further medical checks were planned by the hospital infant neuropsychiatrist. However, since mother's psychic symptomatology persisted, she was referred to an adult psychiatrist for any necessary medication. Home-visits by a community paediatric nurse, specializing in infant neuropsychiatry, were planned.

The first home-visits by the paediatric nurse

The first home-visit took place when Andrea was one month old and Norma, the paediatric nurse, soon realized that Andrea was not present in his mother's mind. Norma found herself concentrating totally on the mother (whom I have called Anna), because of her intense anxieties. Norma's notes read: "Mother starts talking about herself, her sensation of void, the difficulties she finds in reordering her ideas even for very easy things, the confusion which takes her to panic attacks with the anxiety pervading her and preventing her from moving." The intensity of Anna's aggressive feelings and her anxiety that these feelings could be picked up was quite evident. Anna told Norma that she felt like "a female wolf with her cub, which had to protect the cub from everybody". She spoke about "a strange sensation of not having sufficient grip in my hands, I often perceive a persisting pain in my fingers" and added immediately, "All this makes me feel guilty of not being a good mother." During this visit it became apparent that Andrea's mother was likely to have transferred her aggressiveness and destructiveness onto the outside world, and therefore felt she had to protect her child from everybody, and indeed, from her own aggression, by developing a motor deficiency, which might prevent her from acting out this aggression.

ANDREA'S MOTHER'S RELATIONSHIP TO HER OWN MOTHER

Twelve days later, Anna called Norma saying that she was desperate and needed somebody's help immediately—she was alone at home and she did not feel well. The nurse was able to visit her promptly, almost "on demand", and when she arrived at the house, Anna's mother was there. She had gone to help her for the first time since Andrea's birth. The nurse wrote in her notes: "Andrea's mother is frightened by a feeling of numbness in some parts of her body and her movements seem slower. Then she starts talking about her delivery experience and she bursts into tears, she relives those endless moments full of grief, of not being able to push owing to her shortened uterus, which did not expand sufficiently." This session seems to have taken Anna to be born again as a daughter faced with her mother and as a mother faced with her own child (Racamier & Taccani 1986) and it activated that process of overcoming what we have called "evolutionary bereavement" connected to her "pregnancy crisis". The "shortened uterus" seemed to represent a limited internal space even in the maternal uterus and Norma, during this session, was seen almost like a midwife called out for emergency when the delivery was very close.

During the following session, the nurse wrote down: "The conditions of Andrea's mother are improving little by little, the medication prescribed by the psychiatrist makes her sleep better and her mother's presence helps her to control her extreme anxiety."

THE RELATIONSHIP BETWEEN ANDREA'S MOTHER AND HER OWN FATHER

The old conflicts Anna had in the past with her own father seemed to have created what Cramer and Palacio Espansa call "the parental conflict" (1993). Anna, in fact, identified herself with her child, who became the carrier of her infantile claims but, from time to time, she also identified him with her father, as it later emerged in the therapeutic sessions with the family. However, before that, during the fifth home-visit, when Andrea was nearly two months old, Norma wrote: "Anna, with tears in her eyes, relives a memory of her infancy where her father, after arguing with her mother, beat her up. 'I can see him while he takes my mother's head with both hands and bangs it against the wall.' She would have liked to stop him but, petrified, she could not move, she just went on watching them."

Andrea's mother felt almost petrified after the delivery and presented motor difficulties that were so disabling that she was unable to hold a knife, fork, or spoon to eat, as Norma had noted. Andrea's birth brought about a state of paralysis in mother, akin to the one she felt when, as a child, she witnessed her father's violence towards her mother. Curiously, her own child was also inhibited and totally paralysed by a terrified mother. They seemed stuck together. This aroused a great interest within our workshop, especially in the fact that she remembered her father banging her mother's head against the wall, and that Andrea developed hypotonicity in correspondence with the cervical region of the trunk. It was as if, in Anna's mind, her father's violence had been reproduced by her traumatic experience of childbirth. Alternatively, she saw her father in her child and was unconsciously gripped by terror.

Andrea's development, eczema, and hyperactivity

By the time Andrea was four months old, the infant neuropsychiatrist observed (during the hospital follow-up), that his muscular tonicity was completely normal. By six months he was able to keep a sitting position autonomously. At nearly seven months he crawled normally and at eight months he stood up with help. However, during the twenty-seventh home-session, when Andrea was four-and-a-half months old, Norma noticed that: "Andrea looks so precocious in his development that his mother, describing him as "wild", urges him to keep quiet." At this time he became hyperactive and developed a serious skin symptomatology of allergic nature. He seemed to feel endangered when his mother held him. He defended himself from primitive anxieties, such as disintegration and fragmentation, by muscular hypermotility, i.e. by a "second skin" type of defence (Bick 1968; Kreisler, Fain, & Soulé 1974) as he resorted to frail muscular independence in the absence of an established inner object.

Conflict within the couple

Marital issues emerged quite clearly from the very beginning of their baby's life. During the fourth home-session when Andrea was one month old, Norma wrote: "Andrea's mother talks to me about a discussion she had the day before with her husband Luca, who confessed to her he did not wish to stay close to her any longer." Later in the same session: "The day she was discharged from hospital Anna and her husband argued so much that she fainted in the lift." During the following session it was recorded: "Andrea's mother talks to me about the lack of sexual activity in the couple, which was interrupted when the problem of a possible miscarriage arose and this withdrawal continued up to the baby's birth for fear of damaging the foetus. When they got home after the birth, the sexual problems came up again. It was very difficult for both of them to think of a prospective renewal of their sexual intercourse."

Sexual intercourse was regarded as dangerous rather than pleasant and reparative, and this seems to originate from Anna's relationship with her father. Luca's jealousy towards his baby appeared during the fifteenth home visit, when Andrea was three months old. "The night before, Luca suddenly woke up his wife complaining of feeling lonely and neglected". These words, reported by Anna, lead the discussion group to reflect on the fact that it was almost impossible for her to keep triangularity in mind and only duality was possible for her. On another occasion Anna said: "It is very difficult to tolerate sharing the house with my husband, and I am thinking of living in a different place, even in a community where I can live quietly at last with Andrea." When Andrea was five months old, Norma wrote: "Andrea's mother talks to me about her husband in a worried way: 'He frightens me, he says strange things with reference to my mother whom he considers responsible for our problems, the same situation which was experienced by my mother-in-law with her parents is now repeating again. My father-in-law showed so strong an aversion to his wife's mother that his wife was obliged to break off her relations with her mother.'" She referred here to the real experience of her husband's father who had wanted to break any contact between his wife and the maternal grandmother.

Luca seemed to be identified with his father when later on he, too, pushed his wife to stop seeing her mother. The couple's relationship and conflicts seemed to highlight intergenerational, unresolved conflicts, which were passed on to the next generation of Andrea's parents.

These problems were discussed when Norma presented this family to the workshop and expressed her deep feelings of frustration, impotence, and solitude. At this point it was felt necessary to offer parent-child psychotherapy at the local child and adolescent mental health service.

The work with the family

In the first family therapy session (when Andrea was six months old), Anna came to understand how her baby's crying conjured up "ghosts" (Fraiberg, Adelson, & Shapiro 1975) from her past. After communicating that everything was improving, with her usual smiling, calm, and relaxed expression, Anna said to the infant neuropsychiatrist: "I can't really stand Andrea when he starts crying, because he looks at me and I feel so frightened that I am in a sweat." When invited to link Andrea's crying with some memory or circumstance in her past or present, Anna was able to express, at once, that in her mind, Andrea was identified with her own father. She said: "I feel the same sensations I felt when I was a child and my father raised his voice and scolded me or argued with my mother." That session helped Anna to start working through her own past, which brought about an improvement in the relationship with her child. He was, almost "by magic", set free from those feelings of rage, fear, and anxiety, which were linked to his mother's difficulties and were massively projected onto him.

Two weeks later, in the second family therapy session, Anna told the infant neuropsychiatrist: "I think I'm really better because I am not so afraid when I hear Andrea's crying now." However, Anna's usual expression of well being hid a serious, conflictual relationship in the couple, which emerged during the next home visits. It seemed that the ghosts of Andrea's father's past came out at the same time as the mother's ghosts. Both parents were actually present and able to express their deep crisis, due to the feelings of resentment and jealousy Luca felt towards Anna's parents, particularly his father-in-law. Anna said: "My life has become a living hell because, as soon as I wake up, my husband stares at me as if I'm hiding something from him."

During the third session (which took place a week later), Anna talked with the infant neuropsychiatrist about a sense of well being: "I feel much better because I understand that I am not well only because of my fears and nothing else." Luca affirmed that the state of uneasiness in which they were living as a couple was caused by his wife's parents. He thought they had been extremely intrusive and possessive and were unable to understand Anna's needs for autonomy and emancipation. The infant neuropsychiatrist reflected on intergenerational causes, which might have determined Anna's parents' difficulties in accepting her as an adult and in her choice of husband. This touched Anna and propelled her to reach a position of greater maturity, separation, and differentiation from her parents. Luca had later admitted that they had modified their relationship with Anna's side of the family: "We feel better with our child because we have started thinking of him, unlike beforehand, when all our thoughts were totally taken up by the problems with my parents-in-law."

The parents' ability to recover a mental space for their child, who had been the receptacle of maternal projections even before he was born, lead to developmental improvement in Andrea who, even during the sessions, was able to find a space for himself, and in his relationship with his mother. For example, when Andrea was nearly nine months old, he entered the therapy room smiling, then crawled to the window, looked at the infant neuropsychiatrist, smiled again, stood up and walked to fetch a toy cup. He offered it to his mother, pretending to feed her in what was, indeed, age-appropriate play.

During the fourth therapy session (when Andrea was seven-and-a-half-months old), the infant neuropsychiatrist observed that Andrea's psychomotor development was absolutely adequate and normal. Mother sat beside him on the carpet and gave him her attention and at the same time interacted with the infant neuropsychiatrist. Anna also reported that he had started crying when she left him for a brief time and on her return he would cling to her and even refuse his father. Mother could not believe, she said, that she was so important to him. His eczema seemed to have gone, his skin was clear and he no longer needed creams. However, Anna reported that his skin flared up again when he was with maternal aunt.

In the fifth session (when Andrea was eight months old), Andrea's mother mentioned having started to work again, and she wondered why Andrea was missing her so much. She said: "I can't really understand why, when I come back from work, Andrea is always looking for me, he is always next to me and I am not able to separate him from me; if somebody else tries to distract him, he starts crying and he calms down only when I hold him in my arms." From this comment we could see that Andrea was showing ordinary and age appropriate separation anxieties vis-à-vis his mother.

Partial improvement

The intense anxiety and paralysing fear, which had prevented Anna from staying at home alone with her baby, progressively disappeared, and since attending family therapy sessions, she gradually reduced her antidepressant intake until stopping altogether. It is hard to know whether the progress, which was noticed in both Andrea and his mother, also occurred in Andrea's father, whose defensive structure seemed less permeable and modifiable than his wife's. He maintained a position of open hostility towards the maternal grandparents, particularly towards his father-in-law. Such hostility led to a total interruption of the relationship between Anna and her own parents. Despite having improved in the greater attention he was able to give his child, Luca still reproduced some childhood scenario, where his father had cut off connections from his wife's family. This was something, which, in the long run, would not bode well for mental health in this family, especially in view of the premature ending of the therapy. The problems at an intergenerational level were still very entrenched and would have benefited from more therapeutic work, had the parents been able to do so. However due to changes in their working timetable this was not viable and therapy had to be interrupted.

The paediatric nurse's function

The paediatric nurse, thanks to her training in infant observation according to Bick's method and in the Under-Five's counselling model, was particularly appropriate in offering Andrea's mother a non-intrusive experience of "good" mothering. She mainly performed a function of "containment", in Bion's terms, of mother's mental states, by her own psychic availability, and by listening to and participating in Anna's accounts. She contained Anna's dismay, doubts, and anxiety without passing judgement. On her part, Anna felt accepted and understood, and therefore was able to communicate her painful and burdensome life experiences, which had been unthinkable until then. Anna's crying while speaking about Andrea's childbirth took her back to her own birth, and allowed her to "discover" her baby for the first time. When Andrea was about two months old the nurse noted: "Mother seems to acquire a certain physical strength, she says she 'feels an inner strength', she opens up, she trusts other people, she says she has the impression of finding again the 'gentleness' her painful childbirth experience had completely cancelled." And during the same session: "We are walking in the street and Anna smiles at the people we meet, it is as if she has gone out for the first time after Andrea's birth. She looks at him, from time to time, and when she meets people she knows she asks them: "Do you want to see my child?"

During one of the last sessions the nurse noted: "she talks to me of a good Andrea who communicates with her and tries to grasp her nose, eyes, and hair." Andrea's mother said to the nurse during the seventeenth home visit: "When I am with you, I can express myself, I have a chance to get rid of a 'heavy weight', I need to express my pain and you make me feel understood."

The empathetic relationship with the nurse offered the possibility of support and facilitation of the mother's resources and strength, and a new maternal model of identification for mother. This also prepared the ground and fostered in both parents the awareness of a need for more help, which they accepted and became actively involved in the therapeutic alliance with the neonatal psychiatrist at the clinic. Furthermore, through the home sessions Anna was able to relive her childbirth experience, which had led to painful separation from her mother and to remember the experience with her father. This helped her to differentiate the past from the present, and to withdraw her projections from Andrea, projections which had clouded her seeing him as a baby in his own skin. It is quite clear that it would not have been possible to obtain these results with only five therapy sessions without the preparatory work carried through in the earlier home visits.

Conclusions

This infant presented with problems that could be classified as disorders of regulation (Greenspan 1992) and psychosomatic disorders (Kreisler, Fain, & Soulé 1974). However, on closer examination, they were the consequence of the relationship with the mother, whose past "ghosts" (Freiberg, Adelson, & Shapiro 1975), entangled with the father's ghosts, were affecting both the mother-baby relationship and the marital relationship. We could explore the intergenerational line of family dysfunctions going back to both sets of grandparents. Anna had once said that, when Andrea cried, she had felt frightened and sweated just as she had when she was little and her father used to raise his voice to scold her or to argue with her mother. Whether she was identified with the crying and frightened infant of her childhood or whether she saw her father in her baby, it was not possible to disentangle at this point.

However, Andrea had become a strong and active child, permeable to changes, following the changes in his parents who, thanks to the therapeutic work, have been able to recognize his needs, his demands, and understand his problems. We trust that the child's own resources and the love that linked him to his parents could somewhat protect him from the incursion of hostile and unwelcome visitors, despite the interruption of the therapeutic work at a point when some intergenerational difficulties were still lingering. With the therapeutic work and help we have offered both at the family's home and at the clinic, we felt that Andrea's parents were no longer powerless against the "evil ghosts" of their past and were more able to throw them into their "underworld".

Separation difficulties and language problems in four-year-old Giacomo

The second vignette in this chapter is the account of a piece of work by a speech and language therapist with Giacomo, aged four years and three months, and with his mother. Giacomo was the first child of a very young couple and was referred by both the paediatrician and the infant school teacher. His language development was severely delayed, idiosyncratic, "private", and incomprehensible. At nursery he was not interested in taking part in social or physical activities, and was clumsy. He daydreamed and, when spoken to, avoided eye contact. Due to his parents' work commitments, his maternal grandparents had been his main carers during his first two years of life. He was a delicate child who was often ill, easily fell down, and bruised himself badly. Because of his eating difficulties he attended his infant school only part-time. On some days he only drank milk from a bottle and was still in nappies. He appeared passive, uninterested in the outside world, and screeched when annoyed with something. His parents refused to see the educational psychologists suggested by both his nursery school and the paediatrician, but accepted a referral to the speech and language therapist, perhaps feeling less threatened.

When we first met, Giacomo stayed glued to his mother and did not look at me. His mother seemed very anxious and keen, stating that she could not wait for this speech therapy for Giacomo to start. However she was unhappy about the time offered and the distance they had to cover to come to my community-based office. Neither argument had much objective reality but showed me her ambivalence and resistance. I suggested she could stay with Giacomo, if that helped her and him and invited them into my office where I indicated that they might find something to play together, if they wished to do so.

Giacomo chose a construction activity and they did it together while I listened to mother's accounts and noticed her anxieties, which I decided not to verbalize. I only described what they were playing at. At the end of the session Giacomo picked up a bridge from the toy box provided and placed it between them and me. I said—with emphatic pleasure—that by him giving me that bridge he might be giving me a chance to meet him and get to know him. I added that bridges allow people to meet and then to go away and separate. He looked at me for the first time since he had entered the room.

After this session I found myself reflecting on how important it seemed to be not to rush mother to leave Giacomo alone with me. A precipitous separation could have either impeded the work or be seen as a denial of their separation difficulties, which were very present in that first encounter. If Giacomo were made to separate before he and his mother were ready, he may have transferred his difficulty on to me, and then couple up with me closely like he did with his mother, before growing inside himself a capacity to separate and bear triangularity in his relationships. I could pose myself as the third person, as a logo-father figure, who helped them to separate, rather than as another maternal figure whom he could couple with, and then perpetuate his original difficulty. I was quite convinced that the third person was, thus far, felt by both mother and son as an unwelcome intruder, who wanted to un-stick their couple.

During the first phase of this therapy, I noticed that mother was very anxious and showed it by asking many questions about the session and what happened there as well as about her child, his language development, his behaviour etc. She tended to criticize all he did and kept asking him to perform new tasks without being able to contact him emotionally. It was as though they were either fused together or wrenched apart painfully.

Our three-way sessions usually had the following pattern: I observed mother and son interacting and playing together. Giacomo initiated play activities and mother followed him. I made descriptive or interpretative comments on what happened in their play. I also answered mother's questions aiming at reassuring her. For example, she felt concerned about the repetitiveness of Giacomo's play in our sessions and how that affected his learning. I replied that children needed to repeat drawings, games, plays, stories, etc. to gain a sense of comfort and security in the "known" and also to master their abilities and competences. Only then could they move on safely. She was also anxious and questioned me about Giacomo's language delay and baby-like behaviour of which she was well aware. I did not deny the current difficulties but also showed her the minute changes in Giacomo's play and in their relationship. In doing so, I rebalanced her hopeless and negative attitude towards him and kept alive for her his positive evolution, which was noticeable. At times it was a hard task, since mother fed back negative comments made by the paediatrician and the nursery class teacher.

I noticed that, with time, drawing was something Giacomo enjoyed and preferred over other modalities of expression. He seemed to feel safer when drawing. His drawings gave me an insight into his world, which he was not otherwise able to express. For example he often drew a mum, a dad, and a little spider; he coloured and cut out the first two but did not do this with the little spider, which was still stuck and imprisoned inside the paper spider-web. I talked about how difficult it was for the little spider to be born and to come out of the paper/spider web. I added that mum, too, had difficulty in letting her little child come out because she was still unsure about him not playing, drawing, and speaking the way she would like him to, i.e. to be more in line with other children.

Gradually Giacomo's mother welcomed my ideas and showed a different interest in him; she was more accepting and less critical of him. She also began to notice small changes in him. It seemed that, by identifying with me, she was beginning to internalize a different attitude to him. Things seemed to change even at home as I gathered from mother's accounts of what they did or how they interacted together outside our sessions. For example, she bought him some reading books similar to the one we had in therapy as she had noticed how much he enjoyed them. At home she started reading them to him. Visits to the children's park started and she felt more confident about him and less bogged down by negative comments about him. I was very supportive and encouraging of her thoughts, efforts, and successes on their path.

For his part, Giacomo brought some symbolic play like the one with the bridge, which he had already started in the first session. Something which he loved doing was to place his toy bridge between our two wooden houses. However every time I made a toy doll cross the bridge and knock on his house door he refused it access, shaking his head and shutting the door. I did not insist but said that I had to wait outside until he was ready to meet and welcome in the doll, i.e. me. One day, after many dramatizations, and a long wait on my part, he held my arm and showed me that there was a little man waiting outside his house, with the door open ready to let my doll inside. This felt like a real breakthrough.

After the summer break, Giacomo looked more grown-up and more robust. He smiled at me and allowed his mother to go without any resistance. In the session he was more able to communicate with me, even in words! In fact his language had evolved greatly and it was more and more comprehensible. The tone of his voice was stronger, more secure, and far less babyish. He listened and seemed interested when I addressed his speech and gave him exercises. He listened and took in what I had to say without withdrawing and avoiding me as before. He even helped me understand him by using different expressions, when he still struggled with some words. Alternatively he mimicked what he wanted now to communicate. His creativity and initiative in proposing new play activity also increased. His mother, too, continued being supportive, less anxious, and more hopeful. She had become a real ally and I noticed how much she had changed from her original suspiciousness and ambivalence.

In the third year of therapy his language had reached standard skills and he was able to write and read whatever I proposed to him. At school he was fitting in with the class programme, with other children and ate most food with no difficulties. All other symptoms in the area of toilet training and sleep difficulties had gone and Giacomo was, at last, an ordinary, healthy, and robust child comparable to other children of his age, much to his mother's great delight.

What seems to have contributed to this almost unbelievable progress was the slow and patient work with Giacomo and his mother seen together, which was a different modality from more traditional language therapy. Through the joint work with mother and child, mother managed to relax and establish a trusting relationship with the speech therapist; to accept her suggestions, interpretations and reassurances. Mother could identify with someone—the therapist—who related to her child as a separate individual with an inner life and abilities in his own rights. This process lead to a gradual and bearable separation between mother and child and to a healthy individuation of Giacomo. All his developmental milestones, previously delayed, were back on the age-appropriate path.

This therapy seems to have helped mother by containing her anxiety and negative outlook on Giacomo, which enabled her to rediscover her maternal capacities, and to contain the big effect on her of the negative and worrying views, albeit correct, of the paediatrician and the nursery-school teacher. The latter had paralysed her maternal ability and increased her anxiety and sense of failure about herself as a mother and about Giacomo. The family level of anxiety and despair was so intense that they had refused the referral to a more obvious psychological service. This may have pathologized the child even more and left the parents in deeper despair. In view of the severity of Giacomo's generalized developmental delay, it was of great value to this family to have met a language therapist with training in observational skills and understanding of unconscious processes in children and adults. This indeed steered this child and family away from more serious psychological and mental health disorders.

References

Bick, E. (1964). Notes on infant observation in psychoanalytic training. *International Journal of Psychoanalysis*, 45: 558–566.

Bick, E. (1968). The experience of the skin in early object-relations. *Journal of Psychoanalysis*, 49/2: 484–486.

Bibring, G. L. (1959). Some considerations of the psychological process in pregnancy. *Psychoanalytical Study of the Child*, 14: 113–121.

Bion, W. (1962). *Learning from Experience*. London: Heinemann.

Cramer, B., & Palacio-Espansa, F. (1993). *La Pratique des Psychothérapies Brèves Mères-Bébés. Etudes Cliniques et Techniques*. Paris: PUF.

Fraiberg, S., Adelson, E., & Shapiro, V. (1975). Ghosts in the nursery: a psychoanalytic approach to the problems of impaired infant-mother relationships. *Journal of the American Academy of Child Psychiatry*, 14: 387–421.

Giannotti, A., Lanza, A. M., & Del Pidio, F. (1994). Genesi della patologia psicosomatica, ipotesi sul ruolo svolto dalle fantasie inconsce. In: R. Negri (Ed.), *Il Neonato in Terapia Intensiva. Un Modello Neuropsicoanalitico di Prevenzione*, p. 122. Milan: Cortina, 1998.

Greenspan, S. I. (1992). *Regulatory Disorders. Infancy and Early Childhood: The Practice of Clinical Assessment and Intervention with Emotional and Developmental Challenges*. Madison, WI: International University Press.

Kreisler, L., Fain, M., & Soulé, M. (1974). *Il Bambino e il suo Corpo*. Rome: Astrolabio, 1976.

Miller, L. (1992). The relation of infant observation to clinical practice in an under five's counselling service. *Journal of Child Psychotherapy*, 18: 19–32.

Piontelli, A. (1992). *From Fetus to Child: An Observation and Psychoanalytic Study*. London: Routledge.

Racamier, P. C., & Taccani, S. (1986). *Il Lavoro Incerto. La Psicodinamica del Processo di Crisi*. C. Monari (Trans.). Tirrenia, Piza: Cerro. *That Uncertain Job. The Psychodynamics of the Crisis Process*.

Soulè, M., Houzel, D., & Bollaert, S. (1996). Les psychoses infantiles précoces et leur traitement. *La Psychiatrie de l'Enfant*, 19/2: 341–397.

CHAPTER FOUR

Brief mother-father-infant psychodynamic psychotherapy: clinical and technical aspects

Francisco Palacio-Espasa and Dora Knauer
Infant Psychiatric Clinic, Geneva

Introduction

Brief parent-infant psychotherapy is a short-term psychotherapeutic intervention method (Cramer 1974) targeting parents with their child. It has been employed in Geneva according to the technical principles described by Fraiberg (1980). This type of psychotherapeutic intervention was principally created for babies presenting functional symptoms (sleep or food disorders) or behavioral disorders (opposition, aggressiveness, hyperactivity, etc.). At the Infant Psychiatric Clinic, Geneva, the initial research on these psychotherapeutic processes was carried out by a psychoanalytically oriented psychotherapist. Mother-infant dyads were studied during three to ten weekly sessions. The therapist attempted to focus on the elements troubling the mother-infant interactions that were responsible for the appearance of the infant's symptoms. This interactive network was interpreted in relation to the mother's infantile experiences with her own parents and family. This therapeutic approach yielded quite positive results, not only at the level of the infant's symptoms, but also at the level of the mother-child interactions (Cramer et al. 1990; Robert-Tissot et al. 1996).

In 1993, we published the technical details of these brief psychotherapeutic interventions, the nature of the psychotherapeutic process and the importance of focusing on parents' fantasies concerning their child (Cramer & Palacio-Espasa 1993). At that time, we were able to understand how parents took possession of the representation of the unknown provided by their newborn through the projective identifications they passed on to their infant. These identifications were composed of the images issuing from their own parents and other significant people or from images of themselves and their childhood.

In this context, the term "projective identification" does not signify a pathological defense mechanism, but on the contrary, a fully operational mechanism for the development and the organization of the parent-child relationship. This mechanism facilitates the formation of the parents' empathy with the child's needs as well as their adaptation to his or her specific characteristics (Grotstein 1981). We will not make a distinction between the terms "projective identification" and "projection", which will both be employed as synonyms for the process through which parents tend to delegate elements of their psyche to their child. Although we are aware that subtle theoretical distinctions exist between these two psycho-analytical terms, these distinctions do not seem pertinent to the topic examined here.

Parental fantasies, comprised of images from their past that are passed on to their children, have been schematically divided into two categories: anaclitic fantasies and oedipal fantasies. The term "anaclitic" is employed in the sense of the Freudian object relation (Freud 1914), in contrast to a narcissistic object relation. Freud used the term "anaclitic" choice when the object was characterized by nurturing, care, and protection.

This same term was chosen by Spitz (1965) to describe the anaclitic depression that babies present when separated from their mother or from the maternal presence representing security, care, and protection. In this sense, we have demonstrated the contrast between parental anaclitic fantasies focusing on nurturing, caring for, and protecting their child and fantasies about their own oedipal, infantile sexuality, such as fantasies of incest, rivalry, and the authority of the superego. This distinction between parental fantasies may seem artificial, but it actually proves very useful in brief psychotherapeutic interventions since the parents much more easily accept and understand therapeutic interpretations based on anaclitic fantasies than interpretations based on oedipal conflicts that may arouse greater resistance.

While the research programme on brief mother-infant psychotherapy was under way, the father sometimes wished to participate in the sessions with the mother and infant. Of course, the therapist accepted and thereafter worked with this triad. Thus, we became interested in studying the specific characteristics of these brief psychodynamic psychotherapies carried out with the mother-father-infant triad. Many authors have developed parent-infant or parent-child psychotherapies (Lebovici 1995). Certain studies have specifically focused on treating the triad (Daws 1994). All of these works remark on the importance of the father's role as a third party, who can interfere with the emergence of fusion fantasies of the mother-infant dyad. From this point of view, these studies are in continuity with the ideas proposed by classic psychoanalytic literature. In addition to the notion of a third party, the father also fills another classical paternal function, that of "framing" or "protectively surrounding" the mother-infant dyad (Debray 1994). The father's position as a third party in relationship to the mother-infant dyad has even been considered as a guarantee of a "space for the thoughts and representations of the child" (Daws 1994).

We have emphasized that the "third party role" is not exclusively the privilege of the father. Both parents are equally capable of playing this role in relation to the fantasies of exclusive fusion of his/her spouse with the infant (Cramer & Palacio-Espasa 1993). This paper will also emphasize the clinical impression that the father's and mother's fantasy experiences with their infant are quite similar. Both present oedipal and anaclitic fantasies concerning the child that are related to the problems of separation and loss of the object. The narcissistic parental scenario including the infant corresponds to the defense mechanisms erected by the parents to cope with painful feelings stemming from their past experiences of loss (Manzano, Palacio-Espasa, & Zilkha, 1999).

However, the mother maintains closer biological ties with the child, developed during pregnancy, childbirth, and breast-feeding, that augment the intensity of her anaclitic fantasies. A mother-infant relationship of this type would impel the father to experience feelings of exclusion when faced with this "new" couple. At this point, the father more easily falls prey to oedipal fantasies stimulated by this situation in which the mother-infant relationship relegates him to the role of an outsider.

The contrast existing between the conviction with which various authors emphasize the father's importance in mother-infant psychotherapies and the difficulty with which these distinctive elements are demonstrated when the father is present during these treatments has led us to a more systematic review of our clinical practice.

For this reason, we have concentrated on the clinical and technical aspects of these cases, which were examined in great detail in our research on brief parent-infant psychotherapy treatments in which the father participated. Our theoretical and technical reflections will be represented through several illustrative clinical cases that demonstrate the types of difficulties encountered in these clinical situations.

Clinical and technical aspects

In our experience of joint parent-infant psychotherapy, the father takes part in the exchanges with the therapist in the same fashion as the mother. The father speaks just as often as the mother and the therapist do. The time accorded to each party is equally divided through the interventions of the therapist, who helps ensure that the mother, father, and therapist each have equal shares: one third of the time to each participant. The participation of the infant is mostly interactive with both parents and sometimes with the therapist when he or she is confident enough. He or she plays during the session particularly with the parents. When the child is older than fifteen to eighteen months, the play can be symbolic and the language of the child becomes more explicit as he or she relates to his parents. The parents take turns acting as the principle protagonist of the exchange in addressing the therapist. These phases alternate with triadic exchanges between the three partners. The symmetry of the two parents' participation in the joint psychotherapy is also apparent at the level of positive or negative affective expression and in the recall of past childhood experiences involving their own parents and close members of their family. The father invests in the process as much as the mother and brings new intimate aspects of his own psychic life to the therapy. This investment emerges as the result of the therapeutic alliance and facilitates the interpretive work of the therapist. The quantitative contribution of the number of statements made during the process is much larger in a joint treatment than in an individual psychotherapy. We will use a clinical example to illustrate the positive indications of brief parent-infant psychotherapy in a case where the therapist was able to formulate and interpret a common focus for both parents. The psychotherapeutic focus consists in indicating the current conflictual relationship between the parent and child in light of the parent's own childhood and the relationships maintained with key family members. Quite often, while using a common focus, the therapist interprets other subsidiary focuses that specifically apply to one parent or the other.

As we have previously described (Palacio-Espasa & Manzano 1982; Palacio-Espasa 1984), the work of interpretation in brief parent-infant psychotherapy is greatly facilitated by the "positive pre-transference" that the parents establish with the therapist. In this "positive pre-transference", developed by certain parents as an attitude of immediate receptiveness towards the psychotherapist, they project positive images of their own parents linked to libidinal investments.

Generally, this favorable disposition towards the therapist is found in parents who have maintained positive, loving relationships with their children, even if conflictual aspects experienced in the past may generate problems with their child, which then produce symptoms. This "positive pre-transference" leads to a rapid therapeutic alliance. The parents are receptive to the immediate, intense interpretative activity that the therapist exercises in joint psychotherapies. "Positive pre-transference" corresponds to one of the most important criteria indicating parent-infant therapy. However, the nature of this "pretransference" does not truly become apparent until the psychotherapeutic relation gets underway. Thus, it is quite difficult to evaluate before beginning the therapy.

We use the term "negative pre-transference" to designate the defensive attitude towards the therapist maintained by certain parents. This attitude is especially apparent in their resistance to understanding and interpreting their problems with their children in light of their own past. These parents consider the interpretative activity as an accusation and, in some cases of open paranoia, as real attacks. The attitude of these parents may be linked to their projection of negative parental images, coloured by accusing or aggressive characteristics, onto the therapist. Normally, these parents maintain similar negative projections concerning their own child, an element that contributes to the conflicts in the parent-child relationship.

The distinctive difficulty in the practice of psychotherapy with both parents and their infant consists in the fact that the parents can present different pre-transference valencies. For example, one parent might present a "positive pre-transference" and take a very active part in the psychotherapeutic process while the other parent presents "negative pre-transference" and rapidly develops a significant resistance to the therapist's exploration of his/her past. In this case scenario, the "negative pre-transference" of one of the two parents can be the cause of an abrupt rupture in the therapy if the therapist does not notice it at the beginning of the treatment. Thus, the therapist must carry out a therapeutic exploration while continuing to avoid problematic situations with the overly sensitive parent until s/he gains more confidence.

Sometimes, therapists may find themselves rapidly drawn into the middle of a conflict between the couple. Thus, the clinician may be perceived as the ally of one of the partners while becoming the other's accuser. This situation leads to the development of a "negative pre-transference" that is quite unbearable for the parent, who feels accused. In these circumstances, the exploration of parental conflicts becomes extremely difficult and the psychotherapeutic process fails. In other cases, accusing or aggressive conflictual parental images, at the origin of a "negative pre-transference" against the therapist, are first projected by one partner onto the other. At this point, these negative projections generate a torrent of mutual misunderstandings between the two parents and the therapist is drawn into the couple's conflict, to such an extent that he is blamed for it.

The relationship established in the parental conflict concerning the child frequently corresponds to the conjugal problems, leading us to examine the similarities that exist between the ties uniting the couple and those established between the parents and their child. Our hypothesis is that, when choosing a conjugal partner, each parent tends to transfer certain projective identifications onto the other. These narcissistic identifications are defensively erected against the projective identifications of an anaclitic nature similar to those that they transfer onto their child. They are often images of an ideal parent that the father or mother would have liked to have had during his/her childhood and images of the ideal child that the father or mother would have liked to have been. These identifications are often accompanied by complementary, corresponding identifications. The parent also simultaneously projects more sexualized images, from their oedipal infantile past, that are passed on to their partner and child (Kernberg 1991).

Over the course of the therapeutic process with the mother, father, and child, the therapist is confronted with a series of multiple parental projections, of narcissistic, anaclitic, and oedipal nature, that are attributed to their child and reciprocally to each partner. Pinpointing or elaborating these diverse fantasy projections is a necessary step in the effective practice of a brief therapeutic intervention that often proves difficult. Several clinical examples will be presented to illustrate the situations in which a brief, joint parent-infant psychotherapy is indicated and in which the therapist is able to formulate and interpret a "common interpretative focus" for both parents (examples one and two). We would also like to demonstrate how easy it is for a conflict between partners, which is not immediately taken into account, to provoke an intense resistance that can be the source of treatment discontinuation (examples three and four). The last example clearly illustrates a network of conflicts that may appear more discreet and hidden than in the preceding cases, but which required the continuation of treatment over a longer period of time.

Thus, the narcissistic parental images, erected in defence against the anaclitic images, notably those of an ideal parent and an ideal child, are combined with oedipal images into complex parental projections. Moreover, it is not rare to observe oedipal and anaclitic desires of one partner in contradiction with the oedipal tendencies of the other. This tends to create problems in the relationship between parents and children or within the couple itself.

In order to illustrate the principal technical and theoretical notions to which we refer, the first clinical example will be presented in detail with excerpts from the dialogue between the parents and therapist.

Clinical example 1—Antoine

Antoine is twenty-one-months old when his parents consult the Center for his problematic behavior and sleep disturbances.

Antoine attacks and bites other children, as well as adults, refuses to go to bed and presents tyrannical behavior, especially with his mother. From his birth, his mother saw in her child the image of her own father, whose affection she had always longed for.

First excerpt from the first session

Mother: When I saw him after giving birth, I saw the face of my uncle, i.e. my father's brother . . . he scared me . . . he had the same eyes as those in the family of my father . . . my uncle was a very aggressive man, but a very handsome man, very attractive (incestuous parental image).

Therapist: What sort of relationship do you have with your father?

Mother: He was often far away . . . I missed him a lot. When he was at home, he only paid attention to my mother, not to me, only to scold me . . .

Therapist: Is this the reason that you are not really surprised that your son is aggressive? Through him, you can find the close relationship that you always wanted with your father (interpretation emphasizing the anaclitic fantasy of losing the father, more than the incestuous fantasy concerning him).

Mother: Yes, I think so (crying, with clearly expressed emotions).

Moreover, Antoine's mother felt neglected by her own mother, to such an extent that she tried to be the ideally attentive mother for Antoine that she would have liked to have had herself.

Second excerpt from the first session

Therapist: How was your mother with you when you were a child?

Mother: She wasn't violent, but she wasn't really affectionate with her children, particularly with me, the third of her children. She was always preoccupied with my father. When I was an adolescent, I was very impressed by the closeness of their relationship.

Therapist: But as a child, did you suffer from the fact that your mother wasn't closer to you? (interpretation of the anaclitic fantasy of loss and nostalgia for the mother).

Mother: Oh, yes (crying again, emotional).
Therapist: Is this the reason that you are so attentive to your child and so tolerant towards him?
Mother: Quite probably.

Excerpt from the second session

In this session, the father is also present.

On his side, the father is also very tolerant with Antoine due to his experience as a child who was unwanted by his own mother and suffered from her authoritative attitude. He believes that his more aggressive, rebellious brother, although he was unwanted as well, had more easily escaped from the negative influence of his parents.

Therapist: What were you like as a child?
Father: In fact, my mother seemed to be getting ready for an ecclesiastic career, as a nun, very severe. She met my father and the children arrived afterwards. But we were neglected and rejected (anaclitic fantasy). My brother suffered more than I did, but he was very aggressive and he was finally more successful than I was. I felt that I was being crushed by my parents' severity.
Therapist: And you do not want to limit your son's aggressive behavior because you're afraid of crushing him as you yourself felt crushed in your family?
Father: Yes, I think so—he resembles my brother.
Therapist: You think that your brother was more successful than you because he was more aggressive than you?
Father: Yes.

The therapist's interpretations are centered on the "common focus" of both parents, that is to say their desire to be the ideally attentive and tolerant parents that they would have liked to have had. This allows them to find in their son the ideally cherished child they would have liked to have been. In Antoine's aggressive behavior, the mother finds the image of the father that she longed for, while the father could find the image of his brother, who had more successfully endured their family history.

The subject of a latent conjugal conflict was also broached. In fact, following Antoine's birth, the couple had become sexually distant. Occupied by a parental ideal that was too exclusive, the mother had completely devoted herself to her son. The father placed himself in a position of unconscious complicity with his wife in order to offer his son the ideally affectionate mother that he himself had lacked as a child. As a result of the interpretation of the parental problems and the resolution of their latent conjugal conflict, Antoine's behavior, as well as the harmony between the parents, improved remarkably following this brief treatment.

The projective parental identifications in the case illustrated above are concordant. However, this is not always the case; the identifications projected by the two parents onto their child sometimes prove to be complementary. In these cases, the therapist separately addresses his interpretations to each of the two parents, and elucidating their different fantasies towards the infant will not engender "negative pre-transference" onto the therapist. In other words, the brief psychotherapy becomes possible when the parents are capable of listening to their complementary projective identifications in a space of mutual understanding. Here, the presence of the father is a factor facilitating the psychotherapist's work since the two parents reciprocally help each other in the expression of their conflicts.

Clinical example 2—Robert

Robert is ten months old when his parents consult for sleep disturbances (he frequently wakes up at night and has great difficulty falling asleep).

It is very difficult for the mother to be firm with Robert, since she is afraid of becoming quick-tempered and capricious like her own mother was with her. After the elucidation of her problems in the first session, she has succeeded in modifying her attitude towards her child and in being firmer with him.

The father, who didn't come to the first session, presents conflicts that are similar to those of his wife: he feels that his mother was too demanding, leading him to adopt an excessively lenient attitude with his son. He runs to Robert at the slightest whimper during the night. During this second session, the interpretation of a "common focus" was not enough to allow the clinical situation to evolve. It was not until the following session that we learned that the father negatively experienced his wife's firmer attitude towards the child. In fact, he felt confronted with the image of his own demanding mother who also separated him from his father. This had led to an open conjugal conflict since his wife in turn felt that her husband was becoming, towards her, the quick-tempered mother of her childhood.

A "common" interpretation was found for both parents in the reciprocal projective identifications of a persecutory maternal object in the role of the superego. These identifications were the source of the conflicts in the couple. This interpretation made it possible to resolve this conflict and ease the child's symptomatology, since the parents now compel him to develop better sleep habits.

In reality, when the therapist succeeds in interpreting a "common interpretive focus" revealing either concordant or complementary conflicts in the two parents, we observe not only an improvement in the child's symptomatology and the interactions between the parents and their child, but also an easing of the tension in the couple's relationship.

However, the observation of a problem in the couple sometimes leads to the awakening of a "negative pre-transference" carrying with it the risk of a premature discontinuation of treatment.

Clinical example 3—Allan

Allan is fifteen months old when his parents come into the consultation for his sleep disturbances and problems in being separated from his mother. This situation especially perturbs the father, who instigated the request for consultation in our service. From the start, the distance between the partners in the couple is evident and they openly manifest a conjugal conflict. The mother, who admits her need to be very close to her child, does not consider her infant to be symptomatic and is suspicious of the therapy. The father immediately complains of feeling excluded from the mother-infant relationship and thinks that he has lost contact with his wife since the birth of his son (fantasy of oedipal rivalry with his son). Moreover, he is afraid that his son is abnormal since he perceives him as being too dependent on his mother.

When reviewing the parents' history, the mother felt very close to her parents and the identification she projects onto Allan is thus that of her self-image (anaclitic fantasy). As a child, she always felt very close to her mother and grandmother. Her father was also an "affective refuge" for her (incestuous oedipal fantasy). Allan's mother also spoke of her feelings that Allan resembles her father (projection of an oedipal image).

For Allan's father, the picture is very different. His parental identifications are those of a father who is attentive and concerned with the development of his son, whom he would like to be close with, and those of a father who intrusively surveys the mother-child relationship in order to avoid feelings of exclusion. The identifications this father projects onto Allan are images of a child who is too dependent on his mother, as he felt himself to have been. In fact, he left his mother at the age of eighteen in order to study far away from home, running away from a cold, distant mother whom he also considered to be too intrusive. When Allan was born, he felt that his own wife was rejecting and abandoning him, while denying him a close relationship with his son as well (although he is seen to be nostalgic about a closer relationship with his own father).

Confronted with this difficult triangular situation, the parents were unable to listen to the therapist's interpretations concerning the child, showing much more concern about their marital problems than about the child's symptoms. They abruptly discontinued treatment after the third session, seemingly as a result of the "negative pre-transference" emerging from the intricate conflicts between the marital and parental problems. In fact, from the first session, the therapist felt like an object of "negative pre-transference" for each of the two parents. The mother's was mitigated and easier to correct. She viewed the therapist as the image of a demeaning parent with the role of the superego, a role also played by the husband who had requested the consultation for the infant. The "negative pre-transference" of the husband seemed much more virulent and was determined by a negative projection passed on to the therapist. He experienced the therapy's focus on the child's symptoms as demeaning to his parenting skills and as a rejection, thus triggering the rupture in treatment.

Clinical example 4—Gaston and Melanie

The parents came into the consultation for their two children. Gaston, a four-and-a-half year old, exhibits such difficult behavior that he has "already set the house on fire twice", says the father. Melanie, two years old, has presented feeding difficulties since birth. In the parents' history, we discover that the father unexpectedly and tragically lost his own mother when he was two years old. His mother had electrocuted herself when her husband abandoned her in order to marry another woman. Gaston and Melanie's mother describes herself as a child who had close ties with her parents. Especially when speaking of her father, she recounted that "we understood each other without speaking". She presents an infantile attitude towards her husband, whom she seems to invest as the image of an idealized father. The husband seems to project onto his wife the image of the cherished child he always wanted to have been after the early loss of his mother and his painful experiences of a cold relationship with his father and stepmother.

This conjugal equilibrium was unstable due to the rigidity and partiality of the roles taken on by each parent. Problems began to appear when Gaston came into the world. The mother displaced onto him the image of an oedipal father she was very close to, contributing to an over investment of the image of the ideal parent that she had projected onto her husband up to that point. Confronted with the redistribution of his wife's investments, the husband, in turn, had to rework the image of the excluded child that he felt he had experienced during his childhood. As a result, the father feels himself to be an excluded third party and projects onto his son the image of the father who had abandoned him in his childhood as well as the aggressive feelings that he felt towards him. This explains why the father viewed Gaston as a very dangerous child.

This conjugal imbalance was intensified by Melanie's arrival, which the mother immediately experienced as a rival maternal image (oedipal fantasy of rivalry). The unconscious ambivalence towards this image contributed to the infant's feeding difficulties.

The mother's intense feelings of guilt towards her maternal image, projected onto her daughter, provoked major regressive movements. Thus, during the fifth session of therapy, the mother decided to leave her husband and son in order to return to her native country with her daughter to be near her mother. His spouse's departure aroused the father's openly persecutory transference of rivalry towards the therapist, whom he then considered to be responsible for the broken relationship. This ended the parent-children treatment.

Clinical discussion and theoretical considerations

The preceding clinical examples seem to reveal that one of the most distinctive factors of the father's presence in the joint therapy is the apparent frequency of conjugal problems. Over the course of the psychotherapeutic process, these problems can be treated simultaneously with the parents' conflict with their child, or they can represent a source of resistance leading to the disruption of the therapeutic relation. These situations led us to reflect on the similarities existing between the ties uniting the parents to the child and those that unite the couple. The projective parental identifications generate a process of "role giving" (Sandler 1960) to the child accompanied by introjective "role taking" that we call "complementary parental identifications". These different projective and complementary parental identification networks can be normal and extremely constructive in the child's development. On the contrary, they can also present varying degrees of conflict (Manzano, Palacio-Espasa, & Zilkha 1999). In the broad spectrum of these scenarios, we have found that certain scenarios may play a major role in forming the ties uniting the parental couple. This may mean that when choosing a conjugal partner, each parent tends to use the other as a foundation to build certain projective identifications of narcissistic parental images. These identifications are erected as defense mechanisms against the anaclitic images of frustration and abandonment (which are consequently depressing) and are similar to those established with their child, which are accompanied by corresponding complementary identifications. Most notably, these are:

1. The image of the parent, more or less ideal, that the parent would have liked to have had.
2. The image of the child, more or less ideal, that the parent would have liked to have been for his/her own parents.

Such narcissistic images aim to nullify the anaclitic experiences of want or loss. They are interlinked with and filter into more sexualized images of the oedipal father and mother (Kernberg 1991), thus acting as a determining factor in the choice of partners in a couple. The idealization of oedipal images draws its energy from the close defensive relation with anaclitic images, which are feared due to the insecurity and depression they inspire.

According to Kernberg, each parent chooses a partner based on his/her oedipal images: the ideal object of incestuous love and/or the rival object. This author writes that on the couple's stage i.e. in their relationship, six characters are always present: the two partners and each of their ideal and rival objects.

Like the fantasized interactions between parents and infant, when the couple is observed from the point of view of their parenthood, their conjugal interactions show that one parent projects the image of the ideal parent he would have liked to have had onto the other, who easily becomes the image of the incestuous oedipal parent. Attributing the role of the ideal parent to the spouse is often accompanied by a tendency to identify with the ideal child that one would have liked to have been. Reciprocally, this same spouse may also identify with the role of the ideal parent, while attributing that of the ideal child to his/her partner.

The couple's stability will thus depend on the equilibrium with which each partner is able to accept, reciprocally and depending on the circumstances, either the role of the ideal parent or the role of the ideal child for the other. Clinical psychotherapy with both parents and their infant shows that the arrival of the newborn impels both parents to confer the role of a more or less ideal child to the infant. On their side, the parents believe that they must assume the role of the more or less ideal parent for the infant and this movement modifies the previous balance in the couple. This reorganization tends to loosen and weaken the drives uniting the couple while strengthening those of each parent, especially the mother, with the newborn.

Normally, the mother is the one expected to monopolize the role of the ideal parent for the infant while the father may suffer from a feeling of exclusion due to the strength of the ties established between the mother and her infant. In fact, this widespread clinical reality hides another, often neglected situation constituted by the father's unconscious collusion with this intense mother-infant bond. Underlying this unconscious complicity, the father often harbors deep within himself the need for his own child to find the ideal mother that he would have liked to have had himself. This collusion prevails despite the feelings of loss and frustration he experiences due to the weakened bonds within the couple.

As demonstrated in our clinical examples, the mother can also experience feelings of exclusion, loss, and deprivation of the bond with the idealized parental object when the newborn arrives. It is common in clinical psychotherapeutic situations for the two parents to be absorbed by their ideal of parenthood for their infant, who carries the image of the ideal child they would have liked to have been. This is a preoccupation that monopolizes the greater part of the parents' libidinal energy. As a result, the ties uniting the couple are sometimes dangerously weakened. A latent conjugal conflict follows, with both parents feeling emotionally dissatisfied since the rerouting of the ideal images onto the child involves a weakening of the oedipal parental images that the parents previously reciprocally placed on their partner.

When the distribution of roles between the partners in the couple is rigid, with one of the parents tending to adopt the role of the ideal parent while the other takes on the role of the cherished child, the risk that emerges of an open conjugal conflict is much greater.

Conclusions

When looking for the distinctive characteristics of mother-father-infant psychotherapy sessions, we noticed that the father's contribution to the therapy is quite similar to the mother's, both in terms of total speaking time and the emotional and personal role he occupies in the problem of interaction with the infant. Brief mother-father-infant psychotherapy could be carried out only when the therapist succeeded in formulating a "common interpretive focus" for both parents with subsidiary "points" specific to each of the spouses. In these circumstances, the presence of both parents constitutes a motivating factor that increases the chances of a positive treatment outcome.

When elaborating these "interpretative foci", we often witnessed the appearance of conjugal conflicts that then became obstacles to the therapeutic process. In certain cases, we were able to rise above this type of resistance through a psychotherapeutic approach and by working with each parent's projective identifications lying at the root of the couple's conflict.

In the choice of a partner leading to the formation of the couple, we encounter anaclitic projective identifications that are quite similar to those that the parents project onto their children, such as the image of the ideal parent that the parent would have liked to have had and the image of the ideal child that he/she would have liked to have been. These narcissistic parental images serve an anti-depressive purpose as they are erected as defence mechanisms against the anaclitic images. When they are accompanied by oedipal images, they contribute to well-balanced investments in the couple. The arrival of children often upsets this equilibrium, since they draw onto themselves, from both parents, the image of the ideal child that the parents would have liked to have been. The parents are then forced to identify with the image of the ideal parent that they would have liked to have had. When the child monopolizes these ideal images, the affective and sexual bonds uniting the couple are weakened due to the fact that these images carry an intense libidinal potential for both parents. These disturbances can lead to latent or manifest conjugal conflicts. In our opinion, the therapeutic elaboration of these conflicts constitutes one of the most distinctive aspects of joint psychotherapy sessions with mother, father, and infant.

References

Barrows, P. (2003). Change in parent-infant psychotherapy. *Journal of Child Psychotherapy, 29/3*: 283–300.

Cabrera, N. J., Tamis-LeMonda, C. S., Bradley, R. H., Hofferth, S., & Lamb, M. E. (2000). Fatherhood in the twenty-first century. *Child Development,* 71/1: 127–136.

Cramer, B. (1974). Interventions thérapeutiques brèves avec parents et enfants. *Psychiatrie de l'Enfant,* 5/17–1: 53–118.

Cramer, B., & Palacio Espasa, F. (1993). *La Pratique des Psychothérapies Mères-Bébés. Etudes Cliniques et Techniques.* Paris: PUF.

Cramer, B., Robert-Tissot, C., Stern, D. N., Serpa Rusconi, S., de Muralt, M., Besson, G., Palacio Espasa, F., Bachmann, J.-P., Knauer, D., Berney, C., & d'Arcis, U. (1990). Outcome evaluation in brief mother-infant psychotherapy: a preliminary report. *Infant Mental Health Journal*, 11/3: 278–300.

Daws, D. (1994). La spécificité du travail psychanalytique dans les thérapies conjointes parents—enfants. *Devenir*, 6/2, 33–43.

Debray, R. (1994). Spécificité des traitements psychanalytiques de la triade père-mère-bébé. *Devenir*, 6/2: 23–31.

Fraiberg, S. (1980). *Clinical Studies in Infant Mental Health: The First Year of Life.* New York: Basic Books.

Freud, S. (1914). On narcissism: An introduction. In: J. Strachey (Ed. & Trans.), *The Complete Psychological Works of Sigmund Freud: Standard Edition, Volume 14* (pp. 67–102). London: Hogarth Press, 1957.

Grotstein, J. S. (1981). *Splitting and Projective Identification.* New York: Jason Aronson.

Kernberg, O. (1991). Aggression and love in the relationship of the couple. *Journal of the American Psychoanalytic Association*, 39/1: 45–70.

Lebovici, S. (1995). A propos des psychothérapies analytiques chez le jeune enfant. In: G. Fava Vizziello, D. N. Stern, & A. P. Birraux (Eds.), *Modèles Psychothérapeutiques au Premier Âge. De la Théorie à l'Intervention* (pp. 89–98). Paris: Masson.

Manzano, J., Palacio-Espasa, F., & Zilkha, N. (1999). *Les Scénarios Narcissiques de la Parentalité. Clinique de la Consulation Thérapeutique en Psychiatrie Infanto-Juvénile.* Paris: PUF.

Palacio-Espasa, F., (1984). Indications et contre-indications des approches psychothérapeutiques brèves des enfants d'âge préscolaire et leurs parents. *Neuropsychiatrie de l'Enfance et de l'Adolescence*, 12: 591–609.

Palacio Espasa, F., & Manzano, J. (1982). La consultation thérapeutique de très jeunes enfants et leur mère. *La Psychiatrie de l'Enfant*, 25/1: 5–26.

Palacio Espasa, F., & Knauer D. (1998). Conflits de la parentalité à la lumière des cas traités en psychothérapie brèves mères—bébés. In: P. Mazet., & S. Lebovici (Eds.), *Psychiatrie Périnatale Parents et Bébés: du Projet d'Enfant aux Premiers Mois de la Vie* (pp. 413–425). Paris: PUF.

Robert-Tissot, C., Cramer, B., Stern, D. N., Serpa Rusconi, S., Bachmann, J.-P., Palacio Espasa, F., Knauer, D., de Muralt, M., Berney, C., & Mendiguren, G. (1996). Outcome evaluation in brief mother-infant psychotherapies: report on 75 cases. *Infant Mental Health Journal*, 17/2: 97–114.

Sandler, J. (1960). The background of safety. *International Journal of Psycho-analysis*, 41: 387–418.

Spitz, R. A. (1965). *The First Year of Life.* New York: International University Press.

CHAPTER FIVE

The role of the infant in parent-child psychotherapies

A. Watillon-Naveau
Brussels

Introduction

When I started to work with young children and their parents some twenty years ago, my background was essentially psychoanalytical, but I could also make use of my experience as a seminar leader in infant observation following the Esther Bick technique (Bick 1964).

The first case I treated was a baby girl, three months old, suffering from primary anorexia. It was for me a dramatic experience, which I described in an article in the *International Review of Psycho-Analysis* (Watillon-Naveau 1992). Alice and her mother could be helped thanks to my analytical understanding of her mother's discourse and dreams. Although Alice was present during some interviews, she did not play an active role in my understanding of the psychic dynamics that had disturbed the mother-daughter relationship.

It is only with my second case that I became aware of the importance of the child's presence and participation. Let me tell you the story of Lea. She was five years old when her parents consulted me because of her encopresis. During the first consultation, Lea plays peacefully, sitting on the floor between her mother and myself. Father is present but her ten-month-old brother remains at home. I ask Lea why she does not go to the toilet. She tells me that at school, the toilets are dirty and situated far from the classroom. She is afraid.

Father agrees with this hypothesis, but mother does not. She ignores the reason for Lea retaining her faeces but she can give a precise description of how things happen. When Lea feels a bowel movement, she controls herself with such effort that she gets tears in her eyes. If she succeeds in retaining her faeces, the pressure will come back later. If not, she soils her pants.

During the interview we speak of Lea's conception, which happened after a terminated pregnancy. Mother felt that she was not ready to have a child and wanted to wait. She speaks of it calmly and with great equanimity. However, there is some vagueness about the time that elapsed between the abortion and Lea's conception. Father thinks it was a long period, mother does not agree. This hesitation attracts my attention and I bring it up again later. At this point Lea, who has a cold, sneezes violently and her nose begins to bleed. Putting her hand to her nose, she smears her whole face with blood. The father turns pale, I stand up to give Lea a handkerchief and mother takes her to the bathroom for the necessary attention. During their absence, father makes a connection between this incident and the subject of our conversation, namely the abortion. He is very shocked. When Lea and mother come back, I tell them father's interpretation and I add that I also think there must be a link. Mother repeats that the abortion was not a problem for her.

When I meet Lea and her parents, together with her little brother Marc, some weeks later, I learn that, since our first encounter, the encopresis has totally disappeared. There is also a visible change in the relationship between mother and daughter who are now able to have lots of fun together and who seem very close. Lea plays an interesting game with her mother, while her father and I look after Marc. Lea eats a biscuit, and turning her back to her mother, she invites her to bite the biscuit, which she holds behind her. When her mother tries to bite it, Lea quickly takes it away. Sometimes her mother succeeds in biting, sometimes not. They laugh and seem to have a lot of fun. I feel excluded as I suppose the father does too. I have in mind that Lea shows us how free she is now concerning her giving or withholding her faeces. When the game is over, the parents tell me they are very glad of the result, but would like to understand. Father is a psychologist! I explain my hypothesis of a guilt feeling concerning the termination, this feeling having been projected into Lea, who had to retain her faeces, standing for a baby in her unconscious mind. Mother gets angry; she never felt guilty about that abortion. I feel puzzled, anxious, and remain quiet. There is a short silence and mother begins to speak spontaneously of her own mother and her youth. She was brought up by her mother alone and never knew her father's identity. Her relationship with her mother was very bad and, at the age of six, she was placed in an institution. She was ten years old when she learned of her mother's death but only at seventeen was she informed that her mother's death was by suicide. We are then able to understand that the source of the guilt is not the abortion itself but the fact that Lea's mother had chosen her own time for becoming a mother, a freedom that her mother had not had. Some years later I learned that Lea was developing well and never had any toilet problems again.

Lea taught me a lot about the importance of giving attention to the child's reactions and communications, verbal or non-verbal, and to be aware of their link with the content of the parental discourse. The understanding of the interactional dysfunction is due to the conjunction of these two components: the content of the parental story at the moment when the child manifests himself by what I call a "staging" or acting (in French: une mise en scène).

Technique

My experience with Lea and her parents inclined me to set up the following technique. From the start I make it clear that the child's presence is essential for me, and I always try to have the father present, too. The consultation lasts for more than the classical three quarters of an hour; double time is necessary to allow each of the protagonists to find their position and have their say. Naturally there are some toys available for the child, and the opportunity to draw. The interval between sessions is variable; I am attentive to the parents' wishes, and experience has shown me that a week's interval is too short as psychological digestion needs time. These sessions involve moments of great intensity for the parents, the child, and myself. It is interesting to see that children, even very young ones, remember their visits to my office well and recognize it, even after several months. Sometimes it is the child who asks to meet me again.

For example, at the end of their second interview, a particular couple was hesitating about the continuation of our meetings because the situation had improved a lot. They discussed: "Yes, we would like to come back, but not for at least a month. Do we need to fix a date now?" I deliberately said nothing because I had noticed that the child, who was eighteen months old, had stopped playing. She came to me, leaning heavily on me, her back pressing against my legs. I felt the intensity of the pressure and thought of Grotstein's background object of identification (Grotstein 1981). Then I put what was happening into words and the parents, with one voice, asked to fix the next appointment.

This example shows us the child's positive and intense transference, which has been described by many authors. This cathexis is an important therapeutic tool but must be handled with care so as not to arouse jealousy and envy in the parents. I believe that infants readily sense that this benevolent third party, to whom they are presented, will be able to act as a container for their anxieties and for the burden of projection. As the interview proceeds, children certainly notice that the parental projections gradually come to be diverted away from themselves. I remember a little girl who was very shy and anxious. When her mother started to tell me all her anxieties and projected them onto me, the child looked relieved and started to play with pleasure, while I was feeling bad.

This positive transference from the child is also related to the confidence the parents have in the therapist. Once I felt that a mother was rather negative and hostile. Inquiring about this, I found it had to do with the fact that mother's friend—who was not the father of the child—had been in supervision with me. This work had not been satisfying and we had elected to bring it to an end. This could explain the negativity of the mother and the attitude of the boy; during the second appointment, when his mother was not looking, he gave me a heavy kick in my leg.

My technique derives directly from my experience with infant observation. From the start of the first consultation, my attention is directed towards the children while I listen to the parents. I observe their behaviour, when and how they react to the parental discourse, what their games are, their ability to get into an interaction with me, and so on. The parents begin with a description of the symptoms, how they react to them, when they started and how they can explain them. Later I invite them to tell me about the conception, the pregnancy, the birth, the development, and the desire to have a child.

Finally, my interest concerns the childhood of the parents. So different levels are explored: the history of the parents including their relationship to their own parents and siblings, the prehistory of the baby, and his or her developmental vicissitudes. These different levels are explored in an associative way, and by following the actions and interventions of the child. As I mentioned before, the child's interventions can take the form of a kind of dramatization; an enactment, what I call a "staging". With very young children or babies, it can be crying, wakening, or other manifestations. It is most important to be aware of the subject and matter of the parental discourse when children intervene because I consider that this is the way that they can inform me of what is for them an unbearable load.

I consider these therapies to be applied psychoanalysis and, as for a psychoanalytical treatment, the comprehension of the unconscious and the setting that allows this understanding to appear are both important. Winnicott compared the analyst's work with the attitude of a "good enough" mother (Winnicott 1956). He stated that to establish this setting, the psychoanalyst's attitude must be based not only on his theory and training but also on his personality and his capacity for empathy and humanity. For Bion, the setting must create a space where the psychoanalyst's capacity to dream (Winnicott would say, to play) can operate and where the unexpected can appear. This happens when the child acts or stages in reaction to the parental discourse (Bion 1963). We know it is impossible to observe and treat without having theories in our mind but they should, writes D. Houzel, be used to establish and maintain the setting and then be let go of, so that we can be freer to be "surprised" by the material emerging, without holding on to theoretical preconceptions (Houzel 2000).

Following Bick's method of infant observation, I always take very detailed notes after these consultations. I try to reconstruct chronologically what happened and to omit no details. This allows me to understand more about the links between behaviour and words. Before each new encounter with the family, I read these notes to clearly remember what happened.

There are three principal types of events, which the child is unable to mentalize and integrate without help:

1. transgenerational problems.
2. traumatic events.

3. a category of mixed origin: cumulative little traumas to which the parents react inappropriately often because of troubled relations with their own parents.

Transgenerational problems

These concern traumatic events that one or both parents could not digest mentally when they happened and which remained locked up in the unconscious. When children are born, parents will unconsciously try to project this unelaborated trauma onto them. This represents, for children, a load that they cannot get rid of except through symptoms. The work of the therapist is to discover this trauma, to help parents mentalize it, and, as a consequence, to free children of these projections.

These events are not always easy to discover and the staging of the child can be of great help in drawing the attention of parents and therapist to them. But, as it is evident in Lea's case, the concerned parent has to bring forth his or her associations to elucidate the enigma and to become convinced of the role that this event plays for the child. It is most important in all these situations to respect the capacity of the parents to face the consequences of what happened even many years earlier. Here we are also helped by the children who, thanks to their vitality and flexibility, can very quickly abandon their symptoms and restore the initially good relationship between themselves and their parents.

Traumatic problems

When a traumatic event occurs early in a child's life, the consequences will depend on the parents' capacity to cope with that event. If parents react calmly and are able to speak of the trauma, to understand and mentalize it, they will have the capacity to contain and aid their children in overcoming their suffering and anxieties. But when the parents are themselves overwhelmed by the traumatic event, babies and toddlers are too young and insufficiently armed to digest the trauma. In some cases the child immediately shows signs of discomfort; in other cases the symptoms will appear after a second unhappy circumstance for the child, realising what Freud called "nachträglickheit", or "differed action" (Freud 1898a). In some cases parents, even though still shocked by the traumatic event, view it as part of their history, and they are able to speak of it. In other cases, the environment tries to forget, minimize the trauma, or repress it.

For example, Maria's mother attributed all her daughter's symptoms to her first difficult months. Maria was born with bilateral congenital coxarthrosis, and had to be operated on at three months old, remaining in plaster until she was eighteen months old. Although this had been a painful experience for Maria, her mother had been able to care for her with love and patience, and the girl had developed well on the whole. Her brother's birth, when she was two, seemed to have been accepted without too much trouble. However, when I met Maria, at age three and a half, she was very difficult, having presented oppositional and aggressive behaviour over the previous six months. Mother stressed Maria's traumatic early months while her daughter played very calmly near us. Suddenly, in a very low tone mother added: "I do not know if it is important but six months ago I made a suicide attempt, but the children were not told." It was evident to me that mother wanted to bypass this event. At this point, Maria stood up, went to a wooden seat, and started to hit it violently several times.

This staging by Maria helped to overcome mother's resistance and shame in speaking of her suicide attempt and the circumstances that had led to it. At our following meeting I learnt that her eighteen-month-old brother had finally started to walk, on the day of our first encounter. He too had been freed from an unspoken prohibition on walking earlier than his sister.

How do these therapies work?

It is evident that I use interpretations in this work with parents and young children. But can we really speak of interpretation in the psychoanalytic sense of the word?

It is clear that in some cases a link is made between unconscious feelings or images from the parents' internal world and the child's symptoms or the trouble in the interaction. Thanks to the child's "staging" the unconscious can become conscious, but interpretations are never made in the transference. The therapist relies on a very strong positive transference due to the fact that the parents are referred by their paediatrician or, more often, by friends who had previously had a good therapeutic experience with me. This positive investment is used to build up a working alliance and is important to help parents to overcome the narcissistic blow of having to admit at least some failure in their parental role. This narcissistic burden must be handled with care by the therapist, who underlines the positive aspects of the interaction. I never interpret in the transference and feel I am perceived as a benevolent grandmother. When the transference sounds too negative, I first try to clarify it, as I showed in the example of the kicking boy.

An important effect of these therapies is bound to the process of identification. Mothers often identify with me or with the parental image I represent for them. It is a phenomenon we also encounter in infant observation. During the consultation I feel how mother watches me and how intensely she observes the way I interact with the child, particularly when there are conflicts and when I have to put limits to defend my furniture and belongings. It is interesting to see how the child reacts to frustration and how the parents can face aggressiveness and tantrums. Monique Bydlowski (Bydlowski 1997) has described how young mothers are in a particular mental state where the tendency to identify is magnified and where contact with the unconscious feelings and representations is more open. She calls this the "psychic transparency". This particularity allows very direct interpretations and facilitates comprehension but must nevertheless be handled with care because it makes mothers more fragile. These identifications with the therapist, felt as a "good" maternal object (a grandmother) allow mothers to reintegrate the maternal transgenerational ghosts.

I mentioned earlier how the positive investment of the child is crucial. It is nevertheless important to remain attentive to the seduction a young child can make use of. One has to be attentive to his or her countertransferential feelings and the tendency to blame the parents. We must be able to identify with the three persons present, and to encourage parents to express their suffering even in the presence of the child. I am convinced the child perceives the conscious and unconscious emotions of his parents but it can be a very important therapeutic lever to verbalize these feelings—to put into words what has never been said or even consciously thought. This gives the child confirmation of his or her perceptions and can be a great relief. We know the negative influence of family mysteries, of the "ghosts in the nursery" (Fraiberg, Adelson, & Shapiro 1975). It is also important to help parents to undo the denial concerning traumatic events, to make them aware of their feelings, and allow them to be expressed.

This positive investment of the child is, in my experience, not evident with tyrannical children (Ciccone et al. 2003). They are in a general state of opposition, which they extend to the therapist chosen by their parents. It can take me a long time to obtain their cooperation but it seems to me crucial to be in a positive transference or the therapeutic effect will not be obtained.

In trying to understand how and when the symptom appeared, through the story of the child's conception, pregnancy, and birth, by building up the history of the child's development and the past of the parents, a chronology of the family's history is restored. This is an important point, which P. Fonagy has underlined (Fonagy 2001). He shows the importance of being able to make a coherent narration of one's biography. The internal representations of past relationships in the mind of the parents have a significant influence on the child's quality of attachment.

A detailed clinical case

> The first time I meet Daniel, three years old, he is accompanied by his mother. Father cannot join us because of his professional activities, and the twin brother Alex remains at home. The maternal grandfather is a psychologist and he phoned to make the appointment. His intention was to discuss his grandson's case theoretically with me. I explained to him that I needed to see the parents and the child. In the first session Daniel looks at me with interest but refuses to greet me and remains clinging to his mother. It is a very hot day and it obviously annoys mother to have her son sitting on her lap. She tries several tricks to get him down to play with the toys, but Daniel cannot be persuaded and remains attached to his mother. The relationship between mother and son seems tense and cold on the mother's side; stubborn and aggressive on Daniel's. Mother is not at ease and asks what she must do because she has never been in such a situation. It is clear that this consultation is a narcissistic blow for her, as is the attitude of Daniel. I ask her to tell me what bothers her about her child.

She starts to tell me that Daniel is a very complicated child, tyrannical, never satisfied, asking for much attention, and having temper tantrums. When she is alone with him, he can be charming, sweet, and loving. He dominates his twin brother who is calm, obedient, smiling, and very creative. It is Alex who thinks up tricks but Daniel who executes them.

While listening to the mother's explanations, I slowly get Daniel to look at the toys and his interest in the animals brings him to interact with me. He begins to look at other toys but remains tyrannical with his mother. When he wants something he does not ask for it but gives an order and his tone is not gentle. Mother remains nervous and constantly invites her child to show me how clever he is, that he knows the name of the animals, that he is able to count, and so on. Identified with Daniel, I feel irritated and wish she would stop. Daniel looks in a book and I invite him to name the images. In thinking of this, I feel I did the same as mother! Daniel answers for each image: "It is a chair." It is evident that the boy is teasing me and testing limits. Mother is annoyed by this attitude and says angrily: "He knows all these names!" I answer that I have no doubt about it but that I think Daniel is teasing me. Daniel has a brief smile and correctly names the images in another book. Later on he finds building bricks. I build a tower, which he immediately knocks down with much pleasure and looks at me with a question in his eyes. I say that bricks are a funny game because one can build, destroy, and build again. I have in mind the importance of reparation described by M. Klein (Klein 1957). He builds several towers by himself, which he then destroys.

After the description of the symptom, and the history of pregnancy and birth, mother tells me, in a low tone, that she is pregnant but has not told the children. I am always very amazed by the parents who tell me something the child should not know, in front of him, as if he is deaf or stupid or an inanimate object. Daniel's reaction is immediate: he stands up, climbs on mother's knees and hits her chest very heavily while sitting down. Mother says: "Oh, you hurt my belly! I told you my belly hurts." I add that Daniel is perhaps angry towards mummy because there is a little baby in her belly and that he wants to hurt it. Daniel smiles, gets down from mother's lap and goes on playing. He is calmer, gives no more orders to his mother, and seems relieved. He plays alone, concentrating deeply. Mother has noticed the change in his attitude but she thinks it has nothing to do with my intervention. This could be a kind of negation of what she really feels or thinks since I have not said anything about Daniel's changed attitude. She speaks of her obsessionality, inherited from her father, and which she seems to have passed to Daniel. It is the first allusion to the grandfather who phoned me. She tells me she met another child psychotherapist but did not like the lady whom she found too obsessive concerning the setting and too unfriendly with Daniel. It is her father who gave her my name.

Mother describes how Daniel was as a baby: he was an active child, moving a lot, needing much attention. His development seems normal: he sleeps well, eats without problems and is clean. I ask mother how she felt about having twins. She answers she had no choice, but it was difficult because when she was nursing one of the boys, she always felt guilty towards the other. I have to ask about father's opinion of Daniel. He works a lot and is not very present in the family. He is quickly upset by Daniel and loses his temper with him.

After this consultation, I felt rather downhearted and doubted mother would come back for the next consultation two weeks later. However, mother and son arrive on time and I immediately notice the difference in atmosphere: Daniel rediscovers the toys with pleasure. He greets me and is smiling. Mother is calm, affectionate and accessible with her boy. She tells me he has much improved, feels good, is less aggressive at school. She adds: "He has much changed under your influence!" I wonder if she, too, did not feel a change in herself, because I find her attitude with him much modified. She looks at me a bit amazed and tells me she has officially announced to the boys that they will have a little sister. The twins accepted this news with pleasure and asked a lot of questions. Now, every evening they say good-night to the little sister by kissing mummy's belly and if mother asks them for one of their sweets to give to the baby, they give it easily. Father is again not able to come today, but wants to meet me. We fix a date for him with Daniel.

At the following session, mother comes with the two boys; once again the father is not free. I am a bit frightened by this invasion but things go very well. I am aware mother is also testing me: shall I accept her initiative? Daniel and Alex are very nice during the whole consultation. They play together or alone, exploring and sharing. They remain calm and two incipient fights are easy to manage and resolve. Mother looks very proud of her twins. Three weeks later, I finally meet father with Daniel. This consultation brings no new elements, but I have the opportunity to emphasize the importance of father's presence for the children, and of the necessary patience one must have with small children.

Conclusions

The therapeutic affect, in this work of applied psychoanalysis, concerns different levels for the included persons: the child and the parents. The first step for children is to become aware that the settings they find themselves in, and the therapists to whom their parents present them, are able to contain their emotions and understand their problems. Often children very quickly feel that they are considered as human beings, able and allowed to express their feelings, and that the aim of the consultation is to understand what is going on and to lessen their suffering. The load weighing on the children's shoulders can be lifted when the transgenerational message is discovered and accepted by the parents. This is often an astonishing moment for the parents, as it brings previously unconscious memories to the fore. It becomes possible to get out of the vicious circle where the parents get upset by the child's behaviour and the child becomes increasingly anxious and difficult.

Concerning the traumatic events, it is important to recognize them and admit their importance for the child. The aim here is to restore the disturbed parental dream capacity. If the traumatic event is not explained to the child, the perceptive traces left by the event cannot normally develop and be integrated in the child's associative inner world. The staging of the child is for the parents an evident proof that the trauma that they try to forget and negate is important for the child and must be verbalized and explained.

Another level on which this work is based lies in identifications. Mothers are attentive to the way I interact with their child, how I react to opposition, aggressiveness, and tantrums. I suppose they also feel the pleasure I have in playing with children. Shared pleasure and cheerfulness are so important in the parent-child interactions but often waved away by anxiety, anger, and educational intentions.

It is not easy to describe a third level which concerns the non-verbal messages that are exchanged by all the persons present in the consulting room. As I explained, I am very attentive to children's behaviour, mimicry, and looks. Parents sometimes have to stand up in order to intervene with their child, and all these movements can be interesting and perhaps understood. The countertransference of the analyst is used as a tool to help understanding and to orientate the unfolding of the session, but I am convinced that parents and child perceive some of my feelings too.

The twofold attention that observes, comprehends, and interprets the child's behaviour, and which also takes into account the parental suffering, difficulties, and capacities, allows for a narcissistic revaluation. The reorganization of the chronological unfolding of the events, the re-establishment of the topography of the different mental spaces of each protagonist, and the possibility of making links between the events, allow confusion to lessen and, somehow, logic to be gained, which puts things back to their place and restores the transgenerational line of succession.

To conclude, I want to thank all the young children and their parents who trusted my capacity to help them. They taught me a lot and made me aware of childrens' capacity to communicate their suffering, the intensity of their urge to heal and resume their development, their trust in their parents, and in life.

References

Bick, E. (1964). Notes on infant observation in psycho-analytical training. *International Journal of Psycho-Analysis*, 45/4: 558–566.

Bion, W. (1963). *Elements of Psychoanalysis*. London: Heinemann.

Bydlowski, M. (1997). *La Dette de Vie. Itinéraire Psychanalytique de la Maternité*. Paris: Le Fil Rouge, PUF.

Ciccone, A., Resnik, S., Kaës, R., Gampel, Y., Catoire, G., & Meltzer, D. (2003). Les enfants qui poussent à bout. In: A. Ciccone (Ed.), *Psychanalyse du Lien Tyrannique*. Paris: Dunod.

Fonagy, P. (2001). *Attachment Theory and Psychoanalysis*. New York: Other Press.

Fraiberg, S., Adelson, E., & Shapiro, V. (1975). Ghosts in the nursery. *Journal of the American Academy of Child Psychiatry*, 14: 387–421.

Freud, S. (1898a). Sexuality in the aetiology of the neuroses. In: J. Strachey (Ed. & Trans.), *The Complete Psychological Works of Sigmund Freud: Standard Edition, Volume 13* (pp. 259–285). London: Hogarth Press, 1962.

Grotstein, J. (1981). Splitting, the background object of primary identification and other self-object. In: J. Grotstein (Ed.), *Splitting and Projective Identification* (pp. 77–89). New-York: Jason Aronson.

Houzel, D. (2000). Le travail analytique et les modèles théoriques de la naissance psychique. *Journal de la Psychanalyse de l'Enfant,* 26: 57–76.

Klein, M. (1957). *Envy and Gratitude.* London: Tavistock.

Watillon-Naveau, A. (1992). Alice or the vicissitudes of the mother-daughter relationship. *International Review of Psycho-Analysis,* 19/2: 209–216.

Winnicott, D. (1956). Clinical varieties of transference. In: D. Winnicott (Ed.), *Through Paediatrics to Psycho-Analysis.* London: Tavistock.

CHAPTER SIX

Therapeutic consultation: early detection of "alarm symptoms" in infants and treatment with parent-infant psychotherapy

Romana Negri
Italy

History and background

The term "therapeutic consultation" is used here to mean the treatment of disorders of a psychopathological nature, which manifest themselves as difficulties in parent-child relationships. The treatment addresses parents and infants together and usually concerns children from birth to five years of age. The work is not recent. Literature includes a number of pioneering articles that are still considered milestones in terms of methodology and the ways in which treatment is carried out. I refer in particular to Winnicott's "The observation of small children in a pre-established situation" (1941), and Martha Harris' "Therapeutic consultations" (1966). The first writer proposed a setting for the observation of the small child that still represents a model for workers who intend to perform this type of intervention with babies of a few months of age. Mrs Harris's work is extremely illuminating for its understanding of the parental experience and the child's emotional situation. It also seems highly significant in that it delineates the role of the therapist within the consulting room itself. Over a considerable period of time this intervention on very small children has been used by an ever-increasing number of therapists, prevalently with a psychoanalytical orientation (Cramer & Palacio-Espasa 1974; 1993; Lebovici 1983; Pozzi 2003; Stern 1995; Watillon-Naveau 1993). A significant breakthrough came with the experience acquired through the observation of the newborn baby as promoted by Esther Bick over sixty years ago (1964). In the same way, expansion of the intervention has been encouraged by the rapid and efficient results obtained, since it enables elements of a psychopathological nature to be tackled at the onset and at an increasingly early age. My parent-child consultation work started back in the late 1970s and, in contrast to the findings of other authors such as Watillon-Naveau (1993), it concerns above all very small children. This is because I began this work as a consultant infant neuropsychiatrist at the Children's Neonatal Pathology Department of the Treviglio Caravaggio Hospital (Bergamo, Italy).

In my evaluation of infants, particularly in the first six to twelve months of age, it was fundamental for my work to be supervised by Martha Harris (she supervised three cases of Infant Observation I conducted following the Esther Bick's method). In the same way, the Bobath Course for children's neurodevelopment (which I attended in London in 1979 and in 1981) has been highly influential on my work.

The neuropsychology of the infant

The newborn is still at an age when its movements show residual philogenetic features. There is a marked latency period in humans between birth and the maturation of the neuronal and functional postural adjustments appropriate to the extra-uterine condition, which only starts to operate after the second or third month. This phenomenon is less marked in other species of primates and seems to further stress the importance of the mother's role in the development of the human infant. It affects the meaning of the sensuous, physical contact with the mother through acoustic and visual functions, touch, movement, and smell. (In the animal world, for example, the mother sheep accepts its lamb only after recognizing its smell, see Hafez 1975.) This contact cannot be considered merely the most suitable means of facilitating motor integration and development, but must also be seen as part of a wider function of welcoming and understanding the emotional communications that are the foundation for symbol formation, thinking, and the integration of the self by the infant.

Karel and Berta Bobath, respectively a Czech neurologist and a German physiotherapist, both moved to London during the Second World War, and founded a motor rehabilitation centre for children with cerebral palsy. The rehabilitation treatment was based on an extensive knowledge of the sensorimotor development of the child from the ontogenic point of view. The centre, which was named after them, is still active and is famous all over the world. It represents one of the most highly qualified institutes for the rehabilitation of children with cerebral palsy.

The Bobaths considered the infant's neuromotor and sensory evolution from the ontogenetic point of view and in my opinion their consideration on the very beginnings of infant life integrates very well with Ester Bick and Melanie Klein's theory of mental functioning. Starting from a non-integrated condition, which characterizes the neonatal period and which requires the mother's intervention as absolutely complementary to the infant's development, the Bobaths emphasized how infants in the supine position shuffle themselves crosswise. The trunk does not become the main axis until the fourth month, when infants become able to hold themselves in a symmetrical position on their backs and are able to join their hands, watch them, and bring them to their mouths. Only then are their limbs perceived as connected to the main axis, and little by little the upper limbs carry out the function of psychomotor antennae, so useful for the infant's development and knowledge. After the fifth month the upper limbs can explore the middle part, the abdomen, and reach the shoulder from the other side, and so on.

We know that, from the fourth month, the infant, according to Klein, starts living as a more integrated being, facing the depressive position. From this moment on the infant approaches the separation-individuation process both with the help of the mother and through the development of the ontogenetic motor component. Infants starts to put themselves on their sides autonomously, to roll from a supine to a prone position, to crawl on their knees and to start that straightening which will help them hold the upright position and move into the second year of age. The above acquisitions, which show total integration between mental and neurodevelopmental processes, have enabled me to fully understand how, at the beginning of life, biology does not allow us to differentiate between somatic and psychic functions: "The newborn feels with its body and uses it to express itself" (Negri 1983). Newborns avail themselves of all of their physical potential and activity to express deep and intense emotions. It is important to recognize the newborn's tendency to experience the emotions of joy or suffering, well being, discomfort, and uneasiness through bodily sensations. This has been confirmed by the infant observation experience and has led to the recognition of the variability and flexibility of the newborn's posture in response to the behaviour of the mother.

Alarm symptoms

Infants at risk can manifest mental operations with pathological features at a very early stage of their mental development. I have identified from my experience a whole range of features that may be defined as alarm symptoms, since they indicate a psychopathological risk. I am speaking of alarm symptoms (and not of symptoms of psychopathological risk) because the field of the infant mental health is oriented towards prevention and the identification of risk and disturbance is to be considered as crucial. Infancy is a time of rapid change, and the clinician's activity, at every turn, is geared to facilitate favourable developmental changes. The evidence of alarm symptoms is significant when it is followed by adequate intervention able to solve the problems revealed (Negri 1983, 1984, 1986, 1989, 1994, 1998). When the alarm symptoms are the expression of suffering seen mainly in the child himself, the parents' psychological condition is fundamental, from the prognostic point of view. The more the parents are mentally healthy, the more easily and freely they develop what Bion calls the function of "reverie". The extent of the presence of alarm symptoms is also quite significant.

These alarm symptoms are also present, to a lesser degree, in healthy children, whereas they are widely present in the children at risk. Furthermore, while they appear in a transitional way in healthy children, in children at risk they become predominant and can become crystallized parts of the personality. The loss of variability is often the first or one of the first distinctive signs of the disorder: there may be an increase of stereotypy, and a reduced adaptability, resulting in a decrease in both the ability to interact adequately with the environment and to "cope". The concept of variability, as contrasted with stereotypy, is a very useful instrument for differentiating between normal and deviating functions in the early analysis of developmental disorder (Touwen 1989). It means that when the alarm symptoms predominate, they oppose the integration of the child's sense organs or sensory capacity. For the sensory components to integrate they have to be in a state of equilibrium, in a harmonious relationship, which finds its cohesion through the newborn's relationship with the mother.

A vignette from infant observation

> During the first observation session, Francesca, a ten-day-old healthy infant is happily breast-feeding in her mother's arms. This action is accompanied by the baby's hand opening, closing, and then grasping at the mother's hand, which is supporting and offering the breast. In this satisfactory feeding experience, the oral activity is enriched by another component—the hand grasp, which becomes integrated with the mouth function. In addition while the mother is feeding the child, she also talks to her. The sucking experience, when it is associated with the mother's voice, is so pleasurable that eventually the little girl turns her eyes up towards the source of her pleasure and stares at her mother while listening and sucking. Thus the function of the sense organs is further enlarged, as they act not separately but in unison—mouth, hand, hearing, sight—to achieve a full integration.

It is only when the sense organs remain integrated that pathology can be averted. Starting with sense integration at this level of development, the infant passes on to the integrated perception of the other person—usually the mother. We note that at only ten days old, Francesca pays attention to her mother. According to Meltzer attention is envisaged "as the strings which hold the senses together in consensuality" (Meltzer, Bremner, Hoxter, Weddell, & Wittenberg 1975: 13). The visual contact with the mother's eyes is a strongly emotional experience for the newborn, in the context of what Meltzer and Harris Williams (1988) have described as the "aesthetic conflict". This leads the newborn to the perception and introjection of the person as a whole, attracted towards this by a primitive impulsive love, as clearly indicated by the infant's smile (Robson 1967). Sight, therefore, plays a highly integrating role in the healthy newborn (Rhode 1997). Conversely, sight can be used to avert the experience if the infant is faced with excessively painful sensations: he can use his eyes to control or to fix his gaze adhesively to objects. In a situation like this the infant is visibly persecuted by catastrophic, paranoid anxieties, which may lead to a persistent condition of autosensory limitation, an excess of autosensoriality condition.

Autosensoriality condition

Already in the intrauterine life of healthy babies there is an evident interest in their own sensoriality—what Corominas (1983) and Tustin (1986) have defined as "auto-sensuous states". In some cases small babies with a fragile constitution, premature newborn babies who have undergone a long stay in hospital, or those with cerebral pathology may display an excessive interest in sensoriality deriving from stimulations of their own bodies or objects. This attraction may prove "obsessive" and can gratify such babies, who thus suppress their emotional problems, which they find intolerable and disturbing. This prevents the establishment of an adequate relationship with their environment.

It should also be borne in mind that mothers of these babies, traumatized by the experience of premature birth or by the child's pathology, experience anguish. An anguished mother is not seen as such by her infant but rather as a person concerned with herself—rejecting and hostile to her relationship with her baby. This experience strengthens the infant's sense of isolation.

An excess of autosensoriality manifests itself principally through the experience of stereotypes of sounds, gestures, and movements, such as the repetitive protrusion of the tongue. The same significance is acquired by the insistence with which these infants seek sensations deriving from objects to which they are attracted by their colour, shininess, or sound. These are offered to the infants in order to calm them down or stimulate them. There is a further risk that the mothers of these infants, anxious that their babies should recoup their normal stages of development as soon as possible, tend to overstimulate their interest by further using these objects.

Early detection of alarm symptoms

I have been working with the concepts of alarm symptoms since 1977. As a consequence of follow-up checks after discharge, the case analysis of young patients hospitalized during 1977 in the Neonatal Pathology Division of the Hospital where I worked, showed a significant incidence of features, phobias, and other fears recognizable as typical warning symptoms of a psychopathological nature (Table 1).

Table 1 Alarm Symptoms

- Averting the gaze.
- Slipping away of eye-contact.
- Pretending to sleep.
- Spying when unobserved.
- Looking around restlessly.
- Absence of smiling.
- Absence of crying.
- Stiffness of facial expression.
- Absence of mother-child vocal rhythm.
- Rejection of the position of having the back and neck supported.
- Not enjoying being cuddled.
- Tremor (especially during the first two months).
- Hiccupping (especially during the first two months).
- Stereotypes (such as repetitive sounds, hand gestures, etc).
- Abnormal reaction or response to sounds or voices.
- Excessive or strange interest in movements of the tongue inside the mouth.
- Motor restlessness.
- Postural anomalies.
- Psychosomatic manifestations at skin, intestinal (colic), or respiratory level.
- Phobia about having the feet or hands stroked.
- "Little-hat" phobia (fear of having the head stroked).
- Fear of being undressed.
- Other fears.
- Feeding disorders, anorexia.
- Major alterations in biological rhythms (most frequent manifestations: sleep disorders, irritability).

In my opinion, the most significant ones are: averting the gaze together with pretending to sleep, spying when unobserved, and stiffness of facial expression. Again, extremely significant are the repetitive sounds, the absence of mother-child vocal rhythmicity, the absence of crying, anorexia (which is expressed through refusing the breast and, when the baby is bottle-fed, bursting into tears at the sight of the bottle), not enjoying being cuddled, rejection of the position where the back and nape of the neck are supported, and motor restlessness. They all conflict with integration of the different components of the child's body, which leads to an accentuation of the isolation, cancelling the perception of needs and emotions.

The phobias of being undressed and of having one's feet, hands, or head touched, and the "little hat" phobias, are, I believe, particularly related to emotional experiences derived from physical therapies involving drips into the scalp and frequent heel-pricks for taking blood, and in general to the traumas and manipulations to which these young patients have been subjected.

In my experience, the result of treatment is more favourable and quicker (two or three months) in the cases when just two or three alarm symptoms appear. The recovery is slower (four to six months and over) when the presence of alarm symptoms is great both in number and in persistence. When the complete recovery of the baby is not achieved it is possible to observe, with time, a modification of the psychopathological frame, characterized by slighter difficulties for the baby. In the course of my clinical work, and in accordance with Lieberman (2002), it is more difficult to achieve favourable results when the parents show serious personality disorders or mental deficiencies. In these situations, the parents are very often unable to consider their child's problems. The intervention, in these cases, must be performed by people in the extended family. Though in a few cases results were not entirely satisfactory, an early detection of alarm symptoms, at two to three months of age, followed by a proper therapeutic intervention, is an extremely effective means of carrying out preventive action in the field of early psychopathology. In fact, only through a carefully directed environmental intervention is it possible to obtain a "spectacular" remission of the disorder, using Cramer's definition (Cramer 1974; Cramer & Palacio-Espasa 1993).

CONTACT WITH THE BABY'S BACK AND NAPE OF THE NECK

In following both healthy infants and those with psychopathological disorders Genevieve Haag (1988) has stressed the importance, during the early development of newborns, of contact with the back and nape of the neck, and their connection with introjective organs such as the mouth, the nipple, and above all the eyes. The sensorimotor stimulants felt by the infants in these circumstances are very intense: babies lie in the arms of their mothers, their backs are well supported by their mothers' knees, and the soles of their feet are against their mothers' stomachs. This comforting experience will urge newborns to look into their mothers' eyes. Then the words that a mother usually addresses to the baby act as an acoustic envelope, conveying a strong emotional message, which is then completed and integrated by breast-feeding. When the relationship functions like this, integration will be promoted. The child who rejects contact will also dislike being in this position. For this reason, during a consultation, when I see a child who dislikes back and neck contact, combined with a constant strong refusal to meet my glance, I advise the parents to make a definite attempt to re-establish this contact when the baby is lying down to be changed. They can support the baby with the hands behind the neck. I suggest they keep their faces at a certain distance, especially at the start, so that the infant does not experience their presence as something excessively invasive and they can monitor the child's response, stopping when the baby is too bothered, irritated, or tired. It is usually the parents (and the mother in particular), who will do this. Sometimes, however, mothers find it emotionally impossible to make any attempt to do this in cases where they are stressed by the fact that the child reacts so strongly against them. In these cases it is better for the action to be performed by a grandmother or some other member of the family who looks after the child if the mother is at work.

INFANTS SUSCEPTIBLE TO PSYCHOPATHOLOGICAL RISK

Disorders can develop not only in children affected by sensory deficiencies or injuries to the nervous system; some children have a greater need than others for their mother, to function in a way that promotes the integration of their sense organs. In children who are constitutionally less able to integrate, disorders can develop if they have a mother who unconsciously colludes with these less vital aspects of the child. Another situation concerns children of seriously pathological parents who, even before having a child, tend to free themselves of their own pathology by projecting onto the child. The child becomes the receptacle of the parents' pathology (Giannotti, Lanzo, & Del Pidio 1994). Whatever the roots of the pathological situation—sensory deficiency from injuries to the sense organs or nervous system, constitutional factors, or massive projections of parents—it is clear that children are visibly tormented by the paranoid anxieties that prevent them from finding a way out of their persistent autosensory condition.

The parents

During the consultation it is very important to think about the degree of weakening of the life instinct that all newborns at risk of psychopathology undergo. It must also be borne in mind that the newborn tends to experience these seriously persecutory situations as originating in the mother. Given his specific mental apparatus, he is in fact very perceptive of his mother's anxiety that, especially at the beginning, may hinder the adequacy of her response to the infant's complex communications. Therefore the mother's anxiety is experienced by the infant as extremely threatening, and this aggravates the infant's emotional difficulties. This situation has often been confirmed in my work. A discouraged mother once said to me of her baby: "He really seems to dislike me!" Indeed, many children, especially those most seriously affected, seem to prefer their fathers. Awareness of this problem and of the defensive dynamics deriving from it is an important factor in initiating the consultation. It also helps us to understand the deeply depressive situation faced by parents, mothers in particular.

As Martha Harris wrote:

> It is important that the parents come together, jointly responsible for their child, and that they are able to express their problem, their feelings of helplessness as parents, to an "expert" who is supposed to have some experience in dealing with these problems. But not an expert who, from the height of superior

> knowledge treats them as helpless children, instructing them in what to do, or in what they should not have done, thereby confirming their own childish fears of being discovered to be inadequate and fraudulent parents incapable of responsibility and dependent therefore upon some higher authority. The helpful expert in such a situation is one who can play a role analogous to that of the understanding mother with the distressed baby, who receives the projection of the infant's anxiety, identifies with it, and enables it to cope better with pain because it no longer feels alone. A child who does not thrive and respond to the mother's efforts to alleviate his distress, evokes all her own infantile helplessness and loneliness. Such a mother can easily lose touch with the experience that she has acquired, and lose faith in the defence she has built up against her inadequacy.
>
> It seemed to me that I come through to the parents as someone who was interested in them both and in their child; and also as someone who has no magical expertise which would solve their problems for them, but who gives them the hope that talking together and attempting to understand will be able to help in time. This encourages them to go on working upon the problem, to draw upon their own observations and intuitions, their unique knowledge of themselves and of the child, in order to find new methods of coping. (Harris 1966: 48).

In my consultations I invite the parents, who usually hold their baby in their arms, to sit in front of the desk where some toys have been laid out. I try to make them feel at ease, and I observe the infant while the parents talk to me about him. It is important to observe how the parent—usually the mother—holds her infant, and how, while being held, the baby uses his or her organs of perception and performs movements to relate to the environment. At this point I may verify directly the presence of the alarm symptoms described in Table 1. Alarm symptoms can be seen as early as two or three months of age for infants born at term, and at the equivalent age of two to three months for preterm infants. This is very useful in order to guide the intervention during the therapeutic consultation.

My presence, the presence of the parents, and the infant combine to create a complex field of relationships where the therapist and the parents work together with equal responsibility towards the objective of achieving a better understanding of what is happening in the infant. My presence is receptive to the emotional atmosphere conveyed by the parents and their baby. By trying to understand what is happening during the consultation without judging or acting, I encourage the parents' own thinking and help them overcome the effect of the disturbing behaviour in their infant. In this way parents become able to observe their infant closely and also to find the courage to report their findings, thus attaching significance to their intuitions. During the consultation, infants sense the change in their parents' attitudes and respond to my twofold function of stimulating the parents' emotional contact whilst creating a more favourable listening atmosphere in the consulting room. This helps infants to relax their defences and allows parents to understand them better. It is clear, considering all these aspects, that the intervention of the specialist is a particularly delicate and significant one. Disorders of the perceptive functions, vegetative system, conditions of irritability, and motor problems—all the signals I call "alarm symptoms"—need to be taken into account with a special emphasis on the symptom that seems most obviously to affect the relationship between infant and parents.

Daniel's case

The following excerpts from my work with Daniel illustrate the moments in treatment that I consider most important. The child was referred to me by the paediatrician who "didn't like the way he looked" and was afraid the child might be blind. Daniel, aged two months and twelve days, was brought to the consulting room by his young parents. He was their first child, born at term with a normal delivery and weighed more than 3 kg. He was a fine, strong child and his mother held him in her arms looking outwards. His interactiveness was poor, he was drooling, and had an indifferent glance, he made a constant stereotypical noise of the "eh . . . eh . . . .eh . . ." type, his posture was flaccid, and his head dangled. When I tried to establish contact with him, he refused to hold my glance, went red in the face, was spitting, and waving his arms like a boxer. The noises increased and were constant. His attitude showed beyond doubt his rejection of contact. The parents confirmed my theory and mentioned that there had been problems with feeding since birth. He had refused to breastfeed and subsequently also had serious difficulty in digesting. He would have slept all the time if he had not been woken up.

Symptoms of alarm and predictability for an MSDD diagnosis (Multisystemic Developmental Disorder) following the 0–3 Classification.

In Daniel's case we can recognize the following alarm symptoms: failure to hold the gaze, sound stereotypes, lack of vocal rhythmic communication in the mother-child relationship, refusal to have his back and neck supported, and movement stereotypes. The anomalies in his posture can be seen in the frantic movement of his arms similar to the movements of a boxer and in the overall attitude of his body that appears soft and toneless and suggests overall hypotonicity. His mother would often say: "What a couch potato you are!" He also presented eating and sleep disorders. All these suggested a predictive form of multisystemic developmental disorder.

First meeting

During the first meeting the parents appeared stupefied and dumbfounded. As soon as they came into the room they wanted to place the baby on the table for a neurological assessment. After I got them settled in front of my desk, with the mother holding the baby in her arms, I observed him and described what he was doing, i.e. that he would not give eye contact, the boxer-like movements with his arms and the constant sounds he made, which I termed "consolation sounds". I emphasized the fact that he was a beautiful baby. After a while the mother broke her silence and told me that he had avoided eye contact since birth. In the family they had noticed that he looked away and thought he was attracted by something in the room and asked him: "What can you see over there? What can you see over there?" At the end of the session I spoke of my impression that Daniel was a child who, for reasons as yet unknown, shied away from a relationship and chose to withdraw. I told them of the need, on their part, to try to get him actively to hold the glance, to speak to him describing what he was doing, and to hold him close, in their arms. I also said that in most cases, these small babies learn rapidly to renounce their isolation and to enjoy the communication and presence of their parents.

Second meeting

I saw the family again after one week and the change in the child and the parents was already very clear. The baby was two months and twenty days old. The parents were immediately more loquacious; the mother talked about her baby and told him to "look around properly". I emphasized the improvement in the way he held his head, and that the consolation sounds had disappeared and I added: "I wonder what has caused such a rapid change in his attitude?" The mother was animated and told me how he "looked for her with his eyes", and how he "spoke to her", and how Daniel showed increased attention, looked at his hands, etc. She had also noticed that Daniel "spied on her when unobserved"; she related how if the parents were busy talking to other people, he watched them. If they looked at him he would look away. She had noticed that when she offered Daniel a coloured rattle or something similar, he acted as if he expected that the objects would follow his glance. When he looked away, he seemed surprised that the object did not follow his glance and he would then turn his gaze back towards the object, looking for it. When Daniel woke in the morning and was rested, she laid him on his back supporting him with one hand under his neck and tried to hold his gaze, smiling at him and uttering words of affection. At first he appeared extremely bothered by this new approach in the relationship and would rebel. The mother reported that he did not want to look at her and when she saw that he was tired or excessively bothered she stopped.

"Non-saturation" of the intervention

My intervention was restricted solely to observing the child. I tried neither to give too much advice to the parents, nor to make definite remarks on the child's condition. My expression:

"I wonder what could have caused such a rapid change in his attitude?", my holding back from recognizing the cause of the change in the child, and my throwing the ball back into the parents' court, fall within what Ferro defines as "unsaturated interpretation". The aspect of non-saturation intervention (Ferro 1992) is the least coded even in the field of child psychotherapy, yet it is important to recognize how effective it is in promoting activation of both the small child's thought and the parents' reflection during these therapeutic consultations. This is what happened in the second meeting with Daniel where my comment seemed to have provoked deeper reflection in mother. As well as informing me of the changes in the child, she referred to a number of new observations she had made and which I was not yet aware of. "He's looking at me when unobserved" and "Daniel's thinking that the objects follow his glance and not the other way round."

In the same session the mother called his name and he made eye contact for a few seconds. I emphasized the importance of this attitude and the mother also said she thought he was also sitting up straighter. I asked if he liked being cuddled. The mother nodded but added that he liked being alone, especially when he was put to bed. I answered that a child must spend some time on his own too, especially when he was preparing for sleep at night.

The mother observed the saliva dribbling from his mouth and called him "a drooler". Father called Daniel by name and for a few seconds he looked him in the eyes. Again I emphasized the significance of this event. He was still in his mother's arms but seemed to withdraw totally from his environment; his gaze went blank. The mother called him and tried to attract his attention waving a finger in front of his eyes, but in vain. She seemed disconsolate and became quiet. I intervened saying that a child could not always remain in contact and he could be looking around him at all the new things for him in the room.

At this point I preferred not to consider the visible and understandable anxiety that mother was experiencing. I thought that by giving an ordinary meaning (backed up by the child's blank gaze), I was giving her my support, and helping her not to be downcast by observing only the things that were not right with her child. At the same time I took into account the fact that Daniel was present and he could be listening to my comment and be somehow affected. The passivity of his blank stare could be broken through by my words that attributed a significant purpose and a curiosity to his gaze.

After my intervention, the mother again turned to Daniel, reminding him of what they had done together that morning. She told me of his recent progress: he enjoyed his bath, he let her undress him, he stayed awake longer, he communicated to her when he was tired, and he glanced more appropriately. His consolation noises diminished and he showed some interest in his hands, which he put into his mouth, preferring them to his dummy.

Feelings in the relationship with the child

The anguish caused by the child's difficulties frequently leads the parents to a state of intellectual inhibition, to such an extent that (as seen in the case of Daniel's parents), during the first consultation they appeared tongue-tied, made no comments on the child, gave the impression of being superficial, not very bright, and unaware of their child's state. Their communication, when urged by the therapist, was limited to a description of concrete aspects of themselves and the infant. Gradually during the course of treatment, as the child improved and there was greater trust in the therapist, the parents' state of anguish seemed to diminish, giving way to a different state of mind which was expressed even at a physical level.

It can be seen how, especially in mothers, there is a change in their somatic features so that during sessions they seem to become more attractive. This is particularly evident when consultations are videoed, as in the case of Daniel. Together with an improvement in the somatic features there is also a transformation in the parents' communication skills, so that the emotive situation, no longer experienced as a concrete, physical effort, is expressed in words. They become more and more open to feelings and emotions both in the infant and in themselves. Daniel disliked being in the position of having his back and neck supported and for this reason his mother tried to persuade the child to accept this position by placing him at different times during the day on his changing mattress and by trying to establish eye contact and rhythmic vocal communication with him.

A moving moment occurred when, aged three months, Daniel's mother reported that for the first time he smiled at her from his cot and she tried to hold his glance. He looked her in the eyes for quite some time and smiled at her. "For me it was a very moving moment, unforgettable, my eyes filled with tears", she said.

When Daniel was three months and twenty days the parents told me that his main problem was fear. Daniel's fear was the expression of the prevalence of what Klein defined as persecutory anguish (anxiety). Daniel had right from early times proved to be extremely fearful, a "scare baby". "He was afraid of the smallest movement, of anything that approached him, of any change and the slightest thing made him go stiff with fear." Yet again, in this session, it was very significant when his mother spoke of his fear and added that he was fearful like she was and her own father was, too. This opened up the possibility of working on this aspect of parental projections on the infant, in those sessions devoted entirely to mother.

Projections and transgenerational aspects

At a time that felt appropriate and after about ten sessions devoted to the child, I arranged for a number of meetings with mother to examine the problem of fear. Mother had a twin sister, who was very attached to their mother, while she herself was "the image of her father".

I had noticed a sweetness and tenderness, which could be defined as "feminine" in Daniel's father, in contrast to a more rigid, authoritarian attitude in the mother, which could be defined as "masculine". Her father had always shown a strong preference for her, since she reminded him of his twin brother who had died in a car accident. By identifying his daughter with the deceased twin, the father had unconsciously become excessively fearful and was afraid of what might happen to his daughter. These fears were in turn being experienced by her in relation to Daniel so that she was afraid during her pregnancy of having caused the problems recognized in her newborn baby. In the fifth month of pregnancy she had experienced "great fear" as her husband had lost his job when the company he worked for closed down.

TRUST IN THE THERAPIST AND TECHNICAL ASPECTS

Of great importance in the treatment is the confidence and trust which the parents place in the therapist. This means the creation of an atmosphere in the consulting room that inspires both the parents' and the infant's communication of emotional experiences. Daniel's father's comment seemed of considerable importance when he had said: "Goodness, how well we feel here!", thus expressing his appreciation of the therapist and the atmosphere that had been created in the consulting room. I believe that this aspect plays a significant role in the positive development of the treatment of infants at risk of psychopathology and this was surely true in Daniel's case.

The treatment involved weekly sessions up to the sixth month, fortnightly sessions up to a year, and then every two months up to three years of age. Daniel is now seventeen years old, is fine, and is doing well as a high school student.

It is important to bear in mind the many different technical aspects in these consultations, which usually last about an hour and fifteen minutes. In agreement with Watillon-Naveau (1993), I do not follow a pre-established programme but I make appointments on the basis of what emerges in the first sessions and also on the basis of the extent of the child's psychopathological condition. The date of the next meeting is therefore fixed in agreement and discussion with the parents.

Especially in the early period of treatment, I focus my attention mainly on the child since the parents may not yet have confidence and trust in the therapist. If I devote too much attention to them they may, overtly or covertly, fear my judgement and feel guilty about their baby's pathology. Only later will I shift my attention from the infant to work on the parental projections and explore the transgenerational components inherent in the disorder in the infant. This work requires a great deal of time and can take place only when the therapist-parent relationship has been consolidated and founded on deep knowledge and characterized by positive feelings.

Final considerations

I have been developing the work methodology that I have described for about twenty-five years. I think I can say that it has a very significant preventive function in the context of serious symptoms in the baby and in the relationship with his parents, where there is a risk of becoming entrenched in serious pathology. It is a technique that, while not necessarily interpretative, seems to enable parents to use the transference situation with the therapist. During the consultation, the infant senses the change in his parents' attitude and responds to my twofold function of stimulating the parents' emotional contact and generally creating a more favourable atmosphere for listening and understanding. This helps the child to relax his defences and allows his parents to understand the uneasy situation better.

In this way parents, and particularly the mother, can achieve a deeper awareness of the problems, especially when they are able to take back into themselves projections that are affecting the child. Martha Harris wrote that:

> This kind of interview is one which can be conducted by workers without training in psychoanalytic psychotherapy and with varying degrees of sophistication in mental health work and concepts . . . The essential requirement of the interviewer is, I think, a capacity to be interested in, to encompass the total situation without taking sides; to be able to encourage the parents to follow their perceptions, and to use their latent resources without increasing the feeling of helplessness, dependence and failure. Ability to refrain from giving useless advice, to distinguish between helpful advice and interference can come through bitter experience, but it can be taught and encouraged to some extent. (Harris 1966: 51).

The technique used during these interventions, enables parents to make use of the positive aspects that emerge from the transference situation with the therapist and thus to gain a deeper awareness of the problem. This can help both parents and children to overcome the parasitism within their relationship that is preventing the various individuation processes from taking place.

Videoing the consultation sessions

Since 1988 I have been videoing the consultation sessions with infants who present situations of potential high risk. I use this technique with the parents' consent. It is extremely interesting to be able to watch the sessions because this enables a more in-depth examination of the infant's situation as well as observing the communication and the parents' attitudes. Watching and listening to the session afterwards enables me to recognize any mistakes I may have made, for instance in being too hasty in my intervention by interrupting the parents or in missing the infant's initiatives. I also suggest to the parents that we could see some of the films together. They can become more aware of their child's situation too, of his or her improvements and they can comment on this. It is also possible in some circumstances for them to recognize that their anxiety may lead them to intrude on the infant's play, blocking his or her initiative, and not letting him or her be the "director" of his play that has a meaning and represents the beginning of a capacity to think in the baby.

Bibliography and further references

Bick, E. (1964). Notes on infant observation in psychoanalytic training. *International Journal of Psycho-Analysis*, 45: 558–566.

Bick, E. (1968). The experience of the skin in early object-relations. *International Journal of Psycho-Analysis*, 49: 484–486.

Bion, W. R. (1962). *Learning from Experience*. London: Heinemann.

Bobath, B. (1967). The very early treatment of cerebral palsy. *Developmental Medicine and Child Neurology*, 9/4: 373–390.

Bobath, B., & Bobath, K. (1979). *Student's Paper*. London: Bobath Centre.

Corominas, J. (1983). Handicap psichico: applicazioni della psicoanalisi alla psicoterapia dell'handicap. *Quaderni di Psicoterapia Infantile*, 8.

Cramer, B. (1974). Interventions therapeutiques brèves avec parents et enfants. *Psichiatrie Enfant*. 17/1: 53–117.

Cramer, B., & Palacio-Espasa, F. (1993). *La Pratique des Psychotherapies Mères-Bèbès*. Paris: Presses Universitaires de France.

Ferro, A. (1992). *La Tecnica Nella Psicoanalisi Infantile*. Milan: Raffaello Cortina.

Giannotti, A., Lanza, A. M., & Del Pidio, F. (1994). Genesi della patologia psicosomatica, ipotesi sul ruolo svolto dalle fantasie inconsce. In: R. Negri (Ed.), *Il Neonato in Terapia Intensiva. Un Modello Neuropsicoanalitico di Prevenzione*, p. 122. Milan: Cortina, 1998.

Haag, G. (1988). Réflexions sur quelques jonctions psycho-toniques et psycho-motrices dans la première année de la vie. *Neuropsychiatrie de l'Enfance et de l'Adolescence*, 1: 1–9.

Hafez, E. S. E. (1975). *The Behaviour of Domestic Animals*. London: Ballière, Tindal, & Cassel.

Harris, M. (1966). Therapeutic consultations. In: M. Harris, & E. Bick, *Collected Papers of Martha Harris and Esther Bick* (pp. 38–52). Perthshire: Clunie Press, 1987.

Harris, M. (1976). The contribution of observation of mother-infant interaction and development to the equipment of a psychoanalyst or psychoanalytic psychotherapist. In: M. Harris Williams (Ed.), *Collected Papers of Martha Harris and Esther Bick* (pp. 225–239). Perthshire: Clunie Press, 1987.

Klein, M. (1952). Some theoretical conclusions regarding the emotional life of the infant. In: *Envy and Gratitude and Other Works, 1946–1963* (pp. 61–93). London: Hogarth, 1975. Also in: M. Klein, P. Heimann, S. Isaacs, & J. Riviere (Eds.), 1952, *Developments in Psychoanalysis*. London: Hogarth Press, 1975. [London: Karnac Books & The Institute of Psychoanalysis, 1989.]

Lebovici, S. (1983). *Le Nourrisson la Mère et le Psychanalyste*. Paris: Centurion, Paidos.

Lieberman, A. F. (2002). Il trattamento dei disturbi dell'attaccamento nella psicoterapia bambino-genitore. In: J. Martìn Maldonado-Duràn (Ed.), *Infanzia e Salute Mentale* (pp. 119–147). Milan: Raffaello Cortina, 2005.

Meltzer, D., Bremner, J., Hoxter, S., Weddell, D., & Wittenberg, I. (1975). *Explorations in Autism: A Psychoanalytical Study*. Perthshire: Clunie Press.

Meltzer, D., & Harris Williams, M. (1988). *The Apprehension of Beauty*. Perthshire: Clunie Press.

NCCIP (1994). *Zero-to-Three. National Center for Clinical Infant Programs*. Milan: Masson, 1997.

Negri, R. (1982). L'evoluzione della teoria Bobathiana nel trattamento del bambino con paralisi cerebrale infantile. *Giornale di Neuropsichiatria dell'Età Evolutiva*, 2/3: 299–307.

Negri, R. (1983). Introduzione al dibattito: il neonato in neuropsichiatria infantile. *Giornale di Neuropsichiatria dell'Età Evolutiva*, 3/1: 59–70.

Negri, R. (1984). Segni predittivi di schizofrenia infantile nel primoanno di vita. In: C. L. Cazzullo (Ed.), *La Schizofrenia in Etàevolutiva, Fattori di Rischio e Predittività* (pp. 45–52). Rome: II Pensiero Scientifico.

Negri, R. (1986). Riconoscimento e cura della psicosi nel primi mesi di vita. *Psichiatria dell'Infanzia e dell'Adolescenza*, 6: 673–684.

Negri, R. (1989). Problematiche di psicosomatica nel primi mesi: una proposta di intervento. *Quaderni di Psicoterapia Infantile*, 19: 217–231.

Negri, R. (1994). *The Newborn in the Intensive Care Unit. A Neuropsychoanalytic Prevention Model*. London: Karnac Books.

Negri, R. (1998). *Il Neonato in Terapia Intensiva* (2nd ed.) Milan: Raffaello Cortina.

Pozzi, M. (2003). *Psychic Hooks and Bolts.* London and New York: Karnac Books.

Rhode, M. (1997). Psychosomatic integrations. Eye and mouth in infant observation. In: S. Reid (Ed.), *Developments in Infant Observation* (pp. 140–156). London and New York: Routledge.

Robson, K. S. (1967). The role of eye-to-eye contact in maternal infant attachment. *Journal of Child Psychology and Psychiatry,* 8: 13–25.

Stern, D. N. (1995). *The Motherhood Constellation. A Unified View of Parent-Infant Psychotherapy.* New York: Basic Books.

Touwen, B. C. L. (1989). Early detection and early treatment of cerebral palsy: possibilities and fallacies. *Giornale di Neuropsichiatria dell'Età Evolutiva,* 4: 31–38.

Tustin, F. (1986). *Autistic Barriers in Neurotic Patients.* London: Karnac Books.

Watillon-Naveau, A. (1993). Dynamique des therapies psychanalytiques de la relation précoce parents-enfant. *Revue Belge de Psychoanalyse,* 22: 43–56.

Winnicott, D. W. (1941). The observation of small children in a pre-established situation. *International Journal of Psycho-Analysis,* 22. [*Collected Papers, Through Paediatrics to Psycho-Analysis.* London: Tavistock, 1958.]

CHAPTER SEVEN

Transformational process in parent-infant psychotherapy: provision in community drop-in groups

Judith Woodhead and Jessica James
The Anna Freud Centre, London

Introduction

This chapter is about the provision of psychoanalytic parent-infant psychotherapy within community drop-in groups in order to support and repair relationships between parents and infants. The Anna Freud Centre has responded to the need for such innovative services, in ways that are in keeping with its traditions from the establishment of the War Nurseries onwards. Collaborating with health care professionals to establish drop-in groups for parents and infants has extended the Parent-Infant Project's model of parent-infant psychotherapy. The first drop-in group is in a health centre and the second in a hostel for homeless families. The model for these groups is underpinned by principles derived from group analysis and parent-infant psychotherapy, along with neuroscientific, attachment, and infancy research. Early parent-infant relationships are the crucible within which experiences can occur that spark and sustain the development of the infant self. In psychoanalytic parent-infant psychotherapy, experiences of the self arise through, and are transformed by, emotionally contingent intimate relationships with others. Furthermore, at a time of rapid brain development, therapeutic intervention supports the infant in the process of developing "a more complex level of brain organisation" (Tronick 1998: 295).

The Anna Freud Centre provides a parent-infant psychotherapist to form a drop-in team with health care professionals. Creating an inter-professional team, located within existing service structures, is a core principle. Parents are more likely to come to drop-in groups when part of an integrated service where, with their babies, they meet the staff for other purposes, such as developmental checks, immunization, or family support. In this chapter we will provide two detailed illustrations of analytic process that demonstrate the ideas that frame drop-in groups. They are derived from the four central concepts of our model—unconscious communication, emotional regulation, mentalization, and interactive repair. Drop-in groups provide rich contexts for the use of the two techniques we shall focus on—modelling and mirroring. In the recent book *The Practice of Parent-Infant Psychotherapy: Claiming the Baby*, members of the Parent-Infant Project team (Tessa Baradon, Carol Broughton, Iris Gibbs, Jessica James, Angela Joyce, and Judith Woodhead) describe their concepts and techniques and provide full case examples. The theories that underpin our model are also elaborated in the book, notably the work of Donald Winnicott. For clarity, we shall refer to the parent as "mother" throughout, but fathers or both parents at times attend the groups. We shall refer to the therapist as "she".

Establishing an analytic culture within drop-in groups

Busy baby clinics frequently comprise a collection, rather than a group, of individuals, where mothers and babies form a queue and wait, often for a long time, to see a health professional. This experience tends to discourage mothers from forming connections with one another. It can, for some mothers, create a lonely, tense experience where they fear lest their baby cries, is hard to console, needs to feed in public, or is seen to have developmental problems. Especially with poor availability of interpreters, mothers may feel unable to voice questions and concerns, and feel there is insufficient opportunity to understand or digest advice given. Health professionals often express their concern that they lack time and opportunity to observe the relational dynamics of mothers and babies, and address emotional causes that may underlie symptoms.

The drop-in groups offer the health professionals greater opportunity to observe parents and infants in action and to gain fuller understanding of their relationship, while enabling families to become involved with each other in inter-personal ways. They provide the baby clinic teams and families access to analytic principles which the therapists strive to communicate. The aim is to develop a "culture for change" (James 2002) within groups of mothers and babies. An enabling ethos is adopted, encouraging the co-creation of analytic process in drop-in group culture. However, establishing an analytic frame and culture within services that are structured so that parents can drop in and drop out is complex. Responsiveness and adaptability are essential. The therapists' task involves creating, as it were, soft corners in a medically equipped environment—in order to facilitate the representation of unconscious processes in the primary relationship between parent and infant, and the supporting professional network.

The drop-in groups provide a secure place within which ordinary feelings and painful emotions can be expressed—related to loneliness, isolation, depression, fears of incompetence, fears of harming the baby, anxiety at not understanding the baby's needs, and perhaps grief related to giving up previous lives. Mothers may welcome space in which to speak about traumatic experiences, and use the groups to provide emotional containment, but equally well may prefer not to, and they are under no pressure to do so. However the staff group is alert to mother infant relationships, and not only to the difficulties alone that they may bring. They are vigilant to mental states in which a baby may be lost from the mother's mind, and seek to help bring the baby to mind through the interactions and perspectives that the drop-in groups enable.

Aware of the impact of primitive anxieties evoked in early parent-baby relationships, staff welcome parents and babies to groups in a warm way, and voice their recognition of mothers and babies from past groups—perhaps recalling an experience, a favourite activity or toy. Amidst the hubbub of comings and goings, mothers are invited with their babies to take off their shoes and join the staff on floor cushions placed in a circle around baby mats. The circle is not a fixed structure, but changes shape in each session as mothers and babies come and go or move to other places. It prioritizes focus on the infants, face-to-face contact, and interactive engagement. Throughout the group, the therapist and staff members spend long periods just being on the mats with families, making observations together and interacting non-verbally, and at times may move to be with different mother and baby dyads.

In many drop-in provisions emphasis is placed on action and distraction rather than intimate interaction. By contrast, we encourage the use of a small selection of developmentally and emotionally appropriate, non-electronic toys. A surfeit of toys that distract from parent-infant interactions is avoided. Instead, a multiplicity of possible interactional involvements arise within the groups—between mothers and their own babies, mothers and other babies, and between babies, all of different ages and developmental stages. Each mother and baby's repertoire of ways of being with others and understanding others' intentions is implicitly expanded, rather than only through explicit professional interventions.

Every group is regarded as a potential attachment experience, and each moment in a group is seen as an opportunity for supporting each baby's developing sense of self. Attempts are actively made to engage babies in "affective dialogue" (Baradon 2002), alongside and with their mothers. The staff members perceive and internally process unconscious relational dynamics within mother-infant dyadic relationships, and within the context of the drop-in group interactions. In the immediate situation, they may voice what is happening in informal conversational language. Or another mother or staff member may develop the theme. The mother and infant hear other perspectives and see other ways of relating. The drop-in group thus provides a rich context for dyadic and triadic experiences that may enhance mothers' capacities for multiple, new ways of relating with their babies (Woodhead 2005), which bring qualitative changes.

The staff group reflect before and after each group on individual mother and baby relationships and group dynamics. Reflection on the functioning and effectiveness of the provision is stimulated by evaluation, which has become central in the provision of the groups. A research psychologist from the Anna Freud Centre joins the staff groups to carry out evaluation, and meets mothers within, and outside of, the drop-in group sessions. The implicit therapeutic impact of her work is documented in Woodhead, Bland, and Baradon (2006). Through the questions asked, and the videoing of an interactive play sequence, the research process intrinsically enhances mothers' awareness of their relationship with their baby, and they feel cared for through the evaluator's sensitive approach.

Dropping in and dropping out

Families can drop in or drop out at any time during each session, both in their attendance at the session as well as their engagement within the session, recognising from time to time they might want to be on the periphery of the group action. No one knows exactly who will come each week, and the group experience that will arise. The staff need to be able to tolerate these uncertainties, create some certainties within uncertainty, and offer continuity, by carrying forward the history of the group as a shared experience, potentially available even to the most marginalized mothers and to those whose attendance is sporadic. The reliability of the ongoing group—week in, week out—is essential so that it can model good enough parental provision. Each group has a clear beginning time and ending time, even though parents are free to arrive at any time within these boundaries. A clear settling in and middle time is established, followed by a period of preparation for leaving. "Hellos" and "goodbyes" are encouraged between everyone in the group, including the babies.

Experience suggests that the stability yet flexibility of drop-in provision is especially appropriate for the populations of mothers and babies who tend to use the groups. In both settings described below, the groups reflect the diverse demographic status and ethnicity of mothers using post-natal services in London. They include refugees, asylum seekers, and many women, who express feelings of dislocation and isolation in terms of their cultural, ethnic, or professional affiliations. Many have experienced trauma before arriving in London, and may be low in "emotional capital" (Garland, Hume, & Majid 2002). Becoming a mother at a time of loss of motherland, tongue, and family is likely to impact on the relationship with the baby. The health centre is the primary institution they are likely to access to monitor their baby's health and development. The drop-in groups provide a potential attachment object at a time when attachments may have been lost.

New parents may view the centre as a stable part of their lives as they access antenatal and post-natal care, midwives, and health visitors. If emotional difficulties, or concerns about the mother-infant relationship are identified, most mothers have neither the opportunity nor the orientation to be referred to statutory services, and few psychological services specialize in work with babies from pre-birth and in earliest life. With slow referral processes, the baby may well no longer be a baby by the time help is accessed, so that an opportunity is missed for change—and preventive repair—within the early parent-infant relationship. Mothers' access to the inner world work of therapy is securely linked with external world provision—such as medical input, mental health and community support systems and interpreters. When the drop-in groups have a secure place within a network of services, they can provide a resource for the interplay of different ways of being with infants, reflecting the different cultures, religions, and class of all who attend.

The drop-in nature of the groups may be especially important for hard-to-engage families, increasing the accessibility of therapeutic provision in ways that are non-threatening. Those most at risk, and who are the most socially isolated, have least confidence within group situations. Where support offered by professional staff may be experienced as threatening, support offered by peers—other mothers—might be less so. Babies are messy, demanding, and unpredictable and may make mothers feel incompetent, helpless, and ashamed. Groups provide potential for learning and reality checks through comparison with others who also struggle with their parenting. When a group setting offers attuned attention to babies and mothers, their faces ignite, building faith in the possibility of relationship and development of self. With varied weekly membership and numbers of parents and babies, the staff groups retain an image of the drop-ins as solid groups so that parents may drop-in with their babies—and drop out too.

"Drop-in" groups allow parents to regulate their commitment. This may itself be therapeutically important. In the same way that a baby can only cope with a little bit of looking and has to look away when the intimacy becomes too intense, so hard-to-reach parents need to feel that they are able to withdraw—that "dropping-out" as well as "dropping in" is respected. They know the group reliably exists, and can return sooner or later, if they wish to. At the same time the therapist has in mind that they may come back. The culture of the group has continued, and the staff group "remembers" her and her baby. Being remembered models the positive value of connection and relatedness. This may be crucial for traumatized mothers, who have suffered cultural dislocation. The shared experience of having a baby brings them to the drop-in groups, which enables them to build connections amongst mothers and amongst babies, irrespective of ethnicity, cultural background, and language. This models for the babies that emotional connection can be a safe and good experience. When mothers feel more connected with others, it is likely they will be able to offer their babies a more contingent, intersubjective experience of "implicit relational knowing" (Stern et al. 1998) available for internalization within procedural memory. Very often, friendships formed with other mothers within the group are maintained outside the groups. These friendships provide a source of solidarity and mutual support amongst parents, and in turn amplify the probability of positive, shared experiences with their babies.

In short, the two drop-in groups provide a safe context in which parents are helped to reflect upon states of mind in themselves, their infant, and the relationship between them. This includes enabling them to perceive and regulate their own and their infant's emotional states. These processes are illustrated in the following sections.

First illustration: the health centre drop-in group

This clinical illustration describes a health centre drop-in, and then shows how a new mother accesses therapeutic support for her derailed relationship with her son, and how they become part of the group. The drop-in group takes place for an hour and a quarter, and is attended at any one time by either very few families, or up to around ten families, in a room adjoined to a weekly post-natal clinic in a health centre, where mothers come to have their babies weighed, checked, and to consult with health visitors. Some mothers attend frequently for up to six to twelve months, forming a shifting core group who, along with the staff group, create the solidity of the group culture with new mothers. At the time of the group described, the drop-in provision had been running for four years, and the Nursery Nurse and psychotherapist had remained the same throughout, resulting in shared understanding and technique. A Sure Start family worker also joined the team, with the important role of helping publicize the group and sometimes bringing mothers along. In the illustration we see how the new mother and baby bring a potential crisis for the core group of experienced mothers and how the group's capacity to regulate emotion is tested and survived. The importance of this clinical vignette is in the detailed individual therapeutic work that takes place despite the mobile nature of the drop-in.

> The baby clinic had begun. A new mother arrived in the adjacent drop-in group, amidst the buzz of arrivals of babies and mothers who were parking prams and arranging themselves on the floor cushions, talking, settling their babies within the central space formed by the group and interacting with the different babies. The Sure Start worker welcomed her as she walked round the room. She did not have time even to learn their names before the mother poured out that her six-week-old baby would not let her alone for a moment, would feed too much, keep asking for more, and was driving her mad. She said she would have to keep walking round and not sit down in the Group. Another mother said it had been like that for her, but had got better when her baby reached twelve weeks and there were murmurs of shared experience around the group.

Commentary: the therapist realizes that this mother had been referred for individual parent-infant psychotherapy but had not taken up the place. Different professionals had expressed concern. However, as this group does not require referral, the mother dares to come, but needs initially to remain on the outside, and is free to do so. Other parents, who had experienced the development of this group over time, carry and embody its culture for this new mother. The communications of the other mothers suggest she is not alone in her experience of acute feelings in relation to her baby, and that such feelings can be thought about.

> The baby began to cry and unsuccessfully sought the breast. He became distressed, as no breast was forthcoming and the mother's voice sounded harsh. Another mother with a three-month-old baby passed cushions in the direction of the new mother and said she also feels she spends her whole life feeding her baby. A background overall settling-in process was occurring with a

buzz of talk and play. The new mother sat on the cushion and tried giving the baby the dummy, to no avail, and then put her finger in the baby's mouth for the baby to suck on, and he increased his protests. Meanwhile, a different mother was telling about how difficult it was to cope with her six-month-old son's hernia operation, and others were helping her think about the experience; her son lay quietly on his mother's lap, sucking his comforter and others expressed empathy with them both.

Commentary: it is another mother that offers help, by providing a cushion, symbolizing care through informal provision for both mother and baby. All show concern for the crying baby while listening in parallel to the mother of the child facing the operation who uses the group to help her contain and process her feelings and her son's—modelling group process to the new mother. With attention provided at a temperature she can take, the new mother can then tentatively move into the circle of mothers on cushions. She moves from outside to inside. At the same time the buzz of noise takes away the starkness of her baby's screams that were beginning to evoke concern in everyone.

Other babies became unsettled or quiet. The Sure Start worker asked the mother if she could tell a bit more about the feeding difficulties. The mother said he should not be seeking her breast again and others talked about feeding difficulties. The new mother said she had not lived in England long, had no family to help her, and began to weep. Another mother said her own feeling of loneliness, with her family at the other side of the world, was so terrible, and a different mother said that she had struggled for weeks to establish breast-feeding. The therapist spoke of the mother's upset feelings and also spoke directly to the baby, "Oh dear—those pains are hard, and your mummy gets so upset too." The mother began to settle, and the other mothers and babies showed relief. The group attention turned to all the babies and the therapist went to play with two seven-month-olds who were exploring one another.

Commentary: exploration rather than advice about feeding encourages the mother to express her isolation and distress, naming and differentiating her emotions, and discovering they are not hers alone. The baby's experience of pain is mirrored through the therapist's words, voice tone, and facial expression—providing mother and baby opportunity to recognize their own feeling states, and distinguish between their own and the other's feelings. Speaking to and through the baby reinforces that they are two separate selves. Processes of emotional regulation and reflective function (Fonagy, Gergely, Jurist, & Target 2002) are provided and modelled by the whole group, for all to take in.

> Then, a mother helped her settle down more comfortably on cushions and the baby, with difficulty and sobs, latched onto the breast. The mother was not supporting the baby's head with her arm, and the Nursery Nurse put a hand beneath it and stroked his hair while talking soothingly to them. Another mother said that it would not be so hard forever—things would get better. The therapist said aloud from the other side of the room where she was playing with other babies, that sometimes babies seem to want to make their mummies' life difficult, but really are simply struggling to adjust to life, learn all that they need to learn, and find how to get their mummies to fall in love with them. A general discussion opened up of how the babies are in fact trying to communicate their own needs, as separate little persons.

Commentary: mother and baby receive the worker's and the group's scaffolding for the feeding. The therapist reframes the common attribution that babies cry to intentionally annoy their mothers. She indicates that they have selves that are separate from their mothers, have agency, and desires for mothers' love, modelling mentalization, as she emotionally processes the experiences within the present moment.

> The mother became softer towards her baby. She began to say little things to him, saying she was sorry she had been so angry with him. Hearing his mother's gentle, more attuned, voice, the baby's body moulded into his mother's, showing new emotional anchorage. She listened to others, as they spoke of their similar, and different, feelings about the impact of the baby on their lives. By this time the new baby was able to lay in front of his mother,

awake and calm, on a baby mat, a part of the group. He looked towards his mother's face, and she responded to him telling him that she was sorry they got into such states.

Commentary: interactive repair has occurred through the whole group's contribution. The difficulties and ambivalence of mothering can be tolerated. Emotional dysregulation can be accepted, understood, and managed. This process is available for all to internalize, and becomes a part of the procedural memory of the whole group.

Second illustration: the hostel drop-in group

This different kind of drop-in group takes place within a baby clinic in a hostel in which 140 homeless families live in a recently converted building that has individual rooms with integrated facilities. Families in this hostel have a designated health visitor who visits their rooms and holds a weekly baby clinic in a large room in its basement, in which the drop-in group takes place. Sessions last for two hours with fifteen to twenty-five families attending each time for some or most of the time. The parent-infant psychotherapist offers her understanding in this context, alongside the health visitor and other professionals including a nursery nurse and an assistant who weighs the babies. In their discussions before and after the drop-in clinic it is impossible to remember everyone's names and room numbers are often used for identification.

Parents and babies are encouraged to come "just to play with their babies and to get to know each other". Small groups form, usually defined by common experiences such as ages of baby or cultural and racial group. The atmosphere ebbs and flows within sessions and in phases of sessions. The babies are called up in turn to the weighing scales and nappy changing area but, otherwise, discussions are conducted wherever a mother and baby are situated, usually by, or on, the mat. Whilst it is crucial to be sensitive to the realities of homeless people's lives, these cannot be explored in depth within this context as they are in danger of high-jacking the group's purpose of promoting emotionally contingent parent-infant relationships. The illustrations that follow demonstrate the therapist's role in fostering and sustaining a positive group culture.

> A mother and her six-month-old baby arrived first, as the session was just beginning, perhaps hoping to come and leave quickly. The therapist only vaguely recognized them. She greeted them from the mat suggesting the baby might like to try sitting propped up in the foam circle. He was a serious baby and his mother seemed hesitant. She commented about coming for immunizations whilst sitting him down facing away from both her and the therapist. The therapist moved to look towards his face, saying: "That's it, it is a new place, but mummy can sit nearby." Both mother and baby seemed unresponsive, although the mother sat closer and picked up a rattle, which she shook in front of her son without looking at his reaction. The therapist was aware of the mother's annoyance, felt herself unsure and noticed that the baby was beginning to express these difficult feelings, with his body sagging and face crumpling. She said "Oh you are not sure about that." He wobbled over and his mother helped him to sit up again, but still with his back to her. An older baby arrived, crawled over and the six-month-old baby collapsed in tears. His mother picked him up hurriedly and was called out for weighing and they went. The therapist said, into the space of the room, "Maybe you can come back afterwards and we can go more slowly?" She noticed later that the health visitor was encouraging them to stay, but the mother left.

Commentary: it is unfortunate that they arrive before anyone else, without a group situation to scaffold them. The mother experiences the therapist as intrusive, rather than friendly, and she is not able to act on her counter-transference experience in time to contain the situation. The therapist voices the baby's affects, talking through him to his mother, to convey a sense of being able to stay with their fearful responses and that this might be helpful whether or not they return. She also speaks to the others arriving, to demonstrate her belief that this failure can be remedied and that the group will go on. After the group ends the therapist and other workers share their perceptions of this mother and baby, who seem nervous and depressed. The health visitor remembers another mother saying she could come because "you didn't pester me, you were not overpowering". This reaffirms the importance of going gently and the value of drop-in groups where parents can regulate their own pace.

The group atmosphere then developed with the arrival of some regular families, who knew what to expect and settle together with the therapist on the mat. A baby was kicking her legs excitedly as she entered in her mother's arms. She joined with another baby of about eight months and their mothers took off their shoes and sat on the mat greeting each other, with the babies crawling and pulling themselves up onto a wooden frame. The therapist commented that they seemed pleased to be there, and said to the first baby, "Gosh, you are pulling yourself up." This baby's mother looked over briefly and said "He has been doing it for a bit." She had recently started coming each week, but tended to keep clear of the therapist and the professionals whilst beginning to get friendly with other mothers and babies. The therapist caught her baby's gaze and, then when he pulled himself up on her helped him to stand for a few moments and smiled with his mother.

Commentary: the mothers of these eight-month-old babies are building up their trust in the group gradually, and now come for the group itself. One of the mothers is prickly in relation to the therapist, when she shows she had not remembered the baby could pull himself up. The therapist processes this and, retaining her non-retaliatory friendly stance, is able to share moments of mutual delight when her baby climbs onto her. She also notices that the mothers are engaged in livelier conversation than usual.

The therapist then intervened alongside the health visitor to help a mother and her baby with feeding difficulties. A pregnant woman sat with her one-year-old son, who looked sad, on her knee. She talked animatedly in Bengali with another mother. When the health visitor came over, the mother's face became solemn and she said that although she had stopped force-feeding, he was still not eating. A few weeks earlier the health visitor and therapist had discussed her son's feeding, when it transpired that she was holding him down and forcing him to eat. The therapist came over to sit at a small table near the mother and health visitor and engaged the son. She took a dog from a jigsaw that interested him, so he crawled over to the table and she helped him get onto a little chair next to her. They put bits of jigsaw into place, while bits fell on the floor, or went into his mouth, and had a playful exchange as they talked about the animals. The health visitor was talking with his mother about how to make eating enjoyable and help him find his appetite. The therapist showed how he was putting pieces of the jigsaw into his mouth and suggested he could do this with food, which the health visitor confirmed. The other Bengali-speaking mother was watching and her little boy crawled over to get involved.

Commentary: rather than just talking about changing behaviour the therapist and health visitor are able to work jointly and enact what is possible in the here and now. The therapist uses a play opportunity to model and provide experience in the group of what the health visitor suggests. This intervention helps support the baby's sense of self and his mother is seeing him valued as an active participant in the interaction. The therapist has reframed him for his mother as a person with a mind and with agency. Baby-centred turn-taking moments, like these in a group, are also offering messages for everyone about different possibilities for being with each other.

The following situation then arose. An eight-week-old baby was held across his mother's knee and his mother was yawning. The therapist went over and the mother held her baby son into a sitting position and said: "Talk to aunty." He was quiet, his eyes looked glazed and still, but the previous week he had engaged in cooing and talking. The therapist said: "We had a lovely talk last time, perhaps you are tired today?" The mother said she was exhausted and another mother sitting nearby said she was exhausted as well. These mothers were introduced a few weeks previously at the clinic group and the therapist gathered they had been meeting since. They were both single parents and had shared their troubled histories during pregnancy, birth and early weeks with their babies. After the therapist had got involved elsewhere, she noticed the health visitor talking about the eight-week-old baby's skin problems. The mother was looking miserable. The therapist went over and said to her: "It's a lot of work, isn't it? And you are trying so hard." The mother's eyes welled up with tears and the health visitor added: "Yes, we mustn't just focus on his skin, he is such a lovely little boy. You are doing so well with him."

The mother said: "It is just so tiring." The therapist sat quietly with them and the other mother for a few more moments. The baby was going to sleep and the other mother commented: "He looks so peaceful."

Commentary: this mother has developed trust in the group as a place for talking with babies, as well as for talking about difficult experiences. Today the therapist is struck by her low mood and its reflection in her baby's demeanour, also low. She acknowledges this initially through their mutual tiredness but, when realizing the health visitor has been concentrating on skin problems, she tunes into their emotional states more directly. This enables the mother to become tearful, be acknowledged affectively and encourages the health visitor to move the focus from physical issues. Everyone, including the other mother, reinforces the mother and baby's ego-strengths. The health visitor and therapist have had previous experience of babies' skin problems and had found that parents were often unable to see beyond the skin's surface into their babies' hearts and souls. They had discussed this, so the therapist felt secure about intervening and working productively together. At eight weeks this baby is not developmentally ready to take in much stimulation from the group, but he soaks up the atmosphere and benefits from emotionally attuned attention for his mother.

The therapist moved flexibly, in and out of involvement with smaller groupings and pairs of mothers and babies. At one moment, she was mirroring facial expressions, connecting through rhythmic movements and little exchanges involving toys. At another moment, when a five-month-old baby arrived with her father she greeted her across the mat with similar bounces to hers and then another baby was also bouncing. The group ambience had developed with many of its members interacting similarly. The therapist felt a dyad needed help to be closer, so she talked to the mother through her baby: "I expect you are really interested in mummy", and she helped the mother turn her baby round to face her. The therapist supported their face-to-face communication by standing behind them and saying in a slow, high-pitched tone: "Yes, now you can see her and you are talking together."

Commentary: the therapist is helping to create a calm atmosphere where mothers and babies value what they get from each other without having to make adult conversation. Toys or rattles are often used as a symbolic other, enabling people to make contact at a manageable distance. The therapist focuses on an individual dyad and provides emotional scaffolding when she helps a mother to talk face to face with her baby and remains affectively present for them. She does this by talking with them about their experiences, by placing herself where she can be seen, using the quality of her voice and, sometimes, actually touching. Occurring within the body of the group, this form of intimate relating and emotional talking affects all its participants, consciously or unconsciously.

Reflections

The two drop-in groups we have described share much in common. But there are also differences, which are responsive to the networks they are located within, and the families they serve. In both groups, professional disciplines come together and create an atmosphere of liveliness through shared interest in mothers and babies, supported by a therapist from the Anna Freud Centre. The illustrations above demonstrate that emotional regulation is provided through understanding unconscious processes in the drop-in groups, and the use of a mentalizing stance. Opportunity is provided for qualitative changes to occur within mother-baby relationships. The therapist and staff group use modelling to promote the development of reflective function in the mothers, and to support them in becoming more responsive to their babies. Mirroring of emotional states is used to enable mothers and babies to recognize and differentiate their feelings. In turn, parents may internalize these techniques and use them within the groups and within their own families.

In conclusion, drop-in groups can provide informal opportunities for parent-infant psychotherapy for many families who would not otherwise access an analytic approach. Words are not necessarily the predominant focus of the groups. Instead, the dominant focus is on the development of emotional relatedness through the interactions and connections that ebb and flow during each session. The culture that develops is a co-creation amongst all and as such it offers rich opportunities for the representation and acceptance of different ways of being with infants. Experience and evaluation of the drop-in groups suggest that this facilitates transformational process for mothers and babies alike, and contributes effectively to the development of the infant self.

Acknowledgements

We thank mothers, babies, and staff members in the drop-in groups, along with Anna Freud Centre colleagues for their contribution to the development of this work.

References

Baradon, T. (2002). Psychotherapeutic work with parents and infants-psychoanalytic and attachment perspectives. *Attachment and Human Development*, 4/1: 25–38.

Baradon, T., Broughton, C., Gibbs, I., James, J., Joyce, A., & Woodhead, J. (2005). *The Practice of Parent-Infant Psychotherapy*. London: Routledge.

Fonagy, P., Gergely, G. E., Jurist, E. L., & Target, M. (2002). *Affect Regulation, Mentalisation, and the Development of the Self.* Other Press: New York.

Garland, C., Hume, F., & Majid, S. (2002). Remaking connections: refugees and the development of "emotional capital" in therapy groups. *Psychoanalytic Psychotherapy*, 16/3: 197–214.

James, J. (2002). Developing a culture for change in group analytic psychotherapy for mothers and babies. *British Journal of Psychotherapy*, 19: 77–91.

Stern, D., Sander, L., Nahum, J., Harrison, A., Lyons-Ruth, K., Morgan, A., Bruschweiler-Stern, N., & Tronick, E. (1998). Non-interpretive mechanisms in psychoanalytic therapy-the "something more" than "interpretation". *International Journal of Psychoanalysis*, 79/5: 903–921.

Tronick, E. (1998). Dyadically expanded states of consciousness and the process of therapeutic change. *Infant Mental Health Journal*, 19: 290–299.

Woodhead, J. (2005). Shifting triangles: images of father in sequences from parent-infant psychotherapy. *International Journal of Infant Observation*, 7/2–3: 76–90.

Woodhead, J., Bland, K., & Baradon, T. (2006). Focusing the lens: the use of digital video in parent-infant psychotherapy and evaluation. *International Journal of Infant Observation*, 9/2: 139–150.

CHAPTER EIGHT

Babies in groups: the creative roles of the babies, the mothers, and the therapists

Campbell Paul and Frances Thomson Salo
Melbourne, Australia

Infants in groups

Babies and parents spend quite a considerable time in group contexts, and babies have been in group situations or interacting with each other since the beginning of time. In this chapter we look at some ways that four kinds of groups using a psychoanalytically informed group therapy model could be therapeutic. In an earlier paper we discussed the development from 1990 of a mother-baby therapy group particularly from the perspective of the way a baby might take the lead in therapeutic work and is therefore present as an equal member (Paul & Thomson-Salo 1997). Since we started that group there have been many developments, with an increasing acknowledgement of broader social relationships, and of connectedness with babies. In this paper we will consider developments in therapeutic work with infants in groups that retained the idea of viewing the baby as subject in his or her own right. Three others groups grew out of this model that we describe: the Very Premature Babies Group, the Stargate Infant-Parent Group (for infants who were in care for the first time), and the Peekaboo Club (for mothers and infants who had witnessed violence in the first year of life).

The Mother-Baby Therapy Group synthesized developments in the areas of psychoanalytic group work and psychotherapy with parents and very young infants within the first year. We will describe some clinical findings, particularly the interactions between infants and therapists and those between the infants themselves. Interactions that we think contribute to some resolution of the difficulties will be discussed briefly. We think that the Group is innovative in that we have not been able to find any accounts in the literature of a mother-infant therapy group where the focus is as much on the infant as on the mother. There has been growing emphasis on the infant's contribution especially since Klein's (1948; Klein, Heimann, & Isaacs 1952) insights into the infant's internal world, and this is reflected in a rapidly expanding body of experimental work on the capacities of the infant. The idea that very young infants can be engaged in their own right in therapeutic work has yet to be fully explored.

Literature review

Christie and Correia (1987) ran several slow-open groups for neurotic and borderline mothers whose children's problems appeared to be related to unresolved conflicts in their mothers. They described how, as the mothers work through conflicts around ambivalence, there is a freeing of warmth and constructive resources in them and in turn they become freer to allow forward movement in their children. A number of clinicians have described their work with closed time-limited therapy groups for mothers who are depressed after the birth of their infant (Bailey 1981; Holden, Sagovsky, & Cox 1989; Meager & Milgrom 1996). Other clinicians have run groups for depressed mothers where the infants accompany the mothers but the infants have not been engaged as members in their own right. Currently there is an increasing readiness to set up groups for mothers who are depressed, either along psychodynamic lines or more structured groups, usually time limited, and often with a planned programme of topics for each session (Clark, Keller, Fedderly, & Paulson 1993; Conte, Moltz, & Solomon 1990; Gruen 1990, 1993).

Another group with a similar approach to our model was run by Siksou (1990), a psychoanalyst working with a midwife co-leader, which was offered to mothers the week after they gave birth. It is an open group of about thirteen mother-infant dyads with a core of six to ten dyads, and is presented as a group that will help mothers with their difficulties. Initially, when a main theme is the fear that the infant will die, Siksou's stance is a facilitating one, and in time the mothers' identifications become benign and supportive. For the more peripheral members of the group the experience will be one of brief support. In the ongoing work there is no focus on the infant's contribution.

Over the last decade an increasing range of psycho-educational groups for infants and their mothers or sometimes their fathers have been developed by other practitioners, as for example Smith's (2004) PAIRS groups that are time-limited, semi-structured, and build in a separation model. There have also been a number of groups for fathers and infants in varying contexts from antenatal educational classes to fathers in prison.

Rationale for psychoanalytically oriented mother-baby therapy groups

When infants present with a psychosomatic symptom, they often improve without their mothers' issues being addressed and we are interested in trying to bring about change for the infant in the present as well as a more long-lasting change in the mother. Clinical experience suggests that otherwise such infants might present with problems later on, for example, infants with feeding difficulties may present later with anorexia nervosa. We therefore see the group as having a preventive function. In addition, we offer something quite substantial for the infant. Green (1980) argued that the infant may feel with a depressed mother that he or she has a dead mother, and there is the possibility of therapeutic interventions to lessen this effect.

The group is a place where women can share what has been an overwhelming experience, explore their ambivalent feelings and start to redefine their sense of self to include the concept of "mother". It provides them with a place to start separating their past anxieties and conflicts from their view of their infant so that this can become more realistic. Group work may particularly be indicated for those mothers who present as cut-off in a way that might lead to their being difficult to contact in individual work, and also for some mothers who have difficulties with their anger and may therefore feel more supported in a group (Durkin 1954, 1964; Hopkins 1993, personal communication).

Siksou (1990) suggested that mothers in a group can more readily accept confrontation from other mothers than if they were in individual therapy. We have wondered whether the mothers' experience of guilt and feelings of blame is less persecutory in a group, and also whether there is a greater possibility of a therapeutic identification with the baby and other mothers. We have also thought that the therapist's countertransference might be more usefully available in a group.

It seems likely that in selecting women and infants for our Group we reach a population of mothers who need something more long term. The infants are usually three months or older when they come into our Group so we may be seeing pathology that is on the way to becoming established.

We believe the Mother-Baby Therapy Group model has the potential to be applied to a range of different populations. The first criterion is that there is distress in the babies and/or their parents and the parents are able to see their baby as in need. Other criteria are flexible depending on how the group has been set up. Usually parents need to be able to understand what we hope to achieve in the group. Occasionally we have worked with parents who suffer from severe mental illness who find it harder to see what it is hoped to achieve.

Organizational set up of the groups

We will describe the set up and running of the Group as it applies to the original Mother-Baby Therapy Group, and then describe variations in the subsequent three groups. This Group runs weekly and lasts for one and a quarter hours. The infants, referred by various clinicians, present with a number of difficulties, such as feeding and sleeping disturbances, as well as more serious concerns such as failure to thrive and profound gaze aversion. There are four to five mothers and their infants, and the Group is available to them for as long as they feel it would be helpful. It is a slow-open group; six months is an average length of stay. Together we meet the mothers and infants to prepare them for entry into the Group. Our guidelines are that they should feel free to say what comes into their mind; that we advise against socializing after Group sessions to facilitate sharing confidential information in the Group, and we ask for a reasonable period of notice when they want to terminate. We obtain their consent for the Group to be videoed, which we do to help us with what we have missed as we have a special interest in infant-infant interactions, and also for teaching purposes. We are able to make the videotaping arrangements fairly unobtrusive. There has been a brief follow up six to eighteen months after they leave the Group to help us understand what part the Group played for them.

We have not arranged parallel therapy for the mothers in a formal way, though it is available for some. And while there may be advantages in setting up a parallel group for the fathers, we have not done this because of what we felt were boundary problems in entering a therapeutic relationship in another context with the mothers' partners.

It seems helpful to have a male and female co-therapist. We do not have defined roles, but offer ourselves as a thinking parental couple who are different from one another with different contributions that the Group can use from us. Having two Group leaders helps with the experience that, with the infants present, it often feels chaotic in the Group. In the Group room, we provide basically the same few carefully chosen toys each week, to offer as uncluttered a physical space as possible.

Because of its size the Group may appear vulnerable, through illness in the infants or the mothers' difficulty in making a commitment to longer-term therapy when so much in their lives is in flux. The Group is, however, surprisingly hardy, which is linked with the place it has in our minds; the infants are also very much contributing members.

Clinical guidelines

We have four main guidelines in our interpretations.

1. We try to create a space by not providing direct instructions or guidance. We share Winnicott's belief that "the answers" are in the mothers and that there is no single "right" way to parent.

2. We try to interpret group process rather than to work with individual mothers, and, where appropriate, we take up the negative transference. When we work more with an individual mother it is partly to do with viewing her as speaking for other members and also that it would feel somewhat artificial at that moment to make a group comment.
3. We attempt to keep the focus on the infant's communication and the mother-infant interactions as much as on the mother's experience of being a mother.
4. Seeing the infants as being of equal standing in the Group we address comments and interventions to them when it seems appropriate.

Rapid changes in the infants

Rapid change can be a feature of therapy with distressed infants and their families, and can be understood as one outcome of the plasticity of the infant if the environment begins to change. The mother's psychic adaptedness to her infant as well as her wish to get it right are also important. Mothers usually start in the Group with a relatively positive attitude to us. As Gosling (1981) pointed out, very small groups have more benign expectations, fewer regressive features, and less aggressive expression, and where there are more benign expectations, the results seem to be more positive.

> In seven-month-old Ian's first session his body tone was flaccid, he could not sit up, and he looked like an infant who was depressed. Ian. His mother, Mary, was severely depressed. She thought that every time he looked at her she had to smile which led to rather fixed smiling on her part. He did not look at us or the other infants very much, unless we were active in eliciting his gaze or Mary, who had been coming for some time, was persistent in reaching out to touch him and vocalizing to him. He often withdrew into holding or mouthing a toy. By his second session, however, Ian was a transformed child, he sat upright, and was more engaged with the group leaders and Mary; he smiled, moved, and vocalized with pleasure, and communicated what he wanted. It seemed that the new experience of the Group and its interventions had promoted change for Ian and his mother.

Daws (1995) pointed out that in infant-parent therapy small changes have the possibility of setting in motion more widespread changes. It is worth highlighting that in the Group, there are not only the interventions by therapists—the infants cannot fail to be aware almost immediately of the response of the other infants. We think it possible that where infants feel held by the Group setting they may process difficult feelings for one another by projective identification.

Group themes: maternal themes

Schindler (1966) described the clinical finding of the transference to the group as mother, which suggests that the group experience predisposes mothers to be able more quickly than in individual therapy to work on aspects of their relationship with their own mothers, and of the meaning of motherhood. The main themes have to do with conflicts over the losses that they feel they have experienced in relation to themselves, their infants, and their partners, and of a good internal mother. The birth story, the impact of the birth on the mothers' psychosomatic integration and ambivalence about their relationship with the baby's father are prevalent themes. They convey the disparity between societal expectations of perfect motherhood and their own sense of incompetence and despair, as well as being competitive in their neediness with their own children. There is a longing for a reparative relationship with their own mothers; often they have little practical or emotional support from them. Some aspect of these themes may be present in nearly every session and are worked through in each mother's time in the Group.

> In the course of the work Celia's view of Mary changed. She became softer and warmer towards her, and talked with her rather than at her. She stopped dreaming of coffins flying off and came to feel that she was bonded to Mary. She was less intrusive and was happy to let her play with other children, commenting on how well she was doing it. She said with feeling, "The surprise with the new baby is at how much you have to go outside the family for assistance and a lot of family assistance can be pretty damn useless." Talking about hating her adoptive mother and other childhood experiences that she had felt as rejections led in time to the Group helping her redefine her relationship with

her adoptive mother. It was more of a feeling that she had to create rather than recreate an internal good mother. The Group constituted a good mother, in that it was non-judgemental and containing. During sessions she could say things that she felt were trivial or hateful and it was acceptable. By the end of her stay there was an actual reconciliation with her adoptive mother and Celia identified with some of her good aspects.

Infant-infant interaction and infants' themes

Although there is a considerable amount now known about the infant's cognitive capacities it is still not widely thought that very young infants are emotionally interested in their peers. There is, however, from early infancy, awareness not only of the parents but also of peers. Based on Rochat's work (1998) we have come to think that in the group situation the infant sees him or herself reflected in the other infant, the peer, and thereby comes to know who he or she is, a separate person from the other infant.

There has been little research published on infant-infant interactions but pioneering work from Selby and Bradley (2003) illustrates the power of infant-infant interaction in the early months of life. Mueller and Vandell (1979) report that as infants master a particular motor or vocal skill they begin to direct that behaviour to an available peer. For example, with infants who are frequently together, extended looking at the peer in the first two months is reported. Touching the peer is reported at three to four months. From about six months onwards infants become more actively engaged with each other. They smile in response to their peers' coos and vocalizations. By seven to eight months as they become more mobile, they approach, follow and reach for peers. From around nine to twelve months more clearly "social" behaviours develop with increasing frequency. Ten-month-olds have a marked propensity to look at their mother when alone and at a peer stranger when s/he appears. With both mother and peers present, the infant directs more looks, touches and proximity-seeking behaviour to the peer, not the mother.

Around nine to twelve months the "offer" and the social "take" are observed regularly between peers who know each other. The offer is by hand, whereas previously infants have done it by gaze or sound. The "offer" and "take" behaviours are thought to be most important because they maximize the likelihood of evoking feedback from the partner, whether peer or parent. With this feedback the possibility of sustained encounters can be enhanced. During the nine-to-twelve-month period infants who know each other have been observed playing games with each other, such as run-and-chase, peek-a-boo, and ball games. With the acquisition of these behaviours of vocal exchange, offer, approach, and smile, the repertoire for the infant's social encounters is fairly complete. It is clear that interactive play is present in the first twelve months. In stressing that peers are important in installing behavioural organizers, Montagner (1989) highlights the specific importance of the infant's action of offering to others.

Considering the infants' evolving interactive and internal processes in the Group, the infants' awareness of and empathy for the other infants' feeling states seem quickly apparent on entry into the Group. We provide a quiet reflective space and try to keep the focus on interpersonal matters rather than on actual things, to facilitate the development of empathy, and the infants use the space in their own particular way. If one infant in the Group cries other infants can often be seen looking anxious or upset. From a very early age they show pleasure in interacting with other infants, and activities and games are increasingly elaborated with them. From a very early age the infants give clues both that they miss the other infants if they are not there, looking round for them and being low key for a time, and that they remember the activities they had been engaged in with them, by starting off with the same activity.

The Group is a playground where they can work out developmental concerns. For example, after a toddler had pushed over twin girls smaller than himself, we raised with his mother that she had not talked to him about her pregnancy. He then laid a doll in the centre of the floor, and the following week he began the session by laying a doll on the female therapist's lap.

The infants at times express their ambivalence and concern for their mothers. Each mother/infant pair brings their anger and battling into the Group, which provides some containment as they struggle with their difficulties. Infants may hit their mothers, avoid them, or have temper tantrums. If the mother's anger towards her infant comes through in what she says, this resonates with the infant's feelings, and the infant needs to cling to her or act it out in his or her activity. Gradually as mother and infant work out some of these difficulties the infant's concern for the mother can be seen slowly growing. From her longitudinal study of six pairs of same-aged babies (five of whom came into the study aged between six to twelve months), Urwin (1990) reported that as ambivalence towards the infant's mother increased by the end of the first year, there was also increased ambivalence towards the other infant of the pair. We have not seen this as clearly demonstrated in our Group and think that jealousy and other conflicts might be heightened in the way Urwin studied the pair relationship (with the infants playing together but not in the presence of their mothers) whereas the Group setting allows for other possibilities.

Therapeutic interactions and interventions

The fact that the infants' ages range from three months to about a year means that practical aspects of infant care may feature quite considerably, or even dominate, the sessions. Infants sometimes need their nappies changed in the Group; they are fed milk or biscuits or vomit this up; they may be tired; they may sometimes cry inconsolably; they need to be held and walked around by their mothers—all this often gives sessions a very chaotic feel.

Initially we were puzzled about why in some sessions we had not made many transference interpretations, and why we had not more vigorously taken up what could look like attacks on the process, for example if the mothers were late. We did not think that it was simply collusion on our part. The transference may not always be so clear when there is so much happening physically and verbally. And although there may be regressions and anger expressed about their children, the mothers cannot completely put on one side their mothering role as their infants need them to continue functioning as mothers.

The therapists' ability to bear and contain the *actual* as well as the *psychic* mess and pain brought by the mothers and the children, the crying and demandingness, the illness at times in the mothers, and the many difficult feelings communicated by projective identification, is crucially important, and may have a more important function in a group of mothers with their babies than if our Group were composed entirely of adults. Being able in the countertransference to bear the confusion and chaotic states, we provide a containment that acts as a non-verbalized interpretation: what has been brought *is* bearable and knowable. It is noticeable how, after a session where some of the chaos is contained and not acted on, the following session is calmer or leads to further development of material such as a mother's anxiety that she might abuse her child. We hold the child in the mother and the real child, and think about them in a way that allows the mothers to find the answers within them. Our thinking about the mothers helps them to think about the baby. One mother said that she thought we were "reparenting" her and was horrified that we should think that the answers were in her, partly because she did not feel she had any answers and felt what was inside was so bad. By the time she left, she had come to feel there were no "right" answers and no longer felt herself to be the mother of a bad child. The mothers were able to feel we had some faith in their capacities for change and to love and care for their infant.

Whatever rivalry there is for the Group leaders' attention, the mothers can be verbally supportive of one another. Quietly supportive gestures go on between them. It is usually a sign of some internal change when the mothers start reaching out to other mothers' infants.

Apart from providing a containing space for the mothers to project their internal world, which is also a physical space where mothers can watch the play of their children unfolding together, we try to interpret group themes and negative transference when it impacts on the therapy.

We have the expectation that when the infants form significant relationships with their peers this could be as positive a therapeutic experience for them as for their mothers. To facilitate their interactive empathy, the Group toys are arranged between the therapists so that the focus is between us and not all around the room. If children are having difficulty in engaging in the Group we might initially try to facilitate this. We might, for example, make a comment such as, "How would your child feel about another child being away for a week?" We try and create an atmosphere where the mothers talk about how the infants might be thinking about each other.

We do not deliberately offer ourselves as models for the mothers but try to respond from a position of having the infant and her mother at the centre of our thinking. Holding the infant's gaze while we think about and respond to him or her is, we think, one of our most significant interventions. There is increasing awareness of the importance of gaze in early infant communication and interaction (Paul 1991; Riess 1988). It is an enormously significant experience for infants to know that they have succeeded in capturing the gaze of another. We also talk *about* the infants and talk and interact directly *with* them.

The infant's transference and countertransference

Infants transfer onto us and the other Group members' feelings and ideas that derive from their caregivers. The therapists become significant to the infants before the other mothers do and how infants initially behave with the two of us is transferred from how they are with their mother.

Some infants relate positively to us from the first, as though they have left aside the difficulties with their parents, and are ready for what we offer. But it is not the extremely intense and immediate transference that Watillon-Naveau (1993) describes, although over time it can build to that. In Watillon's view, at some point in the first therapeutic consultation the infant externalizes the conflicts with the parents in a dramatization that she can interpret to the parents in order to free development, and the infant senses very quickly that Watillon can act as a container. Her consultations seem, however, to be mainly with older infants, and to constitute brief therapy rather than gradual therapy *with* the infant over time. The children in our Group often end up gravitating towards Campbell Paul partly because he represents an interested and available father figure.

By projective identification we have had to bear very difficult feelings about some infants and their mothers that they could not bear to know about. Sometimes we comment on a child's activity to try and help the mother "see" it, if for example the child is vocalizing more but her mother comments adversely that her language is delayed.

Therapeutic action

What had not previously been focused on before is using the infants' activity as part of the process of the Group. In pointing out the part that the infants' activity plays, we are likely to be addressing one of the following four aspects. Firstly it reflects or illustrates the conflicts and anxieties of the mother(s). Secondly, it enacts for the mother(s), for example where the mothers talk about their difficulties in expressing their anger and the children behave aggressively. Thirdly it helps in a defensive manoeuvre, as sometimes when mothers find a topic difficult the children create a hullabaloo that puts an end to exploring anxiety-provoking material. Fourthly, it counterpoints, for example when the mothers are talking about something sad but the infants seem able to have fun. We increasingly use the children's activity as a basis for a "group as a whole" interpretation (Foulkes, 1964). Not only is it a way of interpreting issues without sounding trite, but it came to seem technically preferable at times to say, for example, "All the children seem to be cross today", rather than saying, "There seems to be an issue of aggression here." It provides a medium for the mothers to focus on what is happening in their own psyches in a way that might otherwise not be so available, and to facilitate changes in their perception.

The presence of infants in the Group as members in their own right faced us with the difficulties that they were experiencing and with the need to consider whether the usual group techniques had to be adapted in view of their developmental status. If we did not respond to an infant who had made an overture to us, would that be experienced by him or her as rejecting? We thought about the times when we initiated a gesture or action, and came to view such times as a communication to the infant and to the Group that we were thinking of the infant's experience and in effect commenting on it. We came to view the responses that the infant evokes from us as enabling us to communicate our understanding to the infant and to let the infant know that we believe that some of the answers are also in the infant. We feel strongly that infants need a response from us that is affirming and growth-promoting. It may be worth clarifying that what we are calling play constitutes very minimal action on our part—we rarely move around in a session.

When Tom, aged seven months, and his mother Brenda joined the Group, he was rigid and unsmiling, with his arms held out at right angles to his body. Brenda had lost her first child in a cot death when she was a year old and had been unable, in anger, to begin mourning. Her relationship towards Tom was a very conflictual one and we learnt that when she looked at him she

> saw her daughter's face. When Campbell Paul moved his own fingers we noticed that Tom watched them. Campbell then touched Tom's hands and talked to him and gradually Tom could mouth Campbell's thumb. Still holding Campbell's hands he was able for the first time to relax his own arms, as if able to loosen a rigid "second-skin formation", and bring his hands together. As he did so he smiled. His mother played with him for the first time, lifting him up in the air and smiling at him. Whereas before his outstretched arms had got in the way of turning round to his mother for comfort he could now use them to find where she was and he began vocalizing.

When a therapist *responds* to something in the child with his or her own activity and this is done in a thoughtful attuned way it has the potential to bring about change very quickly. Rayner (1992) suggested that the pleasure between mother and infant at the height of attunement may be a kind of pre-verbal affective insight, in that what was in one mind is experienced in two, which can then bring about change in the self. This would add to our understanding of relatively quick behavioural changes. We think that an infant's attunement with another infant has a similar potential.

Developments in group therapy: the Very Premature Baby group

A group of parents whose babies had been born before twenty-eight weeks gestation sought to meet together to discuss the experience of having had a premature baby and its impact on relationships within the family. The mothers of the babies had each attended a Maternal and Child Health Nurse centre in the same locality, and a psychotherapeutic group for babies and parents was established, with Rosalie Birkin as the co-therapist, and with the nurse facilitating the process. The mothers had already described to the nurse the trauma that they had experienced while their baby had been in the neonatal intensive care unit (NICU). They described a harrowing and lonely experience. They often felt unable, for a number of reasons, to talk with other families, and yet they could see the pain and distress that their own infant appeared to suffer.

The closed psychotherapy group was established for the mothers and babies, with some separate early evening sessions for the fathers and the babies as well. Guidelines for this group were established. Parents were encouraged to talk about whatever they wished to discuss, but then what was discussed would remain confidential within the group. They were encouraged to play and interact with their babies as they would ordinarily, and we were interested to observe and facilitate interaction between the infants. In this way there were similarities with the community mothers' groups, but we anticipated that the mothers would feel more comfortable with a group of their peers who had undergone similar experiences in NICU.

There were four families and six babies (there were two sets of twins). An analysis of the themes that the parents discussed showed that they included feelings of isolation from their own family and from other families in the NICU. It was clear that the task was one of survival, and they were not keen to share their experiences or talk with other families at times of such intense emotion. The birth story and the account of time in the NICU were avoided in the group as mothers feared it would be very traumatic in the retelling. In time however they felt they needed to know something of each other's experience, so they arranged to present a brief account, in turn, over several weeks. This seemed manageable, and brought them to a shared understanding. Other themes included:

- Fear of breakdown and of damage to the couple's own relationship.
- Ambivalence about their own very vulnerable baby.
- Loss of control over everyday decisions about their baby, and fear of loss of control over major decisions such as whether intervention or resuscitation should occur at particular times.
- Inability to talk with other parents, fostering envy and fear of other babies and their families.
- Fear of their own intense feelings, including anger that seemed to be an intermittent but distressing feeling since it seemed unjustified and the parents wondered how they could be ungrateful and very critical to the staff who gave so much to their children.
- Trauma, and significant post traumatic stress disorder symptomatology, including intrusive memories re-experiencing

> episodes of danger and very powerful identification with their baby's resilience: "she experienced so much but she was a real battler."

The opportunity of this group enabled the observation of the powerful interactions between babies, including the intense relationship that formed between twins. The parents in the group felt it was important that other parents and professionals working with such vulnerable babies should be aware of some of the feelings that they had been unable to tell the staff about at the time their baby was in hospital. A follow-up of this group was developed in the neonatal intensive care unit providing a twelve-session educational and psychotherapeutic group to parents while their babies were in hospital.

The Stargate Infant Parent Group

For a period of time a number of infants were seen as part of an innovative project that provided a comprehensive emotional and developmental assessment program for children when Protective Services had been involved, and they had been removed from their parents' care because of dangerous and abusive actions (see Milburn 2005). We met with some of these parents and infants for a therapy group that ran in parallel with the assessment. This group aimed to provide infants and parents who had been separated an opportunity to be together in a controlled environment allowing for some continuity. We tried to use the same set of guidelines as in the basic model.

Even in the more extreme situations where for example a mother seemed to be colluding in the infliction of massive injuries on her baby, being present in the group with other parents and infants with the therapists helped her see that despite her personality difficulty she still had something to offer her baby. She would still have a relationship with her for the rest of her life, which was an argument for providing help for her now. The mother has to be there in her role as a mother: despite all that happened there is an expectation of responsibility and the capacity to care as a parent and she is still the mother of her abused child. While this group only took place for a short period of time, the staff found it supportive while the families waited for other services to be arranged and infants with a developmental delay began to move forward.

The Peekaboo Club Group

Building on this group experience with parents of deprived, neglected, and abused infants a new initiative was recently launched. We acknowledge the contribution of the facilitator, Wendy Bunston, of the Royal Children's Hospital Child and Adolescent Mental Health Service, Melbourne, whose enthusiasm and drive saw the establishment of the Peekaboo Club. Wendy Bunston had, in the suburbs of Melbourne, provided within the Mental Health Services a child-focused programme for families where domestic violence was a major issue. This tried to help mothers understand the experience of violence in the children's homes. The group therapy model was seen as an ideal way of providing a non-threatening way for mothers to talk about their experience while engaging and playing with their own babies. The group aims to provide the mothers with a safe therapeutic context where issues of violence can begin to be explored in a group where the infants are also related to in their own right, and both mother and infant are provided with experiences of pleasure. Clinicians need to feel comfortable in exploring issues of the violence with the mothers, otherwise these may be avoided. While the numbers are small, there was improvement in how the mothers scored on the scale for depression in pre- and post-test measures and the infants who had been developmentally delayed began to move forward (Bunston 2006).

Reflections

We have wondered whether the Mother-Baby Therapy Group is protective of parents abusing their children at a later date. Providing some mothers with a place where they feel safe enough to raise protective issues and also helping to facilitate being more in touch in a loving way, more empathic, with their infants, may be the greatest single safeguard against later abuse. Research in the area of postnatal depression points to the increased risk factors for neglect and abuse for those parents who experience difficulties in the early months of their infant's life. This highlights the importance of intervention that is early and sufficiently far-reaching. A related question may be whether being in the group enabled this protectiveness by giving more insight into a mother's own emotions and differentiating her own needs from those of her infant and to seek further support from within her family and therapists. The containment provided in the Group is likely to enable some mothers to feel that it is a place where quite considerable disturbance can be held.

We feel that a mother and her infant have been able to benefit from the Group when there is more ease in communicating in the relationship and more enjoyment in doing so. This presupposes that there would be more empathy on the mother's part than there had been on entry to the Group. We have noticed that when mothers leave the Group and reflect on what they have gained from the Group, they often mention a different view of seeing the child, that is, not so much in terms of the child being naughty but a child whose needs can be read and understood.

Conclusions

We have tried to show something of the therapeutic interactions that occur in groups between the infants, the infants' contribution to the group process, and how these might come to have a therapeutic effect. We have also argued that some of the innovations in technique have come about through following the infant.

References

Bailey, V. (1981). Groups for depressed mothers. *Group Analysis*, 165: 165–166.

Bunston, W. (2006). The Peekaboo Club. *The Signal*, 1–7.

Christie, G., & Correia, A. (1987). Maternal ambivalence in a group analytic setting. *British Journal of Psychotherapy*, 3/3: 205–215.

Clark, R, Keller, A., Fedderly, S., & Paulson, A. (1993). Treating the relationships affected by postpartum depression: a group therapy model. *Zero to Three*, 13/5: 16–23.

Conte, B., Moltz, E., & Solomon E. (1990). Training and supporting leaders of mother/baby groups: the P.A.C.E. approach. *Zero to Three*, 11/2: 17.

Daws, D. (1995). Infancy and psychoanalysis, discussion point at the First Colloquium of the Australian Association of Infant Mental Health (Victoria) and the Melbourne Institute for Psychoanalysis.

Durkin, H. E. (1954). *Group Treatment for Mothers of Disturbed Children*. Springfield, IL: Charles C. Thomas.

Durkin, H. E. (1964). *The Group in Depth*. New York: International Universities Press.

Foulkes, S. H. (1964). *Therapeutic Group Analysis*. London: Allen & Unwin.

Gosling, R. (1981). A study of very small groups. In: J. Grotstein (Ed.), *Do I Dare Disturb the Universe? A Memorial to W. R. Bion* (pp. 633–646). London: Karnac Books, 1997.

Green, A. (1980). *A Private Madness*. London: Hogarth Press.

Gruen, D. (1990). Postpartum depression: a debilitating yet often unassessed problem. *Health and Social Work*, 15/4: 261–266.

Gruen, D. (1993). A group psychotherapy approach to postpartum depression. *International Journal of Group Psychotherapy*, 43/2: 191–203.

Holden, J. M., Sagovsky, R., & Cox, J. L. (1989). Counselling in a general practice setting: controlled study of health visitor intervention in treatment of postnatal depression. *British Medical Journal*, 298: 223–226.

Klein, M. (1948). *Contribution to Psycho-Analysis*. London: Hogarth Press.

Klein, M., Heimann, P., & Isaacs, S. (1952). *Developments in Psycho-Analysis*. London: Hogarth Press.

Meager, I., & Milgrom, J. (1996). Group treatment for post-partum depression: a pilot study. *Australian and New Zealand Journal of Psychiatry*, 30: 852–860.

Milburn, N. (2005). Protected and respected: addressing the needs of the child in out-of-home care. The Stargate Early Intervention Program for children and young people in out-of-home care. *Journal of Paediatrics and Child Health*, 42/5: 309–310.

Montagner, H. (1989). Le role d'un espace experimental structure dans l'emergence et le development des systemes de communication des jeunes infants, paper presented at the World Association of Infant Psychiatry and Allied Disciplines Conference, Lugano, 1989.

Mueller, E. C., & Vandell, D. (1979). Infant-infant interaction: a review. In: J. D. Osofsky (Ed.) *Handbook of Infant Development* (pp. 591–622). New York: John Wiley.

Paul, C. (1991). Le bebe qui voit, mais ne regarde pas. *Devenir*, 3/1: 62–78.

Paul, C., & Thomson Salo, F. (1997). Infant-led innovations in a mother-baby therapy group. *Journal of Child Psychotherapy*, 23: 219–244.

Rayner, E. (1992). Matching, attunement, and the psychoanalytic dialogue. *International Journal of Psycho-Analysis*, 73/1: 39–54.

Riess, A. (1988). The power of the eye in nature, nurture, and culture. A developmental view of mutual gaze. *Psychoanalytic Study of the Child*, 43: 399–421.

Rochat, P. (1998). *The Self in Infancy: Theory and Research.* Amsterdam: Elsevier.

Schindler, W. (1966). The role of mother in group psychotherapy. *International Journal of Group Psychotherapy,* 16/2: 198–202.

Selby, J. M., & Bradley, B. S. (2003). Infants in groups: a paradigm for the study of early social experience. *Human Development,* 46: 197–221.

Siksou, J. (1990). Thérapies en groupe des troubles précoces de la relation mere-bebe'. *Devenir,* 2: 35–47.

Smith, J. (2004). No place in the world: unwanted, rejected babies find mothers in Dandenong PAIRS groups, paper given at the 9th Congress for Infant Mental Health, Melbourne, January 2004.

Thomson Salo, F., & Paul, C. (Eds). (2004). *The Baby as Subject: New Directions in Infant-Parent Psychotherapy from the Royal Children's Hospital, Melbourne.* Melbourne: Stonnington Press.

Urwin, C. (1990). Getting to know the self and others: babies' interactions with other babies, paper at 4th European Conference on Developmental Psychology, Scotland.

Watillon-Naveau, A. (1993). The dynamics of psychoanalytic therapies of the early parent-child relationship. *International Journal of Psycho-Analysis,* 74/5: 1037–1048.

CHAPTER NINE

Parent-infant psychotherapy: when feelings of futility are prevalent

Amanda Jones
London

Introduction

The focus of this chapter is very specific. It is written out of a motivation to share some of my difficulties working with babies, who, I feel, have given up reaching out for human contact. The babies I am thinking of actively sever human connection by avoiding eye contact, stilling or startling when touched, and sleeping too much. They are also quiet: the mouth, usually a place of passionate expression is flat, as if the lips are glued together; or sometimes the lips and tongue are floppy, lacking tone. The absence of appetite for interaction is noticeable. Moreover, the babies look lethargic; their eyes are dull. There is no sense of mastery when making a gesture, or manipulating an object. Although these babies look depressed, I do not think this captures the experience of futility and hopelessness they feel. The fifteen or so babies I have worked with who presented in this way were between four weeks and six months old.

I describe an intervention I undertook with a very quiet and disconnected seven-week-old baby to explain what I think was starting to happen in his developing internal object-relational world and then how I helped his seventeen-year-old mother to reach him. This brief introduction is to give a flavour of Nat and Natalie. Although I have changed their names, I have Natalie's permission to share aspects of their therapy. Natalie was referred to the Parent-Infant Mental Health Service by her health visitor. On completing the Edinburgh Post Natal Depression Scale Natalie had said in a flat voice—as if in passing—that she felt suicidal and cut herself. Her health visitor sensitively said that Nat was doing well, but Natalie seemed low. Natalie nodded and agreed to the referral.

In my first meeting with Natalie, it became clear how her mind oscillated: one moment she would be preoccupied by turbulent thoughts and feelings, the next she would dissociate and detach herself. She described how she could feel "calm, my feelings live in another room, I just feel calm". In the first ninety-minute session with Natalie and Nat, I noticed how Nat was awake for the entire time. He sat on his mother's lap facing me. He made no eye contact with either of us and often looked glazed. He made no sounds and no demands; he did not signal to be fed or changed. His body looked stiff; at times he held his arms at strange angles. Although I tried to make contact with Nat, he showed neither curiosity nor alarm at the sound of my voice. He seemed to look through me. In the session, he evoked in me a feeling of inertia and futility. Only later, when not in his presence, I noticed a mounting sense of alarm within me. I became preoccupied that he and his mother would die. I was afraid my wish to help would not be able to reach either of them. Natalie was guarded, telling me she was "fine . . . just a bit low." I felt pushed away. Yet, Natalie also emanated a powerful sense of anxiety: she was hypervigilant, frequently scanning my face and the room. She, too, barely made eye contact. What was also noticeable, for a seventeen-year-old first-time mother, was that Natalie did not want to talk about Nat, or the change in her life since having to care for a baby. All that was on her mind was Nat's father's possessiveness. I felt somewhat isolated. Later, when I describe the work in detail, it will become clear why I thought it important that Nat did not seem to exist in the room in his own right. His identity was faint.

Failing to exist in one's own right

The particular theoretical framework I draw from originates from the psychoanalyst W. Ronald D. Fairbairn (1944, 1952a, 1952b, 1952c, 1958), for he wrote about the serious traumatic sequelae that can follow if a parent, particularly a mother, is for whatever reason, repeatedly unable to relate to her baby as if she loves him for being himself (1952a: 17). Fairbairn's theories grew out of, and in tandem with, the works of Sigmund Freud, Karl Abraham, Melanie Klein, Wilfred Bion, and Donald Winnicott. They have subsequently been developed within what is broadly known as object relations theory. He emphasized the importance of early rejection of the baby occurring in what is described as the early oral phase of development, a time when sucking is paramount. Fairbairn spoke of how sensitive infants are to sensing that their needs are somehow not wanted by their mothers. In other words infants come to feel that they are not really valued and accepted, leading to feeling that their outward expressions of infantile dependence (which I equate with behaving in a object-seeing, loving way), are somehow bad. Bateman & Fonagy (2004: 75) have recently collated research that depicts the detrimental effects of early parental failure to adopt an "intentional stance" towards the baby, a stance in which the parent receives the baby's communications and imbues them with meaning.

Fairbairn went on to hypothesize that infants will adapt by finding a way to internalize a dynamic internal object relationship of themselves interacting with a wanted-yet-rejecting mother. As Nat was very young, he would only have a rudimentary and developing sense of "inside" and "outside", making the experience of rejection much more complicated. Over time Fairbairn suggested that an infant such as Nat would deal with the repeated experience of rejection by repressing the internal relationship of self-in-interaction-with-a-wanted-yet-rejecting-mother such that it would become a dynamically unconscious suborganization of the ego forever after incapable of generating meaning and experience (Ogden 1994: 89). Such an internal relationship would profoundly affect one's perception of future external relationships.

The adaptive function of such a process is that it enables the infant to find a way to preserve the wanted-but-rejecting mother within the self in a way that keeps his mother good whilst retaining a sense that his love is bad (1952c: 90). The consequence is that the infant comes to feel that love relationships with external others are precarious, not to be trusted. It becomes futile to love, hopeless, a feeling Fairbairn considered fundamental in later schizoid pathology. These thoughts led Fairbairn to posit that the way an infant deals with such rejection is to turn increasingly to the realm of inner reality—the preserved internal relationship—and this enables him to keep his longings for his mother within himself. I think this is what I saw starting to happen with Nat.

Fairbairn's (1952d) theory about the processes of splitting that need to occur in order to create such an "endopsychic structure" is highly complex. Grotstein & Rinsley (1994) offer some helpful contemporary explanations, as do Pereira & Scharff (2002). I discuss Fairbairn's ideas alongside the clinical material because it is only when keeping a seven-week-old baby in view that one can make sense of Fairbairn's highly original insights. His insights have helped me to grapple with the following difficult questions:

- What might make a baby give up seeking his mother?
- How does a baby manage to do so?

Although other psychoanalytic discourses and schools would also be able to offer important ideas and answers to these questions, the purpose of the chapter is to look at Fairbairn's understanding of how an infant might become hopeless and withdrawn.

What might make a baby give up seeking his mother?

According to obstetric and paediatric reports, Nat was born a lively baby, hungry for his mother and his mother's breast. For the primary care professionals there were no obvious risk factors: Nat was healthy; temperamentally he was neither noticeably irritable nor unresponsive; there was no overt physical abuse or neglect. The invisible yet powerfully present risk factor was that Natalie could not relate to Nat in his own right, by which I mean she was so besieged within her own mind that she could not value Nat's neediness. Although superficially Natalie looked as if she was managing, Nat's birth plunged her into blackness. Her perinatal breakdown makes sense in light of her own history and her present-day relationships with her mother and Nat's father. Fairbairn was not afraid to name the damage that a troubled or disturbed parent can do to a baby's developing internal world (1952a: 13). Nat's earliest yearnings for his mother had an unexpected impact upon her.

Imagine the following: Natalie, aged sixteen, meticulously planned to become pregnant. She saw becoming pregnant as a way to move out of her childhood home and, specifically, to move away from her own unpredictable mother (who suffered from bipolar affective disorder). The move entailed leaving her five younger siblings whom Natalie had, in effect, "mothered". One of these siblings, Gina, was a twelve-year old who was profoundly handicapped. She neither walked or talked and needed to be fed by a feeding machine. Natalie had been responsible for most of her care and this sister was crucial in Natalie's internal world. There had been five different "father-figures" in Natalie's life: all but one had been violent, both towards her mother and Natalie. Each in turn abandoned Natalie's mother who, it sounded, remained highly reliant on her eldest daughter. There had been no protective paternal provision, either in the form of care or economic support. In her adolescence, Natalie started to take overdoses and self-harm. She was looking for a way out. The idea of becoming pregnant saved her in many respects.

On learning about Natalie's pregnancy and decision to leave home her mother was apparently furious, trying to throw Natalie down the stairs in order to injure the baby and thus keep Natalie "mothering" her siblings. Natalie persisted in her plans and moved in with Nat's father, a volatile and possessive man, some ten years older than her. When Nat was born, Natalie described feeling joy; she said "I'd finally got what I wanted, someone to be there for me, you know—'You can't go anywhere now.'"

For Nat, he entered the world fullterm, the birth was easy and in the first few days his hungry yearnings for his mother were met. There was a complicated resonance between them: consciously, Natalie did want her baby; but what had never been thought about were the unconscious meanings of her need for a baby. On day four, Natalie described how "everything went black". She started to self-harm again and have suicidal thoughts. In reality Nat could not be there for her and I think Natalie started to attack her own body to protect Nat from her disappointment and anger. Nat's cries were now heard as maddening and unpredictable demands, resonating with her experience of her mother and presumably Natalie's own unmet cries as an infant and child. Natalie's urge was to block Nat out; to move away. Although she managed to physically tend to Nat's needs, like she had with her own siblings, what I think Nat sensed was as follows:

- His need for his mother's comfort and his excitement for her nourishment and presence met with either:
  - Natalie's tense arms and facial muscles, handling Nat physically, perhaps quite abruptly, but not holding him emotionally. In other words she was unable to imagine what he might be feeling and unable to assuage the torrents of bodily sensations that caused him to cry (Winnicott 1955: 147–148).
  - Or Natalie said she would leave the room, absenting herself, leaving Nat with an ever-present unmanageable feeling.

If such experiences repeated several times a day Nat would need to resort to complex processes of splitting and repression, as described above. It would be too unbearable to experience his mother as somehow rejecting his infantile dependence and love. I hypothesized how Nat would become more and more focused on inner reality, withdrawing his energy and attention from external relationships. This seemed to be happening within two months of life. Symington (1994) suggests Frances Tustin's (1972) description of the "black hole" experience builds on Fairbairn's formulations, and that indeed it could be occurring at such an early stage of life.

Natalie's history made it hard for her to relate to Nat as a real, live baby with needs of his own. As Fraiberg, Adelson, and Shapiro (1975) so vividly depicted: the ghosts from Natalie's own past haunted how she related to her baby.

The story of how Nat moved from a state of futility to feeling love and need

What follows is how Natalie and I worked hard to enable Nat to become a needy infant. It is relevant that I call them Nat and Natalie: in reality his name is also part of her name, a clue as to Natalie's vulnerability to relating to Nat as an extension of her needs.

I have found in several cases that using the visual aid of video can powerfully penetrate a parent's perception of who or what their baby stands for in the parent's mind (Jones 2005, 2006a, 2006b), and render visible defensive processes operating between parent and baby. I borrowed Dr Beatrice Beebe's (2003) idea of asking to film five minutes of parent and baby interacting sometime during the therapy session. I use a small handheld camera to do this. In the following session, somewhere near the beginning, I invite the parent to watch the interaction with me. When filming, I simply ask the parent to be with their baby, as their mood feels; when watching, I invite parent/s to free associate, to say whatever comes into their minds when watching themselves. The video material can stimulate a rich associative process. I carefully track the sequence of comments and non-verbal language that the parent expresses whilst watching the tape, and what it leads to thereafter in the session. The material that follows will show how the visual material helped Natalie notice how unconscious forces emanating from events and relationships from her past unwittingly influenced how she related to Nat (Faimberg 2005). I do not use the video to point out positive points; of more interest to me are what a parent sees and their emotional response when watching themselves. I say almost nothing about the interactions. The technique comes alive when I describe the case material. In many of the sessions with Natalie and Nat, I took five-minute clips of videotape one week and then watched the video with Natalie at the beginning of the following session.

First session

In the first session Natalie described her feelings for Nat like so: "It's all mechanical, it's like he's an object, I don't feel no love for him."

I described earlier how Nat sat silently on her lap facing me for the entire ninety minutes of the session. When I filmed them, for long seconds it was like filming a still photograph. Natalie's face looked frozen. Nat was similar—the only active movement he made was when his mother lifted him and tried to look at him face to face: Nat looked away. I felt tired, and my mouth felt heavy. It was especially hard to think when I turned the camera off. We all seemed frozen. When I watched the film on my own, I became preoccupied with death. I identified with something occurring between them.

I asked three questions in the first session that elicited important information. Firstly, I asked whom Natalie considered her closest attachment figure. She named her disabled sister, Gina. As a child

Natalie slept in the same bedroom as Gina. She would frequently put her ear to Gina's mouth to check she was breathing, and even her mouth to Gina's mouth to feel her breath to make sure she was alive. Natalie said she had fragments of memories suggesting that her stepfather's violence might have damaged Gina as a baby. I had asked whom Natalie considered supportive for her. Instead of naming a partner, parent, aunt or friend, she named Gina, someone whom she had felt responsible for keeping alive. It surprised Natalie when I asked more about her relationship with Gina; she let down her guard and gave me a glimpse of the kind of feelings she needed to keep at bay. She said,

N: "When she's sleeping I often lay my head on her chest . . . Ummm, like if I listen to her heartbeat, and I think if her heart keeps on beating then she's gonna stay with me, if her heart keeps on . . . beating . . . or like if I hear her breath, like if I hear . . ."

A: ". . . then you know she's alive . . ."

N: ". . . then I know she's alive. If she keeps on breathing, she's not gonna die, if her heart keeps on beating then she's not gonna die and so, that's just what I feel like."

When describing Gina, Natalie became fleetingly animated, less flat. She made brief eye contact with me. But then Natalie flattened her feelings in a way that left me reeling. One moment I was intensely in touch with the agony of the image of her listening to her sister's heart, the next moment Natalie jumped subjects and the emotional tone changed. It became flat.

The second question I asked was what Natalie thought life would have been like when she was Nat's age, seven weeks old. She said:

N: "I probably felt starved and deprived . . . I wasn't eating. I wouldn't eat. They tried to take me away from my mum they thought she was abusing me . . . but she wasn't. When they bought me to the hospital, they saw for themselves that she wasn't abusing me. That's *just the way I was*. I didn't want to eat."

Natalie had been hospitalized in her first few months of life, when critically dehydrated and malnourished. At this time she and her mother often slept in doorways. Linking this back to Fairbairn's ideas about trauma in the early oral phase, perhaps Natalie had also withdrawn into herself, like Nat, and possibly slipped in and out of futile states. Harrow (2002: 187) notes that, "When . . . failure occurs in the early oral phase, the infant feels that it is his love that is at fault . . . Love becomes an unacceptable (to the object) bad oral greed". It sounded as if Natalie, like Nat, had suffered in this way.

The third question I asked related to the state Natalie had been in when she arrived at the session. She had been ten minutes late and she was palpably anxious and edgy. Later I asked if she worried about being late, she nodded. I asked if she noticed the feeling anywhere in her body; she spontaneously grabbed her neck and then recounted a chilling memory from when she was about five. Whilst Natalie was trying to get into a room where her mother was screaming for help, her stepfather had picked her up by her throat and thrown her down the stairs. I had felt giddy whilst listening, but when I asked what she felt telling me, she said: "My feelings live in another room . . . calm, I just feel calm."

From what Natalie had told me, I think the internal relationships activated in her mind since the birth of her baby possibly included the following:

1. A trapped, helpless near-death child, akin to her sibling.
2. A starved and deprived baby who found it hard to exist.
3. An unpredictable, damaged mother whom Natalie could neither rescue nor protect.
4. A violent parental couple who had positioned Natalie as constantly frightened.
5. There was also a dissociated, numb child who could not let her feelings live in her body.

With such roused relationships it made sense Natalie was suicidal and that deeply entrenched defensive processes would need to be available to manage her interpersonal reality, especially with Nat. There was the likelihood that she would, at times, regress into schizoid states when caring for Nat. When in such states, Nat would probably feel profoundly unwanted and helpless to reach his mother.

Second session

Although I worried Natalie would not come back she arrived early for her second session. I felt a sense of hope. I knew I would have to show the first clip of tape and possibly take more film. First, I asked how Natalie felt about watching the tape. It is important to explore what internal relationships are stirred by the thought of being watched and to explore them before proceeding. Natalie said, "I feel like so self-conscious . . . my body . . . so self-conscious . . ." I let her talk about her unhappiness with her body and then linked this to how she might also feel unhappy with the feelings and thoughts she had. Given her infantile experiences, I said that maybe she worried that watching herself would make her feel more starved of hope than she already felt. She nodded. I also said she might expect to be judged by me. Again she nodded saying she always expected to be criticized. After this she said she wanted to watch it. This is a small example of how Natalie let herself feel something with me, her self-consciousness, and together we made sense of it so that Natalie could experience the feeling changing. She then wanted to see herself on film. Psychoanalytic writers would call this a micro-episode of *containment*. I reminded her about trying not to censor what came into her mind.

Natalie's emotional response surprised me. She smiled the moment she saw Nat, the first full smile I had seen. The emotion she felt, on seeing Nat on film was pleasure. Natalie said:

N: "He looks cute! He looks *so* sweet . . . I like recognise him there as *my* baby, but (pause) he looks different there than he does when he's with me, when I've got him *here*." (She pointed to Nat on her lap.)

What happened so she could experience seeing Nat in this way, as her son, and not an object? At its most simple, I think Natalie felt she existed. Perhaps us talking about her worry I would judge or deplete her helped her feel that feelings could exist and be recognized. I recognised her in her own right and somehow this diluted some fusion between her and Nat so she could recognize him differently. The distance of the observer position (Birksted-Breen, 1996; Britton, 1989) and the construction of a triangular space between us seemed to help her see that she had a live, undamaged baby who was actually not her and not ill like Gina. In the first session I described how she said of Nat, "It's all mechanical . . . it's like he's an object . . ." It was as if Natalie had been in the grip of feeling inert and dead and that this feeling-state evoked a similar state in Nat. He was a very quiet and lifeless baby. I think something about lifelessness—the deadening of infantile needs—had been in play between them and this shifted whilst we watched the video together. Natalie could wonder aloud how it was she could feel a live sense of pleasure watching her son when with me, and yet dead when alone with him. Perhaps Natalie had been handling Nat with her own feeling of deadness and Nat felt this and eventually started to stifle his cries as if taken over by an unspoken requirement not to exist in a needy way. This would be an example of the defensive process of projective identification being used by Natalie to manage her emotional reality (Bion 1959, 1961, 1962; Cimino & Correale, 2005; Klein, 1946; Likierman, 2005; Sandler, 1987a).

On the actual film, even though Nat was silent, Natalie had said to him "sssh, we're dancing." Just after we stopped watching it, I asked . . .

A: "What do you make about what you said to him then? The, 'Sssh! We're dancing'?"

N: "If we're dancing you can't cry. You're not allowed to cry if we're having fun. *No noise, no noise* . . . He can't cry."

Then she said,

N: "Look at him now! He's starting doing what his auntie Gina does. He's starting sticking out his lip. His auntie does that a lot."

We had started to explore something that touched on the possibility that fun somehow blocked out distress; which suggested a defensive need to deny distress and shut up. Then Natalie's associative process moved to Gina. She linked Nat and Gina. This gave me information that feelings to do with Gina would probably be important in relation to Natalie's depression and her relationship with Nat. As the weeks went on, I learnt how Natalie cared for many of her own neglected needs through the way she looked after Gina, thus keeping Natalie's distress quiet. It enabled her to deny having any needs of her own which let her feel in control and not so helpless. The birth of Nat challenged this dynamic because Natalie left home, and Gina. Natalie told me in session two that she had a baby so finally she could,

N: ". . . have someone *there for ME*. Someone who *'you can't go nowhere, you can't leave now, you can't go anywhere.'*"

It was clear that, like with the quote about needing to hear a live heartbeat to feel reassured, Natalie needed her baby to be her attachment figure, the one—like her sister—who would never leave her. At this point, there was no concept of her being a mother who needed to be there for her baby. The effect of Nat's infantile love was overwhelming for Natalie and I think she became emotionally frozen, unfeeling, in order to cope. For Nat this was dangerous. As part of his therapy, he needed to feel it was safe to cry and to want. In the second session, when I took the film toward the end, Natalie was gentler with Nat, looking at him with more expression, but he still could not look at her. I did not anticipate what would happen next.

Third session

The next week there was a big shift. Natalie's hungry needs had come alive. She could not stop kissing Nat. She was no longer abandoning Nat in her interactions, but the other side of the dynamic came alive: intrusion and fusion. Natalie's oral needs had come alive, it was if Nat was experienced as an ever-present breast. We took some film at the beginning when Nat was coming awake. Natalie was not aware of how she took him over. Her kissing was rapid and all comments were about him being there for her. It was hard not to say "stop it!" Even though I felt anxious for Nat I held on to my hope that Natalie, with my support, would be able to explore what was starting to happen. She used watching the clip from the week before to do this. Whilst watching she said, in the following order, how:

N: "I think he needed his own space, sometimes I think he needs space.";

"He doesn't want to be held the whole time.";
"sometimes I want to hold him, but he seems not to."

I asked if she could feel rejected, she nodded. Then she said, in a way that touched me,

N: "I look better there, more confident, better, more happy. Everyone's going to see this video, everyone!"

Given her own history of neglect as an infant and child, me merely responding to her communications seemed to kindle a sense of efficacy for her; what she said elicited a response. It was very basic, very powerful. I link it to Fairbairn's pivotal point about recognition—Natalie was starting to come alive because she was starting to have a present-day experience of feeling valued by me, and of all her thoughts and feelings being acceptable to me. Perhaps this helped her to start recognising Nat as a separate individual. As she continued to watch the video she noticed how she hugged him tightly and how he startled. She was able to say:

"*Look*—mummy's proper smothering *you* there."

Natalie went on to talk about her need to be hugged, held, and kissed. At this point she sighed, she looked angry. She said:

N: "Whenever I wanted to hug someone I could hug Gina. Because she can't say no, that's why. She can't say no, and (said more quietly) I know she likes it."
A: "It's hard to have that feeling . . . and to feel it now with me?"
N: "Yes . . . I just want to cry every single time . . . it really hurts, every single time, it always hurts . . . It hurts . . . I feel it here [she put her hand to her neck]. In here it feels like it's just going to burst."

Her involuntary body communication signaled how serious this was. In this third session, Natalie was talking about the opposite pole to her dissociated calm states, which was the pain of her yearnings for hugs and kisses; and her fury when her yearnings were rejected. The pain of such feelings clearly felt life-threatening for her. But for Nat, his mother's yearnings meant that she was starting to use his body in an intrusive and controlling way. So although the deadness had changed, the aliveness now showed in the only way it could.

In individual adult-treatment the pace of the emerging material would probably be very different. In psychodynamic, systemically-sensitive parent-infant work the presence of the parent-infant transferences makes otherwise deeply warded off material more readily available for exploration.

Fourth session

In Session Four, we watched the video of the kissing, and worked with how Gina and Nat could easily become conflated into one. It was hard for Natalie to separate this out. She said:

N: "You [to Nat] look like your Auntie Gina—you just watch people."
(She continued to watch and the kissing started). (She was silent and then said . . .)

N: "*Mummy's gonna kill you with kisses one day,* you get too much kisses."

A: "What makes you say that?"

N: "Cause that's the way I kiss my sister. I kiss her all the time, I kiss her and then I sit down, and kiss her again. I really want to kiss her."

A: "Let's just think about it a bit more, what do you feel"?

N: "**. . .** that's how I show I love them more".

A: "But you said something about "kill him with kisses" . . ."

N: "He probably don't like it that much, but I do it anyway, [to Nat] mummy's does it anyway",
[Natalie paused] ". . . He tenses up sometimes, *like pulling himself inwards . . .*"
[then she said, as if from nowhere] *"You look JUST like your auntie now."*

The significant moment, I think, was when she was remembering how Nat would "tense up". She could momentarily be in touch with his body as his body, not hers. Perhaps she then remembered that her sister, too, would also tense and try and pull away. This would have been too unbearable for her to know before now. This reflection led to her seeing Nat as looking "just" like Gina. It was important that Natalie could say, "He probably don't like it that much" and then recognize how she ignored his cues. Natalie was starting to put into words how helpless in a sense

Nat was, and how he defended himself by *pulling himself inwards.* This vividly depicts a schizoid withdrawal into inner reality. It seemed that when Natalie was kissing Nat she was in a way kissing Gina; and when she was kissing Gina she was, in a way, trying to master, and kiss better, all the pain of her own helplessness, deprivation, and hurt. Natalie's comment, "Mummy's gonna kill you with kisses one day . . ." opened a door. She had seen the danger for herself at a point in time when she could see it. A little later she said,

N: "Like if I talk about something I don't like, I always kiss him anyway . . . it like . . . brings me back to something . . ."
A: ". . . back to"?
N: "To like being more loving, *I don't feel like I hate anyone.*"

So perhaps the action of kissing also kept at bay Natalie's fears about her own aggressive and hateful feelings. It was Natalie's insight. Most importantly for us Natalie could allow us to start thinking about her kissing. She could start to use her mouth to talk about it, especially what it meant in relation to her feeling empty and alone; and also when she felt full of hate. As this happened Natalie started to address a core wound: the feeling of being helplessly trapped in an impossible situation and no help comes, a feeling she so identified with in relation to Gina. In such a world crying makes no sense. With the help of the video and my mind, Natalie came to recognize how, without meaning to, she induced states of helplessness in Nat, such that he too could feel helplessly trapped in the impossible situation of having to manage his mother's needs whilst his own infantile love was neglected. It became possible for Natalie to talk about her desperate need to control neediness—hers and Nat's.

I had the role of managing Natalie's needs. External reality was also difficult. Natalie had to separate from Nat's father and for some months she and Nat lived in a refuge. During this time she described the pain of not being able to sleep in our clinic, or come home with me. Separations felt especially cruel. In the transference between us I said often how Natalie might experience me as crazy and cruel to offer help and a sense of safety, and then limit it; especially when she felt at risk of dying, or not managing.

Yet, as Natalie could talk and think with me, her mouth—with Nat—could be more responsive to him as a separate person. It showed both in the change in relation to her kissing, but also in how she talked with him. She talked to him as a "you", a subject in his own right. Nat started to flourish: he became passionate about his mother's face, reaching for her, touching her. His capacity to smile caught light and they fell in love.

Although by the thirteenth session Natalie and I had much work still to do, the change in Nat's capacity to be passionate about his mother demonstrated how, from a baby's point of view, parent-infant psychotherapy can facilitate rapid and critical change. In this session Natalie unearthed the ally to our therapy, the good internal relationship, which had been lost from conscious memory. Whilst taping them, I felt moved by their interaction. They were having such fun together. After filming, I asked:

A: "I wonder if there was somebody who might have felt good about, who you might've been attached to, when you were little?"

N: "You know when you get a feeling, there is someone . . . but I can't remember . . ." (She looked confused, scrunching her face . . .) "I think it was just my Nan. Never my dad, my dad's mum."

A: "Just keep thinking about her . . . see what comes to your mind."

The details that flowed were astonishing. Tiny details of evidence of care, the way her Nan would slice up banana for her; make her brightly coloured dresses. Although she died when Natalie was eight, what had survived, although not available to her conscious memory, was the feeling of being loved, cared for, and recognized. I think the loss had been so overwhelming for her that her Nan became "lost" to her conscious mind. As Natalie mourned her Nan's loss with me, it restored in her consciousness what she had valued about their relationship. I think her Nan is why Natalie could recognize care and containment, and use it, in the therapy relationship.

I want to end on a note from Nat's perspective. When Natalie said in the second session: "No noise, no noise, you mustn't cry,"

I described how this contributed to Nat inhibiting his distress-calls. During the therapy, Natalie started to feel physical pain again, especially the pain of physical hunger, which she never consciously felt before. At the time when Nat started to crawl and move he inevitably hurt herself. I saw Natalie unconsciously trying to teach him not to cry, not to make a sound, to act as if pain does not hurt, that he does not need help. This was the hardest defence to shift: the denial of pain and the want for a response. One week, when Nat banged his head, my body jumped, Natalie's was still. Nat wanted to cry, looked at his mother, registered her restraint, stilled, and stopped himself. There was silence. For the rest of the session we talked about this and what stopped Natalie comforting him. The next week Nat fell again and hurt his head. Again he stilled himself and looked at his mother. But on this occasion, my body did not jump, instead Natalie's whole body moved and responded to help him. I watched as she gathered Nat up stroking his head where the bump had happened. Natalie then said, very softly, and with tears in her eyes, "It's ok, it's ok . . . you can cry, I know it hurts . . ." At that point Nat burst into tears. I think this was possible because he was in touch with a mother who could both feel his pain with him and help it. With this, something of Nat's propensity to withdraw inwardly changed: he could cry; he no longer behaved as if he needed to manage it for himself. From then on his tears flowed easily and noisily. He came to use his mother's comfort and recover. I think when Nat could cry, it meant that the unconscious demand to shut up cries for help was no longer like a stranglehold. It was no longer necessary to stifle natural cries or needs.

Discussion about the clinical work

All therapeutic processes are complicated and Natalie and I worked together for over two and a half years. At first I helped her to feel feelings in bite-size portions. I was mindful to try and help her digest the feeling with me and respected her need to then toughen up after. After some months, she could gradually tolerate experiencing more feelings both with me and with Nat, especially dread, anxiety, anger, and terror. Amidst Natalie's feelings, the video material helped us keep Nat's in view. Natalie came to recognize when, how, and why she could sometimes lose sight of him. This recognition led to a change in Natalie's defensive use of projective identification: for example, once she could own her own neediness as hers, she stopped relating to Nat as if he needed to be kissed the whole time (Cimino & Correale 2005).

I think this depth of work was only possible because I worked with mother and baby together. In individual treatment I do not think Natalie's defensive processes would have been so open to change: the perinatal period offered us a unique opportunity to bring to life and maximize Natalie's healthy narcissistic investment in Nat and, recursively, we brought to life Natalie's own sense of importance and value. I think this was predicated on a heartfelt, although deeply complicated, desire to connect with her baby. For Nat, by the thirteenth session, he was allowed to be more of a separate person, to move away from her, to take the lead, and by the age of fifteen months this was even more apparent. Although Natalie's parental ghosts still exist, they are now kept more in place by an experience of herself as a mother who can be predictable and safe with her son and this has helped her self-esteem. She does not feel so afraid of helplessness any more: her own or Nat's. To put it as simply as possible, Natalie and Nat are no longer in a defensive dance together and this is, perhaps, what parent-infant psychotherapy can help with.

Conclusion: the move from futility *to feeling safe to feel love*

In his paper "Schizoid Factors in the Personality" (1952a), Fairbairn wrote about an existential domain of schizoid isolation, which can develop in the early oral phase. Without mitigating circumstances it can become akin to a default position within the personality, there to regress to when the self feels under threat. At seven weeks Nat would have still been achieving the most intimacy through feeding and sucking. But given Natalie's feelings it is likely that, whilst feeding, Nat would be taking in the literal milk from the bottle as well as indigestible mental states belonging to his mother (Fairbairn 1952a: 10–11). These states would be expressed in various ways: through Natalie's musculature and facial expressions, her vocal tone, the feelings in her eyes, and so on. Would Nat simultaneously perceive—albeit in a rudimentary way—that somehow his love and want were indigestible to his mother, wrong or bad? Natalie, too, had this vulnerability for she had nearly died of dehydration and malnourishment when Nat's age.

The notion of this being traumatic for the baby makes sense for developmental research has now empirically verified that newborn babies are inherently socially-striving and object (other)-seeking (Fonagy, Gergely, Jurist, & Target 2002). Something significant and worrying must occur if an originally communicative and lively baby starts to appear as if he does not mind what goes on around.

Although Fairbairn was working with adult patients and extrapolating backwards to conjecture how adult schizoid processes might have formed in infancy, I wonder if babies like Nat are present day clinical examples of the formation of such pathology in action. I said earlier how my emotional response trying to reach Nat was to feel futile and hopeless. This is an unusual and telling response when meeting a little baby. Fairbairn stated that the "*characteristic affect of the schizoid state is undoubtedly a sense of futility*" (1952b: 51). He wrote that "the schizoid state . . . represents the major disaster which may befall the individual who has failed to outgrow the early oral phase of dependence" (1952b: 53). For Fairbairn, failure to outgrow the stage of infantile dependence was often associated with the infant's experience of being neglected, rejected, or deprived by the parent in the early or late oral stages of development.

But the actual question as to how Nat started to cope with his predicament of his needs being negated cannot be answered with any certainty. The works of theorists such as Fairbairn (1952a, 1952b, 1952c, 1952d), Klein (1946), Winnicott (1955, 1958, 1964, 1971), Sandler (1960, 1987a, 1987b), Tustin (1972, 1986), Stern (1985, 1998), Fonagy & Target (1996, 1997) and Target & Fonagy (1996) help me to tolerate this uncertainty and keep me motivated to continue trying to understand complex and upsetting clinical phenomena. I offer the possibility that Nat's futility developed in the context of him starting to identify with the rejecting aspect of his mother, and that her capacity to detach and not imagine the mind of the other had helped her to adapt and survive in an abusive and neglectful environment. For Nat, though, this identification would render him at risk of developing an enduring internal object relationship that would, unconsciously, sabotage future intimate relationships. I think the therapy prevented this from happening. Nat is now three years old and living with his mother and new partner. The new partner comes from an ordinary, loving family. He treats Natalie with the love and respect she deserves. In light of this, Nat has attached to him with his now characteristic enthusiasm and affection. But he is also not afraid to be jealous and angry.

Parent-infant psychotherapy can be immensely risky work, but when allowed in—as I was with Nat and Natalie—it can be especially rewarding because the therapeutic relationship can make it safe to feel love again.

Acknowledgements

I would like to thank Angela Joyce, child and adult psychoanalyst, for helping me to make the link with Fairbairn and for her supervisory skills. I also thank Juliet Hopkins for her clinical wisdom and academic rigour. Finally I thank Nat and Natalie.

References

Bateman, A., & Fonagy, P. (2004). *Psychotherapy for Borderline Personality Disorder: Mentalization-based Treatment*. Oxford: Oxford Universities Press.

Beebe, B. (2003). Brief mother-infant treatment: psychoanalytically informed video feedback. *Infant Mental Health Journal*, 24/1: 24–52.

Bion, W. R. (1959). Attacks on linking. *International Journal of Psycho-Analysis*, 40: 308–315. [*Second Thoughts*. London: Heinemann, 1967].

Bion, W. R. (1961). A theory of thinking. *International Journal of Psycho-Analysis*, 43: 306–310.

Bion, W. R. (1962). *Learning from Experience*. London: Heinemann.

Birksted-Breen, D. (1996). Phallus, penis, and mental space. *International Journal of Psycho-Analysis*: 77: 649–657.

Britton, R. (1989). The missing link: parental sexuality in the oedipus complex. In: R. Britton, M. Feldman, & E. O'shaughnessy (Eds.), *The Oedipus Complex Today: Clinical Implications* (pp. 83–102). London: Karnac Books.

Cimino, C., & Correale, A. (2005). Projective identification and consciousness alteration: a bridge between psychoanalytis and neuroscience? *International Journal of Psycho-Analysis*, 86/1: 51–61.

Faimberg, H. (2005). *The Telescoping of Generations: Listening to the Narcissistic Links Between Generations*. London: Brunner-Routledge, New Library of Psychoanalysis.

Fairbairn, W. R. (1952a). Schizoid factors in the personality. In: W. R. Fairbairn, 1952d (pp. 3–27).

Fairbairn, W. R. (1952b). A revised psychopathology of the psychoses and psycho-neuroses. In: W. R. Fairbairn, 1952d, (pp. 28–58).

Fairbairn, W. R. (1952c). Endopsychic structure considered in terms of object-relationships. In: W. R. Fairbairn, 1952d, (pp. 82–136).

Fairbairn, W. R. (1952d). *Psychoanalytic Studies of the Personality*. London: Tavistock with Routledge & Kegan Paul.

Fairbairn, W. R. (1958). On the nature and aims of psycho-analytical treatment. *International Journal of Psycho-Analysis*, 39: 374–385.

Fonagy, P., & Target, M. (1996). Playing with reality I: theory of mind and the normal development of psychic reality. *International Journal of Psycho-Analysis*, 77: 217–233.

Fonagy, P., & Target, M. (1997). Attachment and reflective function: their role in self-organization. *Development and Psychopathology*, 9: 679–700.

Fonagy, P., Gergely, G., Jurist, E. L., & Target, M. (2002). *Affect Regulation, Mentalization, and the Development of the Self*. New York: Other Press.

Fraiberg, S., Adelson, E., & Shapiro, V. (1975). Ghosts in the nursery: a psychoanalytic approach to the problem of impaired infant-mother relationships. *Journal of the American Academy of Child Psychiatry*, 14: 387–422.

Gergely, G., & Watson, J. (1996). The social biofeedback model of parental affect-mirroring. *International Journal of Psycho-Analysis*, 77: 1181–1212.

Gergely, G., & Watson, J. (1999). Early social-emotional development: contingency perception and the social biofeedback model. In: P. Rochat (Ed.), *Early Social Cognition: Understanding Others in the First Months of Life* (pp. 101–137). Hillsdale, NJ: Lawrence Erlbaum.

Grotstein, J. S., & Rinsley, D. B. (Eds.) (1994). *Fairbairn and the Origins of Object Relations*. London: Free Association Books.

Harrow, J. A. (2002). Towards a theory of the self: Fairbairn and beyond. In: F. Pereira, & D. E. Scharff (Eds.), *Fairbairn and Relational Theory* (pp. 183–196). London: Karnac Books.

Jones, A. (2005). *The Process of Change in Parent-Infant Psychotherapy*. Ph.D. thesis, Tavistock.

Jones, A. (2006a). Levels of change in parent-infant psychotherapy. *Journal of Child Psychotherapy*, 32/3: 295–311.

Jones, A. (2006b). How video can bring to view pathological defensive processes and facilitate the creation of triangular space in perinatal parent-infant psychotherapy. *Infant Observation*, 9: 109–123.

Klein, M. (1946). Notes on some schizoid mechanisms. In: *Envy and Gratitude*. Hogarth Press: London, 1975.

Likierman, M. (2005). *Melanie Klein: her Work in Context*. London: Continuum.

Ogden, T. H. (1994). The concept of internal object relations. In: J. S. Grotstein, & D. B. Rinsley (Eds.), *Fairbairn and the Origins of Object Relations* (pp. 88–111). London: Free Association Books.

Pereira, F. P., & Scharff, D. E. (Eds.) (2002). *Fairbairn and Relational Theory*. London: Karnac Books.

Sandler, J. (1960). The background of safety. *International Journal of Psycho-Analysis*, 41: 191–198.

Sandler, J. (1987a). The concept of projective identification. In: J. Sandler (Ed.), *Projection, Identification, Projective Identification* (pp. 13–26). Madison, CT: International Universities Press.

Sandler, J. (1987b). *From Safety to Superego: Selected Papers of Joseph Sandler*. New York: Guilford Press.

Stern, D. N. (1985). *The Interpersonal World of the Infant: A View from Psychoanalysis and Developmental Psychology*. London: Karnac Books.

Stern, D. N. (1998). *The Motherhood Constellation: A Unified View of Parent-Infant Psychotherapy*. London: Karnac Books.

Symington, N. (1994). The tradition of Fairbairn. In: J. S. Grotstein, & D. B. Rinsley (Eds.), *Fairbairn and the Origins of Object Relations* (pp. 211–221). London: Free Association Books.

Target, M., & Fonagy, P. (1996). Playing with reality II: the development of psychic reality from a theoretical perspective. *International Journal of Psycho-Analysis*, 77: 459–479.

Trevarthen, C. (1979). Communication and cooperation in early infancy: a description of primary intersubjectivity. In: M. M. Bullowa (Ed.), *Before Speech: The Beginning of Interpersonal Communication* (pp. 321–372). New York: Cambridge University Press.

Trevarthen, C. (2001). Intrinsic motives for companionship in understanding: their origin, development, and significance for infant mental health. *Infant Mental Health Journal*, 22/1–2: 95–131.

Trevarthen, C. (2005). First things first: infants make good use of the sympathetic rhythm of imitation, without reason or language. *British Journal of Child Psychotherapy*, 31/1: 91–113.

Tronick, E., Als, H., Adamson, L., Wise, S., & Brazelton, T. B. (1978). The infant's response to entrapment between contradictory messages in face-to-face interaction. *Journal of the American Academy of Child and Adolescent Psychiatry*, 17: 1–13.

Tustin, F. (1972). *Autism and Childhood Psychosis*. London: Hogarth Press.

Tustin, F. (1986). *Autistic Barriers in Neurotic Patients.* New Haven, CT: Yale University Press.

Winnicott, D. W. (1955). Group influences and the maladjusted child. In: *The Family and Individual Development* (pp. 146–154). London: Tavistock, 1965.

Winnicott, D. W. (1958). *Collected Papers: Through Paediatrics to Psycho-Analysis.* London: Tavistock, 1958. [Reprinted as *Through Paediatrics to Psycho-Analysis.* D. W. Winnicott, London: Hogarth Press and the Insititute of Psycho-Analysis, 1975. Also reprinted London: Karnac Books, 1992.]

Winnicott, D.W. (1964). *The Child, The Family, and The Outside World.* London: Penguin, 1964. [Reading, MA: Addison-Wesley, 1987.]

Winnicott, D. W. (1971). Mirror-role of mother and family in child development. In: D. W. Winnicott, *Playing and Reality* (pp. 111–118). London: Tavistock, 1971. [New York: Methuen, 1982.]

Winnicott, D. W. (1988). *Human Nature.* London: Free Association Books.

CHAPTER TEN

The health visitor's role in promoting well being in families

Maggie Harris
Bedfordshire, England

Introduction

I am a health visitor and work in the UK where health visitors are registered nurses with post-registration training. We are based in the community and traditionally work with all newly born infants and their families in whatever context we encounter them: at home, occasionally in a hospital, and through an open service at community clinics.

We operate on four core principles:

1. The search for health needs.
2. Stimulation of awareness of health needs.
3. Influence on policies affecting health.
4. Facilitation of health enhancing activities (CETHV 1977).

We prioritize our work in order to maximize preventative care and promote health and general well being for the whole family. However the models of prevention and the framework for health visiting continue to follow a medical or treatment model. This is not always appropriate when considering the emotional health of the family, particularly of infants.

The health visiting service in England is continually undergoing organizational change. Resources for the health visiting service have been reduced in many areas, necessitating the formation of multi-skilled teams including general nurses, nursery nurses, and health care assistants. Working within a climate of change has been a challenge for the profession. This is magnified when working with vulnerable children. We need to ensure that we create robust teams that do not replicate the vulnerability of our clients. Consequently, the support for the teams within the organization becomes equally important.

The diverse nature of my role allows me to work in a variety of ways. There have been different interpretations of our public health role in terms of health promotion and health monitoring and whether to work collectively or individually, the former being more prevalent today. Traditionally health visitor input is based on quantity of contacts. But I prefer to emphasize the supportive nature of the contact and the quality of the relationship. Health visitors and other community health staff have many opportunities when they come into contact with families to observe, for example, how the mother holds her baby when she feeds; how she places the baby on the scales to be weighed; how she soothes her distressed baby while talking to others and how, in turn, the baby responds to her.

I believe other members of the multi-skilled team, with appropriate training and support, can intervene effectively with families too. This view is supported by the work of Barnes (2003) who reviewed different models of early intervention and identified factors associated with enhanced infant mental health outcomes.

Primary factors:

- Shared decision-making between parent and therapist / intervenor.
- Quality of relationship between the parent and the intervenor.
- Cultural awareness / sensitivity.
- Flexible settings / hours.
- Crisis help prior to other intervention aims.

Barnes pointed out that, if the primary factors are not addressed, the importance placed on the intervention by the client may be compromised, making it difficult to achieve changes in behaviour (Barnes 2003: 392). Health visitors are generally accepted into people's homes without stigma. When the "primary factors" described by Barnes are optimized, the rapport with the client and the relationship with the family become important particularly in the context of mental health issues or traumatic life events.

There has also been progress in a community development approach that incorporates a principle that "seeks to be preventative rather than curative" (Luck & Jesson 1996). This implies a move away from a treatment model of working. However, while it is important to work with community groups to meet community health needs, individual health needs cannot be dismissed. By seeing every family when an infant is born the health visiting team works with individuals and families who make up communities.

I undertook the Infant Mental Health course to Master's level at the Tavistock Centre in London which has changed my thinking and ways of working to promote emotional well being with families. I believe not only that an understanding of psychodynamic concepts can assist in the early identification of emotional problems and adverse patterns of relating between parent and child, but also that the health visitor can intervene early and work to promote good emotional development within the family. Knowledge, particularly of Bowlby's attachment model, has helped me to identify parenting qualities and styles of attachment that can predict likely outcomes for infants and can be used to explain the health visitor's role in terms of being a secure base that can be relied upon when needed. Fonagy's "self reflectiveness" (Fonagy, Steele, Steele, Moran, & Higgitt 1991; Fonagy, Steele, Steele, Higgitt, & Target 1994) helps me to think about my effect on the family. Another concept, Bion's theory of container-contained, can be used as the rationale for the health visitor's containing role, not only with families but also with the other health practitioners in the team.

I will discuss the role of the health visitor in relation to infant and family mental health. I will use the casework of two families: in one a baby died and the other a baby had a profound global disability. I will also show the importance of the space for thought given by the work discussion group at the Tavistock Centre, which enabled me to adapt to a more therapeutic style of working. This was part of the Infant Mental Health Master's course held there.

Some useful psychodynamic concepts that health visitors can apply in their work with families

John Bowlby formulated an attachment theory, influenced by ethological principles and evolutionary theory. Bowlby believed that early separation or disruption of the emotional bond between the mother, or her substitute caregiver, and a child had a lasting effect on the subsequent psychological development of the child. Bowlby understood there to be a developmental pathway that was followed by individuals and the extent to which s/he became resilient to stressful life events was significantly determined by the pattern of attachment developed during the early years (Bowlby 1988).

The condition of attachment is fundamental to a secure base. Mary Ainsworth (1982) used the term "secure base" when describing the feeling of safety provided by an attachment figure to a child. Holmes explains the term as follows: "Children will seek out their secure base at times of threat—danger, illness, exhaustion, or following a separation. When the danger has passed, attachment behaviour will cease, but only if it is there to be mobilized if needed will the child feel secure." (Holmes 1993: 224).

Bowlby believed that the experience of the infant's ongoing pattern of interaction and attachment becomes mentally internalized by the child as the "internal working model". This model is a transactional and complementary representation of both sides of a relationship and is mainly concerned with the expected availability of the attachment figure based on the history of the relationship.

Different patterns of attachment behaviour seem to be specific to the relationship. Fonagy et al. (1991) demonstrated that a child could have a secure attachment to one parent and an insecure pattern to the other. The templates for these patterns of relating are laid down in infancy and continue to be used as basic organizational strategies throughout the lifespan.

A secure base is, therefore, a childhood developmental need that continues throughout life and applies equally to adults. "We all feel 'at home' with those whom we know and trust, and within such a home environment are able to relax, and pursue our projects, whether they be play, pleasure seeking or work." (Holmes 1993: 224). It is fortunate that most parents are able to establish emotionally secure environments for their children. But for others the task is less easy and it is with this recognition that I have tried to adapt my role as a health visitor to support them.

In her paper "Ghosts in the nursery" Selma Fraiberg (Fraiberg et al. 1987) described the strong intergenerational connections between the parent's early childhood experience and their relationship with their own children. The connections are the unconscious thoughts and feelings, i.e. the "ghosts" from their pasts, that influence the way parents perceive and react to their babies. Fraiberg acknowledged that "history is not destiny" and that the "narrative of the parental past" is not necessarily predictive of how they will be as parents. What stops some parents from inflicting their painful past on to the child? Fonagy suggests it is self-reflectiveness, i.e. the ability of the mind to understand the mental world of the self and others in terms of beliefs, regrets, values, or purposes that enables a parent, who has an adverse history, to protect the child from its repetition. In these circumstances I see it as part of my task to facilitate a discussion of the parent's past and to promote changes in thinking.

Containment of emotions

The formation of emotional and imaginative thought is integral to Bion's model of containment (Bion 1962). According to Waddell (2002: 28), "The mother brings not only her straightforwardly nurturing and loving qualities to the baby, but also her thinking self." The new infant does not have the capability to make sense of his or her environment. He or she relies on the quality of the carer's communication, i.e. the capacity to recognise and hold her own emotions and to actively hold the infant's projected emotions. If the carer is able to think about and process the infant's emotions without being overwhelmed by them, particularly when the infant is distressed, then both carer and infant reach a state of "reverie", as described by Bion. I frequently observe this when a baby is crying vehemently and the mother does not attempt to explain the cries as "he needs his feed", or "her nappy needs changing", or "he's teething" but talks soothingly to the baby about how he or she might be feeling and adjusts the baby's position and gently strokes or cuddles him or her and the infant settles. However, there are times when a mother does not have this capacity, as for example in post-natal depression. In traumatic circumstances the capacity to contain emotions can be lost, i.e. the mind fails to process emotional stimuli into meaningful thoughts.

Resilience and security

Some individuals seem more able to manage stressful or traumatic events. This resilience is not just due to a strong constitution or temperament. According to Fonagy (Fonagy et al. 1994: 232), resilience is "... a set of social and intra-psychic processes which take place across time given felicitous combinations of child attributes, family, social and cultural environments ... Resilience is normal development under difficult circumstances."

Fonagy found a strong association between resilience and security. He suggests that security during the first two years predicts many features of resilience in the older child. "There is thus a prima facia case that *resilient children are securely attached children*, i.e. that secure attachment is part of the mediating process where resilience is observed." (Fonagy et al. 1994: 235).

Attachment theory and the secure base phenomenon, in addition to Bion's concept of containment, can be applied to a therapeutic process when working with all ages. Health visitors are not "psycho-analysts", yet I suggest that they can work therapeutically, i.e. they could identify families where there are "ghosts in the nursery" or obstacles to the provision of a secure base. We could offer containment, become attachment figures, and provide a secure base for those families. As with the infant, the client needs containment, and to feel safe to explore difficult experiences or emotions. I suggest this can be provided by a trusting, sensitive, and consistent relationship with a member of the health visiting team.

The practitioner will need time to reflect on their effect on the family and to have a clear understanding of their role with the client. Some practitioners may find it difficult to contain another's pain and may revert to practical solutions to divert the client and themselves away from the pain. This will need to be addressed if we are to be effective. It may be that some members of the team take on more supervisory and containing roles and become the secure base for their colleagues.

My task with two families who had premature babies was to accompany them on traumatic and painful journeys as they endured different types of loss.

Loss of hopes and expectations

Prematurity has many risk factors associated with physical and mental health, growth, and development of the infant. McFadyen (1995: 172) suggests that some premature babies "may need to be 'claimed' or called into life by their mothers and into a relationship in the face of overwhelming anxieties and very real external threats to their existence." The babies I will be discussing did survive their time in the Neonatal Intensive Care Unit (NICU). However, they remained vulnerable to external and physiological stresses. Perhaps their mothers were able to bring them to life but for one it was not enough. One later died and the other suffered a physiological insult and developed a profound global disability. In each case there was a mourning process as the catastrophic loss of hopes and expectations was realized. In the former the mourning was due to a death and there was a sense of finality. In the latter the loss was less clear and the reaction was that both parents had an ongoing depression. Freud described two aspects of grief that helped me to make the distinction between these two families. Freud (1917b) made the distinction between "normal" mourning as non-pathological and melancholia as a "pathological disposition". Freud was clear that mourning was painful and that it had a process and a purpose in that he talked of the "work of mourning". He referred to a gradual transition of emotional "detachment" by reliving memories and expectations. It is only by accepting that the loved "object", or attachment figure, is no longer alive that the mourner is free to make new attachments, i.e. the process of mourning is a separation of self from the object.

Freud described the mental features of mourning as: profoundly painful dejection; cessation of interest in the outside world; loss of the capacity to love; and inhibition of all activity. In normal mourning "... time is needed for the command of reality-testing to be carried out in detail, and that when this work has been accomplished the ego will have succeeded in freeing its libido from the lost object." (Freud 1917b: 252).

Freud described melancholia, i.e. depression, as having the same features as mourning with the addition of a lowering of self-regard feelings. He identified mourning as a reaction to the loss of a loved object and made another distinction between the two states. In mourning there is nothing about the loss that is unconscious, whereas melancholia is related to an object-loss that is withdrawn from consciousness. Freud elaborated on the difference by adding that in mourning it is the world that has become poor and empty whereas in melancholia it is the ego itself.

Freud's paradigm of mourning implies that mourning is a transitional phase and has an optimistic outcome, a letting go of the deceased. In addition there is a conscious awareness of the loss, and self-esteem is not diminished. But Hindmarch (1993) suggests that the parents of infants who die have a burden of "shadow grief" that may resolve but is more likely to be experienced as "enduring sorrow" that is both natural and normal. Grief may appear to be resolved initially only to reveal itself at times of stress or reminders during the life cycle. Bowlby (1980) like Parkes (1972) identified several phases through which mourning moves, influenced by both internal and external features. Healthy mourning stages include: numbness, guilt, anger, yearning, searching, despair, disorganization, acceptance, and reorganization. Lewis and Bourne (2000: 53) integrated Parkes and Bowlby's ideas on normal grieving and suggested simply that, "Normal recovery from a loss involves taking in what has happened, and sorting out mixed feelings and lost hopes so that memories of the dead recede to a healthy perspective."

Parkes and Bowlby also recognized that children grieve too. As part of the normal developmental process of separation infants and children experience loss. The child's age, attachment organization, i.e. experience of separation and loss, will determine his or her grieving process. Bowlby suggested that for children to experience a healthy mourning process, they need to be given the opportunity to discuss the loss, be involved in family grieving, and be given accurate information about the loss. In this way the family shares thoughts, emotions, and ideas and facilitates the child's processing of painful thoughts. The child can then develop a capacity for reflective thinking, emotional regulation, and resilience.

My work with the families also includes older children, whose lives were affected by the traumatic events. I saw it as my task to keep them in mind too. The names have been changed for anonymity.

The first family

Sarah and Peter had two girls Tracey, aged six, and Susie aged four, when the twins Molly and Chloe were born six weeks prematurely. Molly was of low birth weight and had been more vulnerable during the pregnancy.

I had known Sarah since Tracey's birth. I began routine visiting as soon as the twins were home at four weeks. At the time the family appeared to be coping well and Molly seemed to be progressing satisfactorily. Molly died suddenly four weeks later.

The family were offered the CONI scheme (Care Of Next Infant). This is for families who have suffered an unexpected child death. It is modified to suit the individual family needs with the aim of preventing another death (FSID 1998). The parents see the health visitor weekly either at home or in a clinic and keep a CONI symptom diary for around six months. Chloe also had a monitor to detect movement during sleep and was weighed regularly. During the home visits I checked the diary and advised on physical health. I observed the interactions and facilitated emotional expression. The regular home visiting enabled me to build up a trusting relationship with the family.

The initial grief reaction

After Molly's sudden death, Sarah explained that Peter cried initially then slept for long periods, grieving alone or talking to his brother. Tracey talked to her mother about Molly and had angry outbursts, whereas Susie showed no obvious signs of grief. Chloe was said to miss her sister.

Sarah cried as she described to me the emotional pain and anger that had overwhelmed her. I felt the intensity of the feelings and acknowledged her pain. I tried to contain the sadness I was feeling but there were moments when I shed tears with her.

Adjusting to life without Molly

Chloe is fifteen weeks old.

Chloe cried vehemently as Sarah removed her clothes and she was weighed. She spoke to her gently as she dressed her again. Then Sarah sat with Chloe nuzzling into her chest. Chloe seemed exhausted and continued to take deep breaths. Sarah talked to her soothingly and gave her a dummy. Chloe's eyes closed and she soon looked asleep.

Sarah demonstrated her ability to contain Chloe's distress and calm her down effectively. Then she angrily expressed her frustration at delays in the pathologist's investigation.

I said empathically, "It is hard not knowing." Sarah replied, "Yes, it is the not knowing that is doing me in. I have always known that one of the twins would die but I thought it was going to be Chloe not Molly." Sarah talked about how Molly was the "quiet" one, whereas Chloe was less compliant.

When Peter came in Sarah said she would like another baby. Peter retorted, "Oh no, I'm not going through another pregnancy. It was awful." Sarah laughed awkwardly . . . and said, "I know some people may think I am mad but I like talking to Molly. I know she is watching over us all." I responded by saying quietly, "You enjoy chatting to her?" Sarah replied, "Yes. She will always be there protecting us."

My support

The work discussion group became an important support for me as over time I felt exhausted and was learning that mourning cannot be rushed. I gained self-assurance and was encouraged to raise Sarah's awareness of the possible effects of the loss of a sister on the older girls. I did this at the first appropriate opportunity. I subsequently gave Sarah some children's books to read with them about death and Sarah began to talk more about the older girls.

Father's role

Sarah was preoccupied and cared for Chloe intermittently. However, Chloe was developing a close, loving, and positive relationship with her father who was reliable, well organized, and caring. He began telling me his life story and looked sad as he revealed that his mother had disappeared when he was a small boy. Peter did subsequently disclose to me how angry he felt towards her. It appeared that as a consequence of trying not to repeat the past, Peter worked hard with Sarah, whom he said was not interested in sex and he described as "running away from him". Sarah was present and shed tears in silence. It seemed that

I acted as a catalyst for Peter to reflect on his past and for the couple to connect. Peter showed a determination to make the marriage work against all the odds.

A few weeks later, when Chloe was seven months, Sarah was delighted to tell me she was pregnant. This raised my concern that the new baby could be at risk of becoming a "replacement child". Perhaps Sarah's grief was to be relieved by attributing Molly's identity onto the new infant.

Chloe came off the CONI scheme at nine months. Nevertheless my involvement continued. I visited close to significant dates and continued to offer Sarah space for mourning. I did not see Chloe at my visits as she was asleep and it seemed important for Sarah to keep my time for herself. I was not able to observe the mother-child interactive style.

When Sophie was born my continued involvement was assured when she was also put on the CONI scheme to prevent another death in this family. Sarah brought Sophie to my clinic for the weekly assessments at her request. She was ready to socialize and to be like the other mothers. Sophie remained in Molly's shadow in the early months as Sarah identified Sophie as representing the idealized traits of Molly in that she was passive and undemanding. Sophie's good health and ability to survive beyond Molly's age then became significant and Sophie seemed free to be herself.

Chloe made the transition out of babyhood into toddler-hood by walking as soon as Sophie was born. Chloe seemed to have a growing capacity to manage on her own and had an endearing smile.

On one occasion Chloe fell in the clinic and cried. Sarah moved away from her to face me. She looked frightened and did not attend to Chloe in her distress. A colleague checked that she was all right and Chloe shrugged her away as if to say, "I can look after myself." Chloe seemed to know it was painful for her mother to attend to her.

I was shocked by what appeared an overt rejection of Chloe and sought the help of the work discussion group. My difficulty in sustaining a therapeutic involvement with this family was acknowledged. I was encouraged to enable Sarah to think differently about Chloe.

At the next opportunity I tentatively asked Sarah, "How do you think Chloe might feel about the loss of her twin?" Sarah looked puzzled. I added, "Chloe will have a memory of it even though she may not be able to put it into words. Also because she was an identical twin she will always be a reminder of Molly and that is sad and difficult for Chloe and you." Sarah looked at me very sadly. "Yes it is difficult, I had not thought of it from her point of view." She smiled at Chloe. There was a reciprocal smile and coy look from her. I hoped that my remarks would be enough to make a change.

The CONI scheme was discontinued when Sophie was six months.

I visited a few months later at Sarah's request. Sarah talked easily about Molly and her belief that she was watching them. I suggested that she found it comforting to think that Molly was there. She agreed. Sarah acknowledged that some people found it difficult to accept her way of thinking and added:

"Molly is a fighter. She fought to stay alive during the pregnancy and her time in hospital only to die later. It was as if she stayed alive long enough to keep Chloe alive."

Sarah seemed controlled as she said: "I know the sadness will always be there. Sometimes I look at Chloe sitting at the table and think there should be another child sitting next to her." I asked, "How much do you think Chloe understood about Molly?" She said:

"I imagine she feels as though she has lost something. She always says night, night to Molly and spontaneously waves. She is very close to Sophie, it is as if they are twins." I said tentatively, "But they are not." She looked angry as she said she is often stopped in the street and asked if they are twins. I imagined this was her wish. A photograph of the twins was prominently displayed as if to confirm to Sarah that she is the mother of twins.

Chloe sat on her mother's knee. She fiddled with Sarah's locket around her neck. Sarah said smiling, "Oh yes that's Molly, do you want to see her?" Chloe nodded. Sarah opened her locket to show a photo of Molly on one side and a lock of hair on the other. I said, "Chloe is that your sister?" She looked at me and smiled. Sarah said Chloe often looks at the picture. Sarah then said that Molly wanted to go to sleep now and so they must shut the locket. As Sarah shut the locket I said, "Molly has gone now, hasn't she?"Chloe looked at me again and smiled.

I have been alongside this family as they survived the loss of Molly. Sarah continues to experience "shadow grief". This seems like a more manageable phase in her lifelong mourning. However the family appear to have developed resilience and secure attachments and consequently a more cohesive family has developed.

The second family

I did not know them until Ben was born at thirty weeks. He was to stay in the NICU for six weeks. During that time I visited the hospital to support the parents Nina and Jim, and their daughter, Vicky, who was two.

The family had moved from another area. I understood Nina and Jim to have experienced depression after Vicky's birth and I hoped to promote a more positive outcome with this baby. Ben made steady progress and began to breastfeed. I had occasion to see Nina feeding both children when Vicky found it difficult allowing Ben to feed on her favoured breast. Nina was patient and we were all optimistic about Ben's progress.

Ben developed a life-threatening infection and became very ill. Both parents were devastated. Nina was already deeply disappointed over the circumstances of the birth and blamed herself. My role was to be more therapeutic as Nina became depressed, showed a loss of self-esteem, and stopped breast-feeding Ben. Jim responded by taking on more parental responsibilities. I visited regularly.

BEN AT SEVEN MONTHS

Nina and Vicky greeted me warmly. Ben was supported in a reclining baby chair and was looking around as if scanning and trying to focus on the activity around him. His arms were by his sides and his legs held slightly flexed. He straightened his limbs and held them rigidly for a few moments. I spoke to him and gently touched his arm. It felt stiff. Ben's eyes were wide open. He looked in my direction but did not engage . . . Nina brought me a cup of tea, organized a bottle for Ben, and began feeding him. Vicky prepared some red playdough sausages for me. I asked how Nina was feeling about Ben. Nina said, "I know Ben is not doing what he should. But now he has started to make little baby noises and crying less. I am beginning to enjoy him; he is more like a baby."

Nina said Vicky was not breastfeeding now. Vicky looked at her mother and began fiddling and lifted her dress revealing her tummy and I asked if she had stopped completely. Nina looked embarrassed and said, "No, of course not, she still has a little suck but it is just comfort." Vicky then moved very close to her mother and looked up at her and said, pleadingly in a tiny voice, "Just a little one, a little, little suck." I felt the tension between them and I rescued Nina by asking Vicky if she did any paintings at pre-school. Nina looked relieved. Vicky went off and collected some paintings.

A couple of months later Nina explained how Vicky was able to say when she wanted a feed and accepted her mother saying that there was no milk left.

Nina described the fuss Vicky made at preschool and that she stopped crying as soon as she went out of the door. Vicky looked worried and said, "Mummy stay, Mummy stay." I said, "Leaving Vicky is difficult for both of you." Nina replied that the first time she left Vicky she waited by the phone expecting a call to collect her but it never came. She went back early but could not hear her crying.

Some time later Nina revealed how she had cried and clung to her own mother when she had to go to school. It seemed she was reliving the memory of her childhood separations and the parenting that she had received. Also Jim told me how he had always feared leaving Vicky in case something happened to her.

At nine months, Ben was diagnosed as having a profound global disability.

Ben at one year

Jim's parents had been staying and had brought two other grandchildren. They had left early that morning.

Jim recounted how difficult the weekend was for his nephews with his mother telling them not to do this or that, and if they did, something terrible would happen to them. I suggested that this might have been how he experienced his mother as a child. Jim's defences against the memory of his childhood were very strong. He looked at me nonchalantly, opened his hands in a helpless gesture and said, "It was possible but I don't know."

My work with this family was very frustrating and hard to sustain. I felt stuck. There was a seesawing of one parent being very depressed while the other appeared more resilient as if one was compensating for the difficulties experienced by the other.

The work discussion group supported me by listening and showed a positive interest in the family. The discussion focused on the parents' fear of separating from the children. I understood that Jim's denial of his childhood memories suggested a consistently painful relationship with his mother. It seemed that Jim's determination not to repeat his past was manifested by a total investment in his family. Vicky was not allowed to experience frustration and could not be left with others.

Nina and Jim became very anxious when Vicky was due to start nursery school. Nina could not sleep and Jim was unable to return to work until this traumatic hurdle had been surmounted. Vicky on the other hand seemed relieved to go to school and did not make a fuss. Later she drew me a colourful picture of her school friends and her teacher and another one of home showing Ben as a large face dominating the paper.

Ben at 18 months

Nina was sitting on the floor in the middle of the room with Ben on her knee. Vicky was kneeling next to her playing with a collection of stones. Nina said Vicky's teacher had had a baby and the baby had started to sit up. She said Vicky knows that Ben won't be able to sit up. Vicky then said something about death. I looked puzzled and Nina explained that Vicky was learning about bereavement at school. She said, "I don't understand it—they are too young."

I replied that on the contrary I thought it was very relevant and that their situation was like being bereaved. Jim agreed and said that he had lost the child that he was expecting. Vicky looked sad. I said, "It is sad that Ben can't sit up and do all the things that babies do." Vicky replied thoughtfully, "Yes it is. Yes." She moved closer to Ben, stroked his head and kissed him. I felt sad.

I went on to talk openly with the parents about how Vicky had lost a brother that she would not be able to play with. Nina agreed and Jim continued with his wish for a son that would play with Vicky. Tears filled Nina's eyes. Jim said that Ben was like an empty shell. Nina became defensive and told Jim that Ben did have a personality and she was not prepared to talk about Ben in this way.

It was not until it was confirmed that Ben was not able to see, that Nina began to acknowledge the full extent of Ben's disabilities and allowed herself to openly reflect on the child that she had lost. She looked deeply depressed as she said: "Ben has nothing there. There is no brain. I look in the garden and think that he should be out there playing with Vicky on sunny days . . ." There was a long silence I did not interrupt. Nina looked at me and said that she did not know how she was going to cope. I said that the night carers were for her and not just for Ben and that she was important too. I acknowledged that part of Nina might not want Ben but that was difficult to admit. Nina looked sadly at me and said quietly, "Yes." There was another silence. I was feeling sad. Ben, who was with a day carer and could be heard to laugh, interrupted us. I reminded Nina that Ben did show emotions and communicated his likes and dislikes. This lifted Nina's mood and she began to talk more positively about Ben.

I did become a secure base for this family as they slowly recognized that Ben's condition was global. As each deficit was confirmed there was a renewed sense of loss. I worked hard with the family and I hope that by discussing feelings openly and honestly with them and in Vicky's presence I have helped the family to communicate with her and to begin to develop a reflective capacity.

Conclusions

As a health visitor I was in a good position to intervene with these families at the time it was needed rather than wait for adverse patterns of relating to become established and which might need a more specialized intervention later.

Thinking of Barnes' "primary factors" (see Introduction) I worked in partnership with the parents at all times. I was able to establish an open, empathic, and enquiring quality that built trust and provoked thought. I tried to be sensitive to the family cultures. Furthermore I was aware that death can be a taboo subject in western European culture. The timings of appointments were always mutually agreed and I was available to the family at times of crises.

I used the psychodynamic theories of Bowlby and Bion in addition to Fonagy's work as a framework of thinking based on observational skills and reflection, integrated with a person-centred style to establish a containing relationship. The support from the work discussion group at the Tavistock Centre was crucial in that the discussion enhanced my understanding of both families and my part in the relationships.

I suggest health visitors can use themselves as a therapeutic resource, a "secure base" for intervention and support with families. Observational skills, self awareness, and knowledge of adverse patterns of relating between the caregiver and child will enhance this role. However lack of training and lack of self-confidence to intervene in infancy need to be addressed if more health staff are to work to promote emotional well being in infants.

Training programmes such as the Infant Mental Health Diploma and MA at the Tavistock Centre or the more practice-based Solihull Approach (Solihull Primary Care Trust, & University of Central England 2001) will help health visitors and other community staff to think differently, to understand the parent-child styles of relating they observe, and to become aware of the intergenerational link of past experience with present behaviour.

References

Ainsworth, M. (1982). Attachment: retrospect and prospect. In: C. M. Parkes, & J. Stephenson-Hinde (Eds.), *The Place of Attachment in Human Behaviour* (pp. 3–30). London: Tavistock.

Barnes, J. (2003). Interventions addressing infant mental health. *Children & Society*, 17: 386–395.

Bion, W. R. (1962). *Learning From Experience.* London: Heinemann Medical Books.

Bowlby, J. (1980). *Attachment and Loss, Volume 3. Loss: Sadness and Depression.* Harmondsworth: Penguin Books.

Bowlby, J. (1988). *A Secure Base. Clinical Applications of Attachment Theory.* London: Routledge.

CETHV (1977). *An Investigation Into the Principles of Health Visiting.* London: Council for the Education and Training of Health Visitors.

Fraiberg, S. H., Adelson, E., & Shapiro, V. (1987). Ghosts in the nursery: a psychoanalytical approach to the problems of impaired infant—mother relationships. In: L. Fraiberg (Ed.), *Selected Writings of Selma Fraiberg* (pp. 100–136). Columbus, OH: Ohio State University Press.

Freud, S. (1917b). *Mourning and Melancholia.* In: J. Strachey (Ed. & Trans.), *The Complete Psychological Works of Sigmund Freud: Standard Edition, Volume 14* (pp. 243–260.). London: Hogarth Press, 1975.

Fonagy, P., Steele, M., Steele, H., Moran, G., & Higgitt, A. (1991). The capacity for understanding mental states: the reflective self in parent and child and its significance for security of attachment. *Infant Mental Health Journal,* 12/3: 201–218.

Fonagy, P., Steele, M., Steele, H., Higgitt, A., & Target, M. (1994). The Emanuel Miller Memorial Lecture 1992: the theory and practice of resilience. *Journal of Child Psychology and Psychiatry,* 35/2: 231–257.

FSID (1998). *Report on 5000 Babies using the CONI (Care of Next Infant) Programme.* London: Foundation for the Study of Infant Deaths.

Hindmarch, C. (1993). *On The Death of a Child.* Oxford: Radcliffe Medical Press.

Holmes, J. (1993). *John Bowlby and Attachment Theory.* London: Routledge.

Lewis, E., & Bourne, S. (2000). Pregnancy after stillbirth or neonatal death: psychological risks and management. In: J. Raphael-Leff (Ed.), *"Spilt milk" Perinatal Loss & Breakdown* (pp. 53–59). London: Institute of Psycho-Analysis.

Luck, M., & Jesson J. (1996). Evaluation of community health development. In: S. Cowley (Ed.), *Public Health in Policy and Practice. A Sourcebook for Health Visitors and Community Nurses,* pp. 261–289. London: Baillière Tindall.

McFadyen, A. (1995). Reflections on special-care babies and their early experience. *Psychoanalytic Psychotherapy,* 9: 57–174.

Parkes, C. M. (1972). *Bereavement: Studies of Grief in Adult Life.* London: Tavistock.

Solihull Primary Care Trust & University of Central England (2001). *The Solihull Approach.* The Solihull Primary Care Trust & the University of Central England. Birmingham: School of Primary Health Care, UCE in Birmingham.

Waddel, M. (2002). *Inside Lives and the Development of the Personality.* London: Karnac Books.

CHAPTER ELEVEN

"It wasn't meant to happen like this": the complexity of mourning great expectations

Lynne Cudmore
Tavistock Clinic, London

Introduction

In this chapter I will discuss some aspects of my clinical work in the perinatal service, part of the specialist service for the under-fives age group, based in the Child and Family Department at the Tavistock Clinic in London. The majority of the individuals, couples, parents, and families that I meet struggle with the emotional aftermath of living through traumatic experiences that have occurred during pregnancy, the infant's birth or the months following. The experience of feeling catapulted into a disaster area where they had previously had great expectations of joy is one they share. There is an inevitable emotional fallout for each individual internally and externally; on relationships within the family, between the parental couple, between parent and infant and with already existing children. Trauma always involves loss (Levy & Lemma 2004) so these experiences need to be mourned if development is to occur; loss has to be acknowledged, grief expressed. But a mourning process might be inhibited by trauma if there is a breakdown in symbolic functioning, the capacity to reflect on lived experience (Garland 1998). The losses that my patients describe can be actual, such as the death of a child, or the loss of an "inside" baby because of a very premature birth; and also symbolic, such as the loss of a sense of self as good and strong, the loss of hope, trust and faith in a benign world. Working through these different layers and aspects of loss is painful to bear and rarely linear. Many factors, both internal and external, influence the meaning that is generated from the experience of "it wasn't meant to happen like this".

The nature and quality of a person's internal resources will profoundly affect the way in which they respond to external life events and the nature and quality of external relationships will also profoundly affect their response. There is always a dynamic interplay between internal and external relationships. For some people the depth of psychic pain engendered cannot be borne and losses cannot be mourned. When this happens not only is the individual parent burdened but it is likely that children too will be burdened by their parent's undigested loss and indeed the burden may fall on children yet to be born. For this reason an intervention that focuses on the parent's experience can be beneficial for children.

Many of our patients, who have been traumatized by what they have experienced as catastrophic events occurring in the perinatal period, describe having lost a sense of being in a safe place, internally and externally, meaning has collapsed. They are often lost for words; they cannot put their story into words or describe their emotional experience. In the language of attachment theory they cannot construct a narrative or mentalize their experience (Fonagy 2002). The idea behind offering help to parents is to provide a sense of what Winnicott (1965) described as "a sense of being held" or Bion (1962) described as "being contained". It offers the possibility of a dialogue, a conversation, of sharing an experience with someone, who can try and understand, out of which a narrative might be formed, given shape, and meaning constructed.

I will begin by sketching the backdrop to the development of the perinatal service and then discuss ideas about trauma and mourning that have helped to guide me as I have tried to understand what my patients were describing. Finally I will discuss two cases, the first where an infant was born prematurely and in the second where an infant died.

The perinatal service

The Under-Five's Service in the Child and Family Department at the Tavistock Clinic has, since its conception in the 1980s, seen families whose difficulties have arisen because of "out of the ordinary" experiences that have happened to them during the perinatal period. There has been a commitment to the importance of attending to these experiences that can have such serious repercussions on the quality of the relationship between the parental couple and between parents and infants and as they grow their child. It is now widely recognized that traumatic beginnings for parents and infants can have long-lasting consequences that might be mitigated by an early response and intervention.

Three years ago a new initiative that focused on this area of work was launched and it was part of my brief as a child psychotherapist, who is also trained as a couples psychotherapist, to develop this. The combination of specialized experience in the team led us to publicly highlight a range of areas in which we might offer help. These included couples or parents with difficulties concerning conception, or who had had an abortion, or for whom an infant had died, been born prematurely, been ill following birth, or suffered from a congenital condition. We developed links with local GP's, health and community centres, and the multidisciplinary staff on the special care units of two local hospitals.

These close working links with potential referrers have been important for two reasons. Referrers have an opportunity to think about the case with us, and explore whether a referral to this service might be helpful and whether the timing of the referral is right. Distress can be generated in the professional system because of the agonising nature of the family's situation. A referral can often be made in haste as a way of getting rid of this distress as a response to the professional's own anxiety and difficulty holding a painful situation. If a referral is made to relieve the professional's anxiety the chances are the family will not engage. We have found that "handovers" need to be handled with great sensitivity because families feel so vulnerable and might have made strong attachments to those professionals, who were first on hand when their baby was born or died. For example I am thinking of one family where a baby who had spent a long time in a special care unit was dying and had returned home to die. Immediately the baby died the palliative care team referred the parents to us without properly discussing it with them. I think they could not bear the immense distress the baby's death had generated for them and feared that this would spill out when they saw the parents. The newly bereaved parents arrived for their appointment at the Clinic, yet another institution, bewildered about the referral but compliant. When I began exploring their feelings about coming to see me, it was clear that they didn't want to engage with yet another professional from yet another setting, and the offer of help was too early for them. They needed space and time alone, away from what felt to them at that point to be further intrusion. This idea of the helper as intruder was perhaps the more negative side of their view of professionals, who had also been experienced as devoted and caring. I felt that they needed time to see what resources they could bring to bear on their situation. Bereavement, even a death as shocking as the death of a child, does not necessarily need a professional response.

Families are not just seen at the Tavistock. Sometimes I might go to the special care unit to meet a family and so provide a bridge to the service here, a "reaching out" that is really necessary for some. Sometimes the referring professional will bring a family here for their initial meeting. The idea of "reaching out" is also behind what is called "outreach" work. Once a week I work alongside a health visitor who runs a baby clinic in a local health centre. Here I come across many complex scenarios of families referred by the health visitor or I meet mothers, fathers, and their infants in the waiting area, or by the "weighing scales" as Daws (2005) has described. The informality of this setting means that I see many families who would not normally find themselves talking to a child psychotherapist. These are families whose distress and anxiety is so much under cover that it is unlikely that they would have raised concern in the professional network or referred themselves for professional help, but when they tell me their story they describe very traumatic situations. For example, I see mothers with babies born very prematurely, who ostensibly are coping but are experiencing sleep problems with their babies, and no link has been made with the separation that mother and baby endured when the baby was incubated. Feeding problems are common and often stem from a persisting anxiety that the infant will not survive, an anxiety that cannot be laid to rest. Just recently I met a Nigerian mother whose baby had rolled out the window when she turned her back as she was changing her. She was still traumatized two years later and constantly saw her face when looking at her new baby, seriously interfering with the development of their relationship. Many of these families are newly arrived in this country, have no family around them, have no established supportive networks and are very isolated. When they are faced with a pregnancy or a birth that has been very difficult they are particularly vulnerable because of this paucity of external support. Although I have sometimes tried to transfer some of these cases to the nearby Tavistock Clinic, it has rarely worked. Of course, there may be many different reasons for this but I think that being seen at the health centre feels more ordinary—it is less formal than a clinical setting. It might also be felt to be less stigmatizing to receive help there. It allows for a greater flexibility in the nature of the contact.

We see many individuals and couples where there are no children because a baby has died, either during pregnancy, at birth, or after. Unmourned losses can affect subsequent children, so this work has a preventative aspect. The time frame is also more flexible. Although the Under-Fives Service at the Tavistock has evolved a brief intervention model of five or ten sessions, my own experience leads me to think that the nature of this work especially in the area of loss does not really lend itself to this kind of time frame because it places too much pressure on the process of mourning, which takes time, and which you cannot hurry. It is a process with many vicissitudes. However I think that setting up a therapy structure is particularly important because parents can feel that all structure internal and external has been lost. I have found it valuable to offer sessions where there is a longer interval (at fortnightly, three weekly, or monthly intervals). This can be helpful especially when working with parental couples who are in a state of mind in which they can continue talking and "working" between meetings and where there is less dependence on the therapist to facilitate this function. The nature of the work is probably less active; it is not "doing" work as brief work can sometimes tend to be. I would say it is more about "being there", available, attentive, sensitive, and receptive; being there to notice the obstacles that might occur that impede development and to help "give sorrow words" (Judd 1989), from Shakespeare's Macbeth.

Theoretical background

Traumatic experience is by its very definition shocking, unexpected, and unpredictable. The word trauma is borrowed from the Greek where it refers to a piercing of the skin, of the body envelope. As Garland (1998) has described, "Freud (1920) used the word metaphorically to emphasize how the mind, too, can be pierced and wounded by events, giving graphic force to his description of the way in which the mind can be thought of as being enveloped by a kind of skin or protective shield. Freud (1920) thought this protective shield was the outcome of a development in the brain (and therefore mind) of a highly selective sensitivity to external stimuli. This selectivity is crucial: shutting out excessive amounts and kinds of stimulation is even more important in terms of maintaining a workable equilibrium than is the capacity to receive or let in stimuli" (Garland 1998, p. 9).

For infants this filtering function is usually performed by the mother, through her sensitivity to what her baby is able to manage. She acts to protect her baby from the extremes of experience both environmental and emotional (Garland, 1998). Bion (1962) and Bick (1968) described a mental skin that envelops the mind that protects and enfolds, and within which we feel a sense of safety—a sense of being held. Bion believed that this mental skin—this feeling of being contained—was the result of the mother being receptive to the infant's state of mind and capable of allowing it to be evoked in herself and process it in such a way that in an identifiable form, she could attend to it in the infant. In this way something that in the infant is near sensory and somatic is transformed by the mother into something more mental, which can be used for thought or stored as memory. He believed that her capacity to do this detoxified the infant's unmanageable distress, transforming it into something bearable and meaningful that could be thought about. The nearly sensory-somatic qualities Bion called beta elements and those that become more mental in character he called alpha elements. The infant with a more or less successfully containing parent eventually incorporated that very capacity to think about his or her own anxieties and over time acquired a capacity to think about emotional experience. When there is a traumatic breach in this envelope or mental skin, very primitive anxieties are released internally in both the adult and the child and that sense of being held—contained inside something safe—disappears. The mind is flooded with unmanageable stimulation. The feeling of safety of having something good inside and around one, the sense of protection originally provided by the mother's mind and arms is lost. The capacity for containing, knowing about emotional experience, and thinking about it is ruptured. One way of managing this degree of internal terror and pain is to erect defences such as denial, splitting, or projective identification. The latter can also serve to communicate the distress.

Parents I have met whose child has died, have described to me that they feel they have been attacked internally—it feels like an internal structure has broken down. The loss of a belief in the predictability of the world and in the protective function of one's good internal and external objects means a resurgence of fears about the cruelty and strength of bad objects.

Following traumas flashbacks are common. Garland (1998) describes the sudden gripping sensation that you are not just thinking about what happened in the past but you are actually reliving it in the present (Garland 1998). Freud (1920) understood this phenomenon as a form of repetition compulsion, the ego's attempts to master a traumatic situation. By recreating the event in the mind, the individual attempts to gain control over the trauma and so reduce the impact of the assault on the mind. Garland (1998) believes that the flashback is the experience of the loss of the container—the internalized place intimately related with good early care—in which thinking about something can occur is lost. She describes how the capacity to be able to think about something implies an "I", who is separate from the event or experience that is being considered. Having a flashback seems to indicate that the distinction between "I" and the event has been lost. The individual is flooded with extreme anxiety, and as a result recollection and remembering have been replaced by re-experiencing.

Bion (1967) linked what the mother can do for the baby with what the therapist may be able to do for the patient; she might be able to help transform the unbearable into something that can eventually be thought about, held in the mind and considered, rather than responded to as an overwhelming experience that causes a further breakdown of an ability to think. If the trauma can be transformed into a mental experience able to be digested and thought about, then the experience can begin to be processed. This can lead to a capacity to reflect on the experience and construct meaning and to start a mourning process. In the language of attachment theory "improving the coherency of the narrative" (Fonagy 2002) is central to recovery. Attachment theory has shown that emotional security is powerfully related to the coherency with which adults tell their story as opposed to the actual disruptions of attachment that they have suffered. It is what the traumatic experience has done to the sufferer's mind and emotions that is crucial.

Clinical vignettes

Case study 1

I first met baby Andrea and her mother when Andrea was four months old. I have chosen to discuss this case because of the complicated emotional aftermath that followed her birth fourteen weeks prematurely, necessitating that she spend the first ten weeks of her life in a special care unit. The emotional fallout that followed this could be partly explained by the trauma of the abrupt separation caused by the prematurity and was also related to the damage done to the mother's conception of herself as a mother. Both these factors had destructive repercussions on the marriage, which further destabilized mother and for a time interfered with the development of the parent's relationship with their daughter. Mother was eventually able to find her way out of a very persecuted, aggrieved state of mind, where she felt under the influence of very malign forces, to a more benign and secure state, where she could think about Andrea and her needs. She could enjoy her and their relationship together and also enjoy being part of a parental couple that came together to look after their daughter. I have been seeing mother and baby for a period of six months. I intend to describe the beginning of our contact in detail and then discuss the themes that emerged over time. Names and details have been carefully disguised.

Mrs Baleru was referred to me by the family's doctor a month after Andrea had returned home. He was concerned about mother as she seemed low but had no concerns about the baby.

He told me that mother was Russian and her family lived in Canada.

Mrs Baleru arrived an hour late for her first appointment but had not realized she was late. She was very upset when she realized her mistake; this suggested she had been looking forward to the appointment and to talking to someone. Fortunately I had a little time and suggested she came in so we could arrange another meeting. She looked pale and in disarray—she was disorientated. The baby was strapped to her body and I could not see her face. When I asked about the baby, she said she was asleep, and that on the whole she was doing well, and putting on weight. Mother was clearly not doing well and upon sitting down she started crying. She told me that antidepressants had been prescribed but they made her sick and she had stopped taking them. Andrea had been born at twenty-six weeks, and all the time she had been in hospital, she had been coping but now she could not stop crying and was feeling irritable with her husband and the baby. All her distressed feelings came flooding out. I noticed that the baby did not move in response to all this distress and I wondered whether her immobility was a way of holding herself together in the face of her mother's distress and inner emotional absence from her. We had just enough time for me to explain that I would be able to see her the following week and that I could go on seeing her and Andrea for as long as needed to think together about what they had both been through. She was grateful. She said she needed to talk to someone as she could not talk to her husband—they argued all the time—and her parents were in Canada. She felt lonely. I felt bad about not being able to see her for longer, worried about her and the baby—a week seemed a long time. I wondered whether my anxiety, and feelings of impotence and inadequacy (at not being able to attend to her distress because of being robbed of the time I had allotted them) were a reflection of her feelings of helplessness and impotence at having been robbed of her pregnancy and a more predictable beginning to the transition to becoming a mother.

The next week she was on time. She described being strong in the hospital but now she felt weak. She felt collapsed. I said I wondered if in hospital she had been holding herself together tightly, willing Andrea to live, rooting for her survival, but now all the feelings connected with her prematurity and their shocking, surprising beginning were flooding out leaving her feeling weak and depleted. I encouraged her to tell me what had happened. She described how, when she was twenty-four weeks pregnant, she developed pains in her stomach. The midwife said that the baby was stretching and getting ready to be born. She desperately wished to hold on to her. She was worried that she would die (the year before she had lost a baby at twenty-three weeks) and she had been desperate to be pregnant again, desperate to be a mother. The birth itself was frightening. The doctors did not arrive until after the baby was born and the nurses asked her husband to administer an injection when he, too, was feeling shocked. The baby was whisked away to special care and she was too upset to see her. Her husband also thought she should not see her because the baby looked so strange and was covered in tubes. She thought he was trying to protect her. I talked about the traumatic experience she described, naming those aspects of the trauma I could discern: not being able to hold on to the baby inside her, feeling she might have dropped her, as well as the sudden separation from Andrea, which had left her feeling so empty, surprised, and shocked at the speed of events. She described how the baby was so covered in tubes she could not see her and her foot was bruised from so many injections. I talked about her feelings of helplessness and impotence as she watched Andrea being submitted to invasive and painful experiences, feelings that perhaps mirrored her daughter's experience of great pain, which was hard to watch and bear. As she talked I thought how difficult it must have been for her to imaginatively enter into her daughter's experience—so many feelings must have had to be kept at bay in order to manage the deep anxiety and pain and to survive the experience. Each night she had to wrench herself away from her baby to return home. She said those feelings could return in a flash. She still expected a catastrophe. In hospital it was like being on a roller coaster—one minute Andrea was fine, the next minute she was not. There was never any feeling of stepping on stable ground.

Eventually Andrea had returned home a month ago, but after a week had to return to hospital for a planned hernia operation.

She described how Andrea trembled when she left her for a minute. I felt relieved that she could notice her daughter's desperate need for her and that she could respond. She stayed up for two nights holding her hand, keeping a tight grip on her. She was clearly trembling, too, and for the first time allowed herself to feel overwhelmed by all they had been through together. Her defences started to crumble. She had begun to be more open to Andrea's feelings when she began to be more open and aware of her own experience. Andrea's trembling resonated with her own and she could respond to her and soothe her.

Over the next weeks she came alone to see me. I felt she wanted the time to herself to begin to put words to what she had gone through. She recounted the painfulness of being separated from Andrea, and her conflicting feelings about the nurses looking after her; on the one hand she felt grateful but also sensitive to feelings that they were usurping her role. These more negative feelings she was barely conscious of while she was in hospital. I imagined her to be a very uncomplaining mother, compliant and accepting. We talked about how inhibited she felt talking to Andrea in the presence of the nurses and doctors. The private intimacy, that in more optimal circumstances mother and infant enjoy, felt denied. I realized how her function as the container of Andrea's experience, her function as the giver of meaning, was seriously interfered with. In order to carry on, mother had had to split her conflicting feelings: the hospital staff were preserved as good. The bad feelings, the anger, the rage, the hatred, and her own feelings of inadequacy and failure at not being able to hold her baby inside were projected with a vengeance onto her mother-in-law, who her husband had asked to come to look after them. Mother-in-law was pilloried as the one who discounted her as a mother, not recognising the primacy of the mother-baby couple.

Mrs Baleru said mother-in-law had taken a photograph of Andrea in her arms and cut her out of the picture. She had been beheaded. She described her insides as filled up with hate, and she hated her husband for not supporting her enough and standing up to what she perceived as his mother's rejection of her as a mother. She was thinking of separating from her husband

and could not see how the marriage could survive. The fallout on the marriage and the conflict with her mother-in-law, which rippled through the extended family, took centre stage in our meetings. The rivalrous relationship between mother and daughter-in-law made me wonder if she was struggling with a little girl part of herself that felt that she was being punished by a vengeful mother for having a baby. She told me that her father adored her and she had been her father's princess all her life.

Earlier conflicts were brought to life at the point that she became a mother and brought her baby home. By the time we started meeting, mother-in-law had left weeks before but she was completely preoccupied with her grievances about her. Mrs Baleru's vulnerability, her sense of failure, and her loss were subsumed under a hard and hating part of her personality. I wondered if anger and hatred operated as an anaesthetic to the helplessness, pain, and fear that had felt unbearable. Mourning had given way to grievance. I talked to her about this and the reality that mother-in-law had returned to her home country now but she had allowed her to take up residence in her head, where the fights with her still raged. This comment seemed to bring her some relief and she began to separate the external situation from her own psychic reality, outside from inside.

Around this time I suggested that her husband join her for our meetings. I felt concerned about the disintegrating marital situation; the bedrock for Andrea's development of two loving parents working together to look after her seemed very unstable and I thought their separation would be a further huge loss for her. She said talking about such personal difficulties was not part of her husband's culture. I think by this time it was very difficult for her to envisage sharing our meetings with him. However my concern about her husband and their relationship as a couple and as parents was registered by her and this led to her talking about him in a very different state of mind, much less complaining and more concerned. I heard how badly he had been affected by Andrea's prematurity. He had difficulty breathing, asthma, stomach pains; he was in and out of hospital while Andrea was in hospital. His identification with Andrea was, perhaps, his way of managing the trauma. He was eventually diagnosed by the doctor as depressed.

This made me realize how overlooked the impact on a father of a premature birth can be. He had also been unsure of what his role as a father to a very premature baby was, feeling very much a bystander. Over the next weeks the marriage seemed to start recovering. Rather than just blaming her husband she began to talk to him about how she felt, and how she wanted to be looked after. She had moved into what Britton (1989) has called the "third position"—she was able to stand just enough outside her experience to think about it and she was able to observe herself in her relationship with her husband. Once this step was made she was able to use their relationship as a resource rather than just attacking it. There was a move towards using their relationship as a container, a place to think together about the difficulties they had encountered and were still facing. They benefited from this and Andrea benefited, too.

Whereas earlier I had been concerned that so many other things were occupying Mrs Baleru's mind that Andrea did not have the prime place she needed—she described her as a very good baby who never cried—Mrs Baleru told me that Andrea had started to cry and demand attention. She had also started to gurgle. She seemed to have at last found her voice, perhaps as there was more space for her to be really noticed and heard. Andrea became much more of a presence in our meetings. She was growing into a sturdy baby, and putting on weight, which was a source of enormous pride to her mother. In one meeting I watched them enchanted with each other, completely caught up in each other, stirring feelings of pleasure, envy, and exclusion in me. She became a much more observant mother, who had begun to know her baby. In one meeting Andrea examined my face seriously, when they came in, then burst into tears. Mother told me that she gets worried about strangers and told me how she needed her and her father to soothe and talk to her about the stranger and then she was able to go back and try again, seeming less anxious. With great affection, she told me how attached she was to them, how attached they felt to her, the importance of this, and how they felt a family.

Over the months the experience in hospital has been told and retold, giving myself and mother a much fuller picture of what happened to Andrea and to her parents. The story has changed over time and I think that because Mrs Baleru has been able to grieve for the very difficult beginning—the loss of intimacy with her baby that special care proscribed—she has been able to move on. She still gets occasional flashbacks and hears the monitors but it is fading and she no longer feels depressed. She recently told me a little vignette, which suggested that a link between Andrea and her parents had been forged in the special care unit, despite all the difficulties and the overpowering sense of loss. Andrea recognized their voices very early on and when they went into the unit she would turn her head to listen. Once her husband gripped Andrea's hand and after that whenever she heard her father's voice she turned her hand round and opened it. It was interesting that this very touching observation was only told when mother became more optimistic and less depressed.

Case study 2

The second case example is of Mrs Menzies, whose baby died in utero at thirty-five weeks. Mrs Menzies, a thirty-year-old married mother of a four-year-old little girl, was referred to the service by her family doctor, who mentioned her previous two miscarriages.

As we walked down the corridor Mrs Menzies said she was not sure if she needed to come because she was feeling a little better. She sounded almost apologetic and guilty to be taking up my time, anxious about making a claim. I looked at her and saw that her face looked raw and naked, and that she had been crying. As soon as we got into the room, before I had time to shut the door, she told me that she had been feeling very bad since her baby died and she started to cry. I asked if she would like to tell me what had happened. She gave me the facts: that her baby had died at thirty-five weeks just as she was about to go on maternity leave and really start preparing for his arrival. She woke one morning and felt heaviness in her stomach; she did not feel pregnant any more. She described the terror she felt. A scan later that day revealed that the baby had died. The pregnancy had been trouble free and, because of the deaths of her previous babies, she had been regularly checked. The week before she had had a check up with the midwife and listened to the baby's heartbeat. The post mortem revealed nothing; there was no medical explanation for the death. Mrs Menzies said that a few weeks before the baby had died her husband had been in hospital having a major operation and she had been going to and fro the hospital, busy looking after her husband and getting ready for her maternity leave. She did not know if the baby had died because she was rushing around so much and she had not had her mind on him. She felt guilty and to blame and repeated what she had already said: "If I hadn't being doing so much the baby wouldn't have died, I should have been more attentive to the baby's movements." She seemed to come to a full stop, as if there was no more to be said, no dialogue possible. As she talked it became clear that her life had come to almost a full stop as she was unable to return to work and had found it difficult to function around the home—she felt lifeless. I felt she was identified with a lifeless baby.

After a while I said that in the absence of a medical explanation or cause, in the space left by no explanation, she had found herself casting around for a cause and decided that she was to blame because she was negligent. She said her husband and her doctor kept telling her it wasn't her fault but it made no difference to how she felt. What they said didn't touch her. Her doctor had told her that 60% of such deaths had no explanation. It was also difficult because she had no explanation to offer other people. She couldn't talk to anyone about it. She went into the details of the scan she had had the week before the baby died, reliving and questioning every detail of the observations that she and the midwife had made, going over the movements and the lack of movement that the baby had made in the following week. Had she misread the baby? How could she know about what was going on inside her? Should she have known? Would a better mother have known? Did the stress kill the baby? The questioning was relentless and tortuous. In between the questions, she told me that this was not her first infant loss. In a very different tone, almost light, offhand, and factual, she told me that she had a previous miscarriage and had lost another baby at twenty weeks with a chromosomal abnormality. She felt she had managed these losses "well". She had felt fine, and taken them in her stride.

From her description it sounded as if there had been no interruption in her functioning, indeed these previous losses seemed hardly acknowledged, almost brushed off. I felt as if I was hearing about a pile up of losses none of which had been truly mourned. These deaths did not seem to have touched her in the same way that this last death had. Of course they were earlier and for one of the deaths there was an explanation, but I wondered if previously she had been heavily defended against the pain of these losses. This latest death, however, had really tapped into a very primitive area of her mind where terror and persecution reigned.

I think this trauma had breached the protective shield that surrounded her mind. It is a world that we all carry within from our own infancy but under ordinary conditions is kept out of consciousness, is rendered unconscious so we may be able to carry on our lives. I noticed how in our meeting, I got caught up in trying to find a cause, or an explanation for her state of mind. I began asking her questions about whether she felt resentful and reproachful towards her husband for having been ill, which resulted in her being so very stretched, so she felt there was little time to attend to herself and the baby. She agreed that she did feel angry. She was dutiful, someone who tended to do what is required and, if she is aware of anger and resentment, it is rarely expressed. She expects herself to manage and be in control. These deaths were beyond her control. I said I thought they were but that in fact the way her mind was thinking was that she should really have been more in control than she felt herself to be.

I felt that she was oscillating between two very different states of mind. On one hand she was in touch with a more benign part of herself linked to more benign figures (her husband and doctor), who did not accuse her of negligence, but on the other hand there was another part of herself acting as a persecuting judge that had put her in the dock and leveled accusations against her. When this figure had a grip on her mind, the attacks were relentless. She was guilty and forever damned. No forgiveness was possible. The internal space vacated by the baby had become a courtroom. This persecuted state did not allow for any repair. While in the grip of this state of mind, there was no sense of protection, of having something good and protective inside. Instead she inhabited a cruel world.

I talked to her about this internal activity, the self-reproach, the blame and the guilt based on her fantasy of causing harm and not attending to the baby, and of not being attuned to the baby. In her mind she was a neglectful mother, an inattentive mother whose attention had gone elsewhere. This description did seem to offer her some relief. I felt concerned at my activity level in the meeting: wall to wall talking, interpreting prematurely, jumping in with an idea, as if I could not bear the pain of what she was describing or was too frightened to leave a space for fear that something persecuting would come and fill it. I could not bear the gap myself.

When Mrs Menzies left I realized that there was much I hadn't heard about. Had she seen the baby? What was the baby's name? All these details were not filled in; they were not her concern as she was preoccupied with condemnation. There was little sense of her baby as a separate person who could be known about.

Despite some protest from Mrs Menzies we continued to meet regularly. She began to look better and said she felt better but the reproaches continued. Although I think she valued the opportunity to talk and she realized that she needed to work psychologically, she often approached the sessions with an anxiety that she would not be able to fill the time we had. I thought she had a terrible fear of finding emptiness, as if the session represented a place that could not be filled, the empty place inside, the place vacated by the baby that could never be filled. She talked in more detail about the deaths of her other two babies and described herself as a carrier of death rather than of life. None of the deaths were linked in any way—it was extraordinarily bad luck—but for a long time the meaning for her was that she was fated, that there was always the possibility of a catastrophe round the corner. Over time the persecuting sense of blame and guilt did change into regret for not having noticed and attended to the inside baby enough and sadness for what had been lost. Over time she became less persecutory towards herself, less internally preoccupied; she began to look out and turn towards life.

Conclusion

Working with trauma and loss in the perinatal period is affecting work, but if you are not affected there is something wrong. It is often difficult to tolerate the intense and primitive feelings that are evoked when listening to such painful stories. There is always a danger of feeling overwhelmed and then distancing oneself or over identifying. Garland (1998) has described how real listening involves, in part, making an imaginative identification with the experiences of the speaker. It is important for practitioners in this field to feel "well held" themselves, either through supervision or through discussion with colleagues.

In this paper I have tried to show the importance of helping two mothers begin the complicated task of processing their traumatic experiences. If the help does contribute to an experience of being listened to and understood, if there is an experience of being contained, this hopefully might prevent an outpouring of undigested loss into the infant or existing children, or indeed into children yet to be born.

References

Bick, E. (1968). The experience of skin in early object relations. *International Journal of Psycho-Analysis*, 49: 484–486. [*Collected Papers of Martha Harris and Esther Bick*. Perthshire: Clunie Press, 1987].

Bion, W. R. (1962). *Learning from Experience*. London: Heinemann. [London: Karnac Books, 1984].

Bion, W. R. (1967). Attacks on linking. In: W. R. Bion, *Second Thoughts: Selected Papers on Psychoanalysis*. London: Maresfield Reprints, 1984.

Britton, R. (1989). The missing link: parental sexuality in the oedipus complex. In: J. Steiner (Ed.), *The Oedipus Complex Today: Clinical Implications* (pp. 83–101). London: Karnac Books.

Daws, D. (2005). A child psychotherapist in the baby clinic of a general practice: standing by the weighing scales thirty years on. In: J. Launer, S. Blake, & D. Daws (Eds.), *Reflections on Reality. Psychoanalysis at Work in Primary Care*. London: Karnac Books.

Fonagy, P., Gergely, G., Jurist, E., & Target, M. (2002). *Affect Regulation, Mentalization and the Development of the Self*. New York: Other Press.

Freud, S. (1920). Beyond the pleasure principle. In: J. Strachey (Ed. & Trans.), *The Complete Psychological Works of Sigmund Freud: Standard Edition, Volume 18* (pp. 1–64). London: Hogarth Press, 1955.

Garland, C. (Ed.) (1998). *Understanding Trauma: A Psychoanalytical Approach.* London: Tavistock Clinic Series, Duckworth.

Judd, D. (1989). *Give Sorrow Words*. London: Free Association Books.

Levy, S., & Lemma, A. (2004). *The Perversion of Loss. Psychoanalytic Perspectives on Trauma.* London: Whurr Publishers.

Winnicott, D. W. (1965). The *Maturational Process and the Facilitating Environment*. London: Hogarth Press, 1982.

CHAPTER TWELVE

Ten years of parent-infant psychotherapy in a township in South Africa. What have we learnt?

Astrid Berg
University of Cape Town, South Africa

Introduction

Since 1995 we have run a weekly mental health service in a Well-Baby Clinic in Khayelitsha, a formal and informal settlement outside of Cape Town. This service forms part of the Infant Mental Health Unit of the Division of Child & Adolescent Psychiatry at the University of Cape Town. To our knowledge it is the only such service in the country and probably in sub-Saharan Africa.

The majority of the nearly two million people living in Khayelitsha have come to the city from the traditional "homeland" of the Eastern Cape—a rural area where medical and educational provisions as well as job opportunities are scarce. However, life in the city is not easy either, and the burdens that are carried by many of the people in terms of poverty, illness, and single parenthood are immense. Having a baby is a given for women—is part of their life cycle—but under these circumstances is not always easy.

The question that therefore arose for us when first entering this community was: can infant mental health have a place in the minds of the mothers and clinic nursing staff when the main task is the physical welfare of the child? The answer lies in the response we have had to our being there: a yearly average of 300 infants with their parents have been seen with half of those being repeat visits;

this can only mean that a need is being met. What thus started off as a pilot site has now become an established, integral part of the Clinic.

In this contribution a description will be given of some of the adjustments that had to be made when working in a community where there is much hardship, a language barrier, as well as cultural differences. We have found failure to make the expected weight gain to be a key symptom of multiple origins and that it is a useful presenting problem for an infant mental health team to take note of. Failure to thrive will be examined from three aspects: the collective and larger family dynamic; conflict within the mind of the mother; and the effect of disrupted attachment on the child.

The western tradition of parent-infant psychotherapy

Selma Fraiberg (1987b) movingly describes the conflicts she and her team experienced when they started their treatment of five-month-old Mary and her mother—these were their first patients and they did not have a treatment model available to them; the familiar intervention of a very needy mother having her individual psychotherapy, while the baby was visited in the home by a psychologist, did not prove to be effective. One of the reasons was that this mother could not tolerate the intensity of the individual encounter with a male therapist. Because of the urgency of the situation, Fraiberg and her colleagues had to be innovative and find a way that would work. They modified the old model and they began to use their home visits for their emergency treatment. Thus parent-infant therapy was born.

What started as "psychotherapy in the kitchen" (Fraiberg 1987a: 108) has now become formalized into a clinical category, namely the "new clinical population" of parents and their infants (Stern 2004). This "new" patient needs to be examined and treated in a different way to the "old" one, as we have to do with a dyad, or a triad, in which one partner is absolutely dependent on the other. This lends urgency to the treatment—it has to be effective, otherwise the baby might die—emotionally or even physically.

Fraiberg met this challenge by abandoning the old model; she did not confront the resistance of the mother, but went with it, allowing herself and her team to be led by the mother-infant dyad. If taken in the context of the times in which she worked, and the discipline of psychoanalysis that she was part of, this was courageous indeed; this is perhaps what babies awaken in all of us: the ability to look at the world anew and to dare to act differently.

From the city to the township

When I entered the community of Khayelitsha ten years ago, I soon realized that the model that I knew and had been trained in would have to be revised.

My outer base is at the Red Cross Children's Hospital, the only designated children's hospital in sub-Saharan Africa. My inner base is my training, which has been in the medical and Jungian psychoanalytically orientated model, where the paradigm is about scientifically proven cause and effect; where the keeping of time is crucial; where the boundary between self and other, professional and patient, is clearly demarcated; where acting-out is frowned upon and where the individual is the focus of attention. All of these assumptions took on a different meaning when I entered the community setting.

I realized how different it was to meet the patient where he or she came from as opposed to having individuals out of the community come to the professional in a hospital setting where they indeed "are extracted from their normal habitats and therefore it is difficult to understand and help them in their normal contexts" (Orford 1992: 8). We give little thought to the fact that we are expecting our patients to adjust to our world, to our establishment. When the tables are turned, the perspective changes and it is the task of the person entering the community to adapt and accommodate to its context.

The problem is the problem

The divide between physical and psychological is a western, Cartesian concept. In our city location, the Child Psychiatry Out-Patient building is separated from the main Hospital by the "Rondebosch Common", an open—and in spring-time a flower-filled—field, where people go for walks. Any physical problem has already been dealt with by "the doctors over there", and we are "here" for the emotional problems only. Social problems are referred "elsewhere" to social welfare organizations.

In a primary community health care setting these kinds of distinctions are meaningless. "Working in the community you can't stick to one thing", said Nosisana Nama, a member of my team. The well baby clinic to which the mother brings her child is a place from which she seeks help—be this for a birth mark on the baby's body to severe weight loss; she is not concerned about which system should deal with the problem she presents with. Both of these extremes—the mark on the body and the failing to thrive infant—require the detailed attention of the clinician or the therapist. In our context a link to a medical resource is vital; it helps enormously in the establishment of credibility and trust.

The infant with delayed milestones or a clear physical problem or illness is relatively easily assessed and directed onto the path of the local hospital. It is however the infant who is failing to thrive that poses a particular challenge. Here we are at the interface of soma, psyche, and environmental provision. Is this baby failing to gain weight because of an illness in the body, such as HIV or Aids? Is there sufficient food in the household to feed this young child? Or is the poor weight gain a manifestation of a disordered attachment, of depression in the mother and infant?

It is these questions that need to be kept in mind from the moment the mother walks into the room with her baby on her back or in her arms. Which one of these is in the foreground will determine the manner in which we intervene: the issue at stake is the survival and optimal development of a baby and it is this that will direct our therapy. However, sometimes this needs to be put on hold for a while, as the "bigger" picture first needs to be appreciated, as was the case with Amanda and Sihle. Before continuing, I wish to acknowledge the team of women who work together with me. Since 1995 I have been working with Nosisana Nama and Nokwanda Mtoto, two women who know their community and culture well and who will articulate what is on their minds. In the particular situation I am about to describe, we also had a young woman student from the USA with us. We work together in one room, sitting in a semi-circle around mother and child, with Nosisana and Nokwanda being the main spokespersons with the mother, while I engage with and observe the baby.

Sihle and Amanda

When fifteen-year-old Sihle walked into the room with three-month-old Amanda it seemed as though a child had come in with her rag doll. Sihle is a bright "girl", fluent in English, who presented us with a desperate situation: she lives with her mother, Ina, and her nineteen-year-old sister in Khayelitsha. Both girls have young babies, and Ina, the infant's maternal grandmother, works in a home as a domestic char and only returns to her own family on two days every week. Ina separated from the father of her children many years ago and raised her two daughters single-handedly. Now they have both become mothers themselves. Ina was furious and refused to help Sihle when she went into labour.

It is now three months later and Amanda presents with failure to gain weight and is thus referred to us. Amanda is not well cared for; she looks slightly haunted, is slightly grubby and is being handled by Sihle in an abrupt manner. We provide them with one of our food parcels and ask her to return, all in the room feeling quite despairing of this situation and aghast at the maternal grandmother's treatment of her daughter.

Two weeks later Sihle comes with the father of Amanda. He is a nineteen-year-old youth, living in the backyard of his paternal home. Sihle reports that in the meantime she was kicked out of her mother's home and has moved in with the boyfriend. Quite unexpectedly, Nosisana and Nokwanda start talking to Sihle and her boyfriend at length and in a very stern manner. The student and I do not understand what this is about, and we remain in the background. We try to link with Amanda and observe that she is becoming restless and turning her head to the breast, opening her mouth. Sihle is unaware of this, as are my two co-workers. I suggest that Amanda be given the bottle, which she then gulps down hungrily. However, Sihle expects her to hold it alone, putting her little hands around it, and she does indeed manage this for a while.

Several themes emerge from these two sessions:

I notice the fact that Sihle has given her child an English name. This is relatively infrequent in modern South Africa, where there is now pride in the African language and tradition, and children are usually not called by names that are easy to pronounce for the "whites". Was she trying to break away from her traditions?

Then there was the despair and sympathy we felt for this young girl with her neglected baby and the change into a "talking to" by my co-workers in the second session. Secondly, Amanda's failure to thrive did not have to do with lack of provision; she did have a full bottle of milk in her bag. It had to do with the mother's preoccupation and resultant non-attunement to her baby's needs. Thirdly the young mother needed to have her baby hold her own bottle: a push into premature independence. These themes will be unpacked carefully.

The motherhood constellation in African tradition

The change that took place in the second session had to do with nuances in language and attitude that Sihle expressed. These led Nosisana and Nokwanda to an enactment, something they acknowledged, but did not retract or wish to undo. They were very clear that what was happening in these families was "not right", and were unapologetic and unambivalent about their stance. What was "not right" was on two fronts: Sihle had talked about her mother in a disrespectful manner, accused her of drunkenness and was angry at her for not supporting her with the baby. It was strongly felt that the mother's side of the story needed to be heard and that all efforts should be made to connect with Amanda's grandmother. They hypothesized that Ina had in fact done well by her two daughters, had worked hard as a single mother to raise them; the good English that Sihle spoke bore testimony to this. The pregnancies they regarded as wilful, rebellious acts—there was no excuse for them, as family planning was freely available in the community. On the other front was the paternal side: living with the boyfriend's family was not seen as a solution, but in fact as an indication of how dysfunctional that system was. In traditional culture the family of the father of the baby acknowledges to the family of the mother that their son has taken the childhood of the girl away and a sum of money is paid as compensation. This process is called *inhlawulo* (Preston-Whyte & Zondi 1992). For a grandfather to allow his son to live with his girlfriend and their baby in the backyard is completely against the norms. We could not be seen to be supporting this kind of arrangement.

While my focus was on the mother and her baby, trying to connect them, my colleagues had the bigger picture in mind. After ten years of working in the community and even after thinking and writing about going "Beyond the Dyad" (Berg 2002), I had not given it the priority required. The western training plus my medical focus on the "index patient", that is the baby, blinded me to the importance of the bigger picture. This bigger picture has less to do with a baby born out of wedlock than with an apparently rebellious acting out by a teenager against her mother with the boyfriend's family colluding in this acting out. Through this a number of traditional taboos were violated, the most striking one being the moving in of the mother with the boyfriend. This moving in only occurs if there has been a marriage, with the attendant ritual transfer of bride-wealth—one of its functions being the linking of the two groups of kin (Preston-Whyte 1974). Because this has not happened, and because not even the *inhlawulo* was done, Ina, the maternal grandmother, had been excluded and has become angry. This has resulted in her being lost to Sihle—a loss that is a profound one during this life phase and would be such across all cultures.

Daniel Stern (1995: 172) has given words to a phenomenon that he has come to realize is one, which "most mothers in therapy have known all along". I would add that this is what is known in the collective unconscious of all mothers, namely that during the early weeks and months after the birth of her baby, a new triangle comes into existence, which becomes the new internal organizing principle in the mother's psyche. This triangle consists of the mother, her baby, and the maternal grandmother. Stern wrote (1995: 172), "The motherhood constellation concerns three different but related preoccupations and discourses, which are carried out internally and externally: the mother's discourse with her own mother-as-mother-to-her-as-a-child; her discourse with herself, especially with herself-as-mother; and her discourse with her baby."

The discourse between mother and maternal grandmother is in our experience one that needs to be carried out externally. It is about the real, lived relationship between the two and this is what my co-workers' unambiguous stance spoke to. It is the interrupted attachment between mother and maternal grandmother that we had to address before turning to the attachment between mother and baby. That is underlying the whole "custom"—that the motherhood constellation is primary and indeed comes, for a moment, before the mother-baby dyad. If that relationship is intact, even a teenage pregnancy with no support from the father's side will be managed by the grandmother, and hence by the young mother. It is when this first relationship has been broken that we see the devastated landscape little Amanda finds herself in.

There clearly is pathology in Sihle's family, which needs to be addressed—we were not simply following grandmother's version or reasoning. However, continuing to support Sihle and Amanda in an unconditional, accepting manner, without challenging her oppositional behaviour, would constitute collusion with the transgression of this cultural norm. It was also feared that our support would falsely encourage Sihle in her strivings to be an adult, that it would mask her real dependence on her mother and even result in a second pregnancy. The point made was that ultimately we would not help Amanda.

Another important aspect of community work is the reputation of our service: it is crucial that we are respectful of traditional values, that we adapt to them, and do not import what is foreign and unapproved. The history of South Africa has too many painful memories of white ignorance and thoughtlessness towards its fellow citizens.

Our anxieties regarding Amanda's weight and general care had for a moment to be put aside. Contact with the maternal grandmother has to been established, a gesture she appreciated, and we have been told that Amanda is doing well. Our efforts could now go into restoring the relationship between mother and grandmother. The bigger picture has to be aligned with the community and with tradition before the individual infant can be again in the centre.

More than food is needed

Sihle had food for Amanda, but did not pick up on the hunger cues coming from her baby: her preoccupation with her life situation filled her mind, leaving Sihle on the road to failure to thrive. This is a common presentation and, as stated before, we have found that failure to gain adequate weight is an important, easily identifiable parameter, which in a great number of cases indicates a disturbance in the mother-infant relationship.

When poverty and hardship are so obvious in a community such as Khayelitsha, the assumption is that provision of nutritional support is all that is needed. In fact this assumption is also evident in international guidelines on infant nutrition. For example the Resolution of the Executive Board of the WHO of January 2001 on *Infant and Young Child Nutrition* (http://www.who.int/gb/ebwha/pdf_files/EB107/eer16.pdf) states its deep concern regarding the fact that more than one-third of children under five are malnourished. It urges Member States to take note of a list of requirements that infants and mothers need to ensure adequate feeding practices. However no mention is made of the emotional, relationship-based component of the feeding process.

Examining our figures we found that two thirds of infants referred to us present with failure to gain adequate weight. Amongst this group almost two-thirds had a mental health problem, which was identifiable within one clinical interview. Depression in mother and infant, in turn, formed two-thirds of this group. It is not sufficient to make this diagnosis and treat it, in the case of the mother pharmacologically. The reason for the depression has to be found. Each case has its individual characteristics and requires attention in specific areas. However, there are general themes that have merged within these particular dyads and which we have learnt to specifically enquire about.

This local clinical impression is borne out by findings elsewhere in the world. For example, Diane Benoit (Benoit, Zeanah, & Barton 1989) found that 96% of mothers of infants who fail to thrive were classified as insecure with respect to their attachments, with lack of resolution of mourning over the loss of a loved one being in the foreground. It was postulated that these mothers' preoccupied attachment produced a disordered relationship, which in turn contributed to the feeding disturbance and consequent growth failure.

Although we did not perform the Adult Attachment Interview on Sihle, the intense manner in which she spoke about her mother and the lack of focus she had for her baby do point to a preoccupied attachment. Her expectation that Sihle should, at such a young age, be able to feed herself could be understood in terms of projective identification: just as she had been "kicked out of the nest" prematurely, so Sihle had to take care of herself. Neither of them had reached the developmental stage of being able to do this, and thus the intergenerational transmission of loss had begun.

With Amanda and Sihle the larger family view had to predominate and be taken into account in the beginning of our contact with them. There are however also those mother-infant dyads where what goes on in the mother and baby's mind can be dealt with through working with the couple only.

The father in the mind of the mother

The motherhood constellation, as mentioned earlier, remains the bedrock for the mother-child couple: the support of the maternal grandmother is a sine qua non; if not present then the literal survival of the baby is at stake, as seen in our example above. However, almost equally strongly represented within the mind of the mother is the couple relationship between her and the baby's father. Perhaps it is so starkly in the foreground because of the very absence of men in our communities, absence in the sense of family involvement and in taking responsibility. It is this glaring deficit that has prompted the Human Sciences Research Council of South Africa to adapt a positive strategy through its child, youth, and family development research programme called *The Fatherhood Project*.

"The Fatherhood Project aims to recognize, encourage, and support men's care and protection of children ... The Fatherhood Project acknowledges that men are often absent, neglectful, abusive and sometimes brutal. They may be self-absorbed and taken up with their own interests and careers. We know that some South African men commit acts of extreme violence against women and children. This is the dark side of fatherhood in our country." (http://www.hsrc.ac.za/fatherhood/)

The Project presents images of fatherhood as seen through the lenses of professional photographers, students, and children. Alongside these images are words of children talking about fathers, and men talking about the way they see themselves. It will take some time before the hoped for effects of this project will be seen on the ground.

The mothers, both very young and not so young, that come to us with their babies present frequently with a depressed affect and a preoccupied, cut-off handling of their babies. They do not seem "lost in the job" of getting to know their infant (Winnicott 1964: 27), but are rather "lost with the husband/boyfriend".

Becoming a mother is a rite of passage into adulthood in many African cultures, but many of the men are not in the phase of adulthood and the commitment this brings with it; they disappear as soon as the girl has become pregnant. This is the story we hear time and time again. A systematic observation of urban children born during the year of Mandela's release from prison in 1990 showed that biological fathers live with their children in only two out of five households (Barbarin & Richter 2001).

The reasons for mothers' preoccupation with the men are of course individual but also specific to the cultural, socio-economic situation. Having a family is an expectation most girls in Africa grow up with; single status is generally not acceptable. The hope is that by falling pregnant, the boy would be induced into a commitment. When he literally runs away, this social wish is thwarted, and results in a narcissistic blow that would be inevitable for anyone who is being rejected by an important other. Then there is the economic situation of being provided for. Most of the women we see do not have much choice in this regard as they are often not skilled for any specific job.

The narcissistic injury and economic reality make the anger, which these mothers feel, understandable. Often they themselves are not sufficiently aware of this, and even if they are, have not shared this with anyone in their family or community. The anger towards the boyfriend then gets displaced onto the infant. Many times the mother has, with some encouragement, acknowledged that when she sees her infant, she sees his or her father, and that this makes her very angry. We even had one mother who did not give her child a proper name, because of her negative feelings towards the father.

Perhaps one could argue that the construct of the motherhood constellation can only be so evident, as Stern alleges, if there is no conflict regarding the father of the child. The couple that produced the child is also an internal couple in the mother's mind, which is as important or primary as that of the mother-grandmother dyad. From a therapeutic point of view we have found that giving mother permission and space to talk about her anger and disappointment regarding baby's father provided relief for her and she "felt lighter", in the words of one mother. We then follow-up with supportive counselling; this aims at de-linking the baby from the father. The often-dramatic results keep on astounding us, as is illustrated by the following vignette.

Bukho was an interactive five-month-old baby who presented with failure to thrive. He worked hard to make contact with his young mother, stroking her face and looking at her intently. She responded with hesitation and, after having fed him with the bottle, shook him so vigorously that he regurgitated. She spoke about "this baby" and did not call him by name. Mother was depressed because of a broken relationship with the baby's father. After one session of counselling and support Bukho's weight increased.

Bukho is one of many such examples, each with their own, individual life stories and nuances. The weight increase following the first few sessions is often remarkable. While there is no study with a control group available, in our clinical experience 70% of infants with failure to thrive, who were seen by us, gained weight.

No set practice parameters can be given, as would be the case in organic failure to thrive. However, there are guidelines that could be drawn up, such as:

- An accepting and open therapeutic attitude.
- Detailed observation of the infant and the mother-baby interaction.
- Information regarding the relationship with the father and the maternal grandmother.
- Containment of feelings plus concrete suggestions or advice where these can be given responsibly.

There are times when an abrupt fall-off in weight is noted on the growth chart. Identification of a possible stressor at that time is an item that should be added to the list above. One such stressor that has commonly been identified amongst our patient population is caused by separation of infant and mother.

Disrupted attachment

The disruption of attachment is one of the corner stones of Bowlby's theory. Because of world events, both natural as well as man-made, an increasing number of children have to face the loss of their caregivers. What concerns us however, is a less obvious, more subtle form of disrupted attachment, one that has its roots in our country's past.

The "homeland" system created in 1951 aimed at restricting African mobility between urban and rural areas—families could not live together, but were forced to stay behind in the homeland, while fathers and mothers provided the workforce for the cities. Many young women had to leave their children with their extended families and return to their place of work, the separation often lasting for a year or even many years. Though today every citizen is free to choose where to work and live, the custom has continued. It is regularly part of the course that infants and toddlers are sent to the ancestral homesteads in the rural areas to be cared for by grandparents, thereby enabling the parents to earn a living in the city. Young children and even infants will not infrequently be sent with a stranger to travel twelve hours by train, bus, or taxi to be left with a grandparent in the country. This grandparent is as much a stranger as the person the child travelled with, but there seems to be no obvious concern about this: as long as the child is taken care of, it seems to be in order that this transportation and translocation takes place in this way. If queried, the reply is that this is "how we do it".

The fact that grandmothers and family members are very much involved in the rearing of children is indeed cultural and it is probably so in many cultures. However, I would dispute that the manner in which this occurs is "cultural". Is it perhaps not a re-enactment of generations of traumatic separations? It is for this reason that we have come to not simply accept this custom, but question it with the mother, and ask her to think about it. And it does not take much for her to gain insight into what this may mean for her infant—if this had been a "deep" culturally embedded custom, it would not have been so accessible to being challenged and changed.

From a different angle, but along the same lines, this is the story of Lindelwa, aged two-and-a-half years. This little girl was referred to us because of her poor weight gain. She had been seen at the clinic at six months of age, when her weight had been satisfactory. She then disappeared from the records. In the two years that followed, much had happened to this child: she was sent to the Eastern Cape to be cared for by an aunt, because mother and father were in the process of separating. They had recently reconciled and Lindelwa was returned to her parents the week before this reported consultation. On asking her mother during the first session how she thought Lindelwa was feeling about this she replied: "she does not care about the aunt. She is happy, because she is now with me; she knows I am her mother." Lindelwa was sitting quite comfortably on her mother's lap, but was not relating to her. She easily walked to Nokwanda, who picked her up and she responded and talked to her. When asked who her family was, she named all the persons, but did not mention her mother. She then walked back to her mother, stood by her side and looked sad.

We spoke to the mother regarding Lindelwa's attachment needs and how the relationship with the aunt had been disrupted. Mother could easily understand this and could quite readily accept a different version of her child's inner world. When we saw her one month later, we were struck by the fact that the little girl remained with her mother throughout the session, and was not willing to walk over to us. Mother noted this, understood this to be a good sign, and was pleased. We spoke about Lindelwa needing time to reconnect with her, and that she should not be sent back to the Eastern Cape, to which mother spontaneously added "because of the bond."

Another mother's open admission that she "did not think about what is going on for him", when she told us about her leaving her youngest child with family far away, underlines the necessity for us to be the spokespersons for these children and to help parents to think again about what they are doing. Although Apartheid has come to a formal end, its vestiges remain in what is being repeated, both out of outer necessity, but also helped along with the inner drive of repetition compulsion. It is our task to do what we can to prevent this re-enactment.

So, what have we learnt?

Infant Mental Health has a place and fulfils a definite function in a well-baby clinic in a community setting that struggles with the problems of a developing country. In young and vulnerable children weight gain and weight loss are manifestations not only of their nutritional status, but are also an indicator of the status of the affective bond between infant and caregiver.

There, thus, needs to be an urgent awareness nationally and internationally that more than food is needed, if we wish to prevent failure to thrive in infants and young children.

Practice parameters to treat the emotional aspect of failure to thrive can only be given in very general terms: each mother and infant's story needs to be heard and responded to. The response may be a simple one, but it is derived from the listening and observing by accepting and containing "others".

The motherhood constellation and the father-in-the-mind of the mother are inner representations as well as living, outer realities, which need to be addressed directly and often concretely.

Disruptive Attachment Disorder may manifest as failure to thrive. In South Africa the antecedents responsible for the frequency to which young children are subjected to this stressor need to be acknowledged and remedied.

Because Selma Fraiberg and her team worked in a developed country with many resources, their emergency treatment "in the kitchen" would be followed by an extended treatment phase "back at the office" (Fraiberg 1987a) where the ghosts in the parents' past could be identified and rendered less threatening. In a developing country with an emerging economy, we do not have such privilege; we remain "in the kitchen", so to speak. Despite this, babies and their parents are helped because a space is provided in which a reflective dialogue and informed action between the mother, the baby, and the team of care-workers can take place.

Acknowledgements

I wish to acknowledge the contribution of Nosisana Nama to this paper and to our service over the past ten years. Without her I would not have had the knowledge and insight into the inner and outer worlds of the mothers we encounter. The lively debates we have and the tolerance of different opinions are crucial to our trying to understand and reflect on the material. They are mutually enriching and add immeasurably to the fulfilment of the task that is at hand: the wellbeing of the youngest and most vulnerable members of our society.

References

Barbarin, O. A., & Richter L. M. (2001). *Growing Up in Post-Apartheid South Africa—Mandela's Children*. New York & London: Routledge.

Benoit, D., Zeanah, C. H., & Barton, M. L. (1989). Maternal attachment disturbances in failure to thrive. *Infant Mental Health Journal*, 10/3: 185–202.

Berg, A. (2002). Beyond the dyad: parent-infant psychotherapy in a multicultural society—reflections from a South African perspective. *Journal of Infant Mental Health*, 24/3: 265–277.

Fraiberg, S. (1987a). Ghosts in the nursery. In: L. Fraiberg (Ed.), *Selected Writings of Selma Fraiberg* (pp. 100–136). Columbus, OH: Ohio State University Press.

Fraiberg, S. (1987b). Infant-parent psychotherapy on behalf of a child in a critical nutritional state. In: L. Fraiberg (Ed.), *Selected Writings of Selma Fraiberg* (pp. 137–165). Columbus, OH: Ohio State University Press.

Orford, J. (1992). *Community Psychology: Theory and Practice*. Chichester: Wiley.

Preston-Whyte, E. (1974). Kinship and marriage. In: W. D. Hammon-Tooke (Ed.), *The Bantu-Speaking Peoples of Southern Africa* (pp. 177–210). London: Routledge & Kegan Paul, 1987.

Preston-Whyte, E., & Zondi, M. (1992). African teenage pregnancy: whose problem? In: S. Burman, & E. Preston-Whyte (Eds.), *Questionable Issue—Illegitimacy in South Africa* (pp. 227–246). Cape Town: Oxford University Press.

Stern, D. (1995). *The Motherhood Constellation: A Unified View of Parent-Infant Psychotherapy*. New York: Basic Books.

Stern, D. (2004). The motherhood constellation. In: A. J. Sameroff, S. C. McDonough, & K. L. Rosenblum (Eds.), *Treating Parent-Infant Relationship Problems* (pp. 29–42). New York, & London: Guildford Press.

Winnicott, D. W. (1964). *The Child, the Family, and the Outside World*. Harmondsworth: Pelican Books.

CHAPTER THIRTEEN

Innovation in parent-infant psychotherapy in Japan: the infant reveals family trauma

Hisako Watanabe
Japan

Clinical practice in infant mental health reveals that an infant is capable of actively informing us of problems in his intimate relationships. Often he reveals a family trauma, which the whole family has long forgotten. The past that is not reflected upon will continue to repeat itself (Santayana 1905). An infant evokes unresolved family conflicts. Fraiberg coined this phenomenon "ghosts in the nursery" (Fraiberg 1975). The infant takes on a dual role of an active agency and receptor for the evocation of the unresolved conflicts.

How and why does the infant take on such a role? Recent research in affective neuroscience and psychoanalytic developmental psychology reveal the powerful force at work in infancy and the perinatal period. Soon after birth the infant actively perceives emotional states of the mother (Schore 1998; Panksepp 1998; Trevarthen 1983.). The baby keenly engages in nonverbal dialogue with her through gaze, voice, and gestures. The mother, in turn, intuitively responds in infant-oriented rhythmical, melodious voice, and facial expressions named *motherese* (Trevarthen 1983). The contingency and rhythmicity found within this dyadic interaction led to the theory of communicative musicality by Trevarthen and Malloch (1999–2000). When the mother becomes confused and distressed by uncomfortable feelings when she is with her baby, this will emerge as a less than optimal quality of interaction and communicative musicality (Malloch 1999–2000).

Lebovici described how the infant arouses three different images of the infant, namely the *real baby,* the *imaginary baby* and the *fantasmatic baby* (Lebovici 1988). They derive from three different dimensions of the mother's psychic life. The real baby is the baby she sees as a mature adult. The imaginary baby is the baby her girl-self has long wished for and conceived in her latent thought. The fantasmatic baby is the representation of the mother's self as a baby consisting of projection of her unfathomable deep bodily memories in infancy.

The mother unconsciously conveys to her infant what she expects of him, whom he or she represents and what frightens or pleases her. The infant is exquisitely receptive to her projections and actively resonates to them (Cramer & Stern 1988). Through subtle and repetitive clues of gaze, emotional display, physical exchanges, and intonation of voice, unresolved family traumata come to be enacted leading to intergenerational transmission of psychopathology.

In Japan today, the rapid modernization after World War II has radically changed the lives of people on the surface, while traditional mentality still prevails at the roots of daily life. Ubiquitous are such proverbs as "silence is golden", "shed the past into the water", and "see no evil, speak no evil, hear no evil". People follow them as ways of adapting to the reality of daily life, while on an imaginary level, they fear ostracism and stigma, believing that "a nail that sticks out will be hammered in". At a fantasmatic level, many people still live the nightmare of unresolved wartime loss and trauma, which linger all the more because they are not grieved and put down to rest. Thus past conflicts continue to permeate invisibly into daily life, intruding into intimate relationships through nonverbal interactions, like the aftermath radiation of the Hiroshima bomb. The infant becomes an active receptacle of such permeation. Unresolved conflicts are transmitted down the generations (Ehrenberg 1992; Watanabe 1998). The perinatal period and infancy will provide opportunities for massive transmission of such unresolved conflicts, and the mother-infant dyad as well as the whole family will be affected by them.

The following is an example of infant-parent psychotherapy in Japan, in which mother's postnatal depression proved to derive from her parents' unresolved wartime conflicts. Megumi, a Japanese mother in her mid-thirties, came to see me in depression complaining she was unable to love her baby. She had come home from a foreign country, where she had got married and gave birth to a baby boy. Seven sessions of parent-infant psychotherapy were conducted over three months during her stay in Japan. It revealed that Megumi had been haunted by the ghosts of her own father's wartime abandonment trauma.

Case: Megumi and her baby son Ken

THE FIRST SESSION

When I first met Megumi in the therapy room, she sat silently with a masked face and dead gaze like a zombie. John, her Asian husband, sat by her side holding Ken, their seven-month-old baby. Ken was an attractive baby with eyes full of curiosity. He referred often to his father but seldom to his mother.

Then Megumi broke the wall of her depression and fumed in English "I don't want this boy!" The room fell silent with her harsh voice. Ken's eyes registered fear. The tone of despair in her words struck me and I felt alarmed that I was now in charge of a mother with a death wish. Her words could be implying that she was going to leave Ken behind or commit a double suicide, mercifully killing her baby at the same time, which is a traditional mode of parental suicide in Japan. She could be abusing him, psychologically and neglectfully, if not physically.

I carefully observed Ken. He was a gentle baby with lively curiosity and active referencing to his father. Megumi sat still brooding and muttering, "I'm nobody. I'm no good. I shouldn't be around. Why am I like this?" John perceived Ken's apprehension and sensitively took him out of the room. Then with only two of us left, Megumi started to tell me about herself.

Born and brought up in Japan, Megumi was a highly competent successful journalist in her early twenties. She was not satisfied with this and went abroad to study, acquired an MA diploma, married a competent Asian scholar and settled down to live there for good. When she decided to get pregnant, she anticipated motherhood to be a new territory to be conquered.

But what had actually transpired was that she found herself unsupported right after the delivery. The birth of a baby brought an end to her career—"It's the end of my life!" She panicked and lapsed into a deep sense of useless and worthless self.

Megumi's mother flew over from Japan to help her. Megumi could not welcome her, for she felt stressed having to cook Japanese meals for her. Then John's mother, a stout Asian housewife, came to visit her. She bullied her by saying, "Your milk is not good enough dwindling like this. It should gush." She criticized her baby care and even called her stupid. Megumi felt all the more helpless. When John went away for a week because of his work, Megumi felt totally left out. She was no longer able to look after Ken, who was then four months old.

Megumi was diagnosed as suffering from postnatal depression and was hospitalized in a mother-infant unit of a mental hospital. She continued to get worse to the point of receiving electric-shock therapy, before she met a sympathetic child psychiatrist. She felt relieved and improved with a trustworthy therapist to confide in. Then John had to study for six months in a Japanese university. The child psychiatrist referred her to me for brief parent-infant psychotherapy during her return with her family to Japan.

All this Megumi told me in English in a flat subdued voice. Her eyes never lifted to meet mine and her mask-like face concerned me. She reiterated that she felt so worthless that she wished to disappear. After a while, John returned with Ken in his arms. While John listened to her story, she appeared lost in her world. Ken looked relaxed towards John, but he never smiled nor vocalized to Megumi. She never glanced at Ken as if she wanted to avoid him. The mother-infant relationship was mutually avoidant and Megumi's depression was already depriving Ken of a good enough relationship with his mother.

I understood that Megumi felt trapped by the fear of becoming an uncultivated Asian mother like her own and her mother-in-law. She was ashamed that her mother was a "mere lowly housewife". This was her view of her mother ever since she was a girl. "That's strange", I spontaneously responded when she told this to me. "How come that a girl of six, and not sixteen, distanced herself from her mum?" I started to wonder about Megumi's early life. Could she have been deprived as a baby? "I despised her because she could only cook and clean", she retorted bitterly as if to rationalize her rejection. I then insisted that whatever the reason in the past, now was a prime time for a daughter to depend on her mother immediately after childbirth. Not only was it traditional, but it was a dire necessity for Megumi, who needed bed rest. She listened to me in silence.

This first session left me with a confused feeling of despair and hope. Megumi's frightful gaze paralyzed me. There were moments when I was not sure whether Megumi registered my words or was actually listening. I had to tread carefully not to provoke her into an aggressive outburst or depressive withdrawal. I was not sure whether I was listening to her in the right way. I felt like an infant with a depressed mother suffering from self doubt because of her non-contingent response (Green 1986; Tronick, & Weinberger 1997). I was so preoccupied with Megumi's state of mind that there was little room for Ken and John in my mind. During the two-week interval between the first and the second session, I swayed back and forth between pessimism and optimism.

The second session

When Megumi came with John two weeks later, I felt relieved that she looked a little better. She shyly confided that she sought her mother's help in looking after Ken and found life much easier with her help. She also reiterated how her mother-in-law intruded into her household, forcing changes, which she had to submit to, for example moving the furniture around overnight and without her consent. She could neither say "no" nor complain. John listened and responded saying there were two irresolvable value systems in their household. To this Megumi responded saying she could no longer trust John nor his mother.

She remembered her mother often smacking and yelling at her as a child. "I do not want to follow in my mother's footsteps", she said. Then she contrasted John's mother, who was logical and domineering, with her own mother, who was weak, unstable, and hysterical. Megumi rudely commented, "John did not even know Jeanne d'Arc or Florence Nightingale and other historical people. If I educated Ken as John's mother did, Ken would never be able to read or write. John was made to work like a child slave and was deprived." Her statement was absurd as he was a competent scholar. John disagreed by saying his mother never dominated him and his father was the decision maker of the household.

Megumi went on to talk about her own childhood. Her earliest memory was of a woman wearing a kimono looking down on her with blank eyes. Her mother gave birth to a baby girl when Megumi was just three years old, and she hired a baby sitter for Megumi. She felt neglected ever since and resented that her parents doted on her younger sister, who was more assertive and attractive. "I don't know how to look after Ken. I don't know how to give affection to Ken", she said. Megumi was confused about numerous negative memories of her past but also about her current mother and mother-in-law relationships.

In this second session, I was relieved to learn that Megumi went home and asked for her mother's help straight away. She found life much easier and her mother skillful in baby care. These discoveries uplifted her. It was as if my suggestion at the end of the first session proved to be permission for Megumi to depend on her mother. Yet, still her dead gaze kept me concerned about impending disaster such as suicide. She reiterated her wish to quit this awful meaningless life. I confirmed with her that she was regularly seen by her psychiatrist in another university hospital and was on medication.

The real baby (Lebovici 1988) was an appealing healthy boy, yet Megumi was oblivious of it. She dwelled on her disillusionment of motherhood and life with a baby. She was telling me about her lost dream. This led me to wonder about her fantasmatic baby and her own experience as a baby. She had confided that she never felt positive towards her mother. She had despised her for being nobody, since she was a child. This struck me as unusual. My feedback led her to talk about her upbringing. I suggested that she should have quality time with her mother, which is the traditional form of Japanese postnatal care for a new mother.

I hypothesized that her early infancy and childhood could have been less than optimal. On a reality level Ken was an easy happy baby and definitely the pride of his parents. On an imaginary level, Megumi anticipated an idyllic encounter with her baby that did not happen. Ken could have evoked in Megumi massive feelings of self-denigration and devaluation. She was trying to protect Ken from her badness at the expense of devaluation of herself as no good. I suspected that she could be enacting her own experience of maternal deprivation. I scrutinized my feelings vis-à-vis Megumi. She was like a zombie with flat voice and mask-like face. Her despair and paralyzing sense of worthlessness permeated into me and made me feel incompetent and alarmed. She was unconsciously conveying to me a living hell of having to live in humiliation and with an identity loss.

The third session

When Megumi came to see me three weeks later she looked much better. She said coming to see me made her name her problems and find solutions. She even said she was surprised that her own mother could be so available to her that she wanted her to come and help her again after she returned to her country of residence. This made me feel a little relieved.

The fourth session

Two weeks later, Megumi came to me for her fourth session. With smiles she reported that she was now able to see herself and her mother more positively. She informed me that someone in Japan had remembered her and that she had been offered a job by a publisher to draw watercolour sketches for a book. She did still provoke John into petty rows but, instead of retreating into depressive states, she was now able to tell him that in fact she just wanted a warm hug and reassurance from him. She reflected that under the facade of a modernized woman, she was carrying the resentment and oppression of Asian women at the core of her heart. She realized that like her submissive mother she, too, lacked self-esteem.

The fifth session

The fifth session took place three weeks later. Megumi came and told me how she was better and lively. Ken was now ten months old, healthy, and walking two steps. "These days I really enjoy looking after Ken. When Ken cries, my mum and I look at each other and guess whether Ken has peed or is hungry. But it is strange, just as we rush towards Ken, my dad enters the room and shouts 'Where is the newspaper!' or 'Bring me a cup of tea!' My dad is a typical Japanese man. I am fed up with his chauvinistic attitude. I don't like my mum's submission. But the timing of his intrusion is so exquisitely punctual that it feels so funny!"

She then went on to elaborate on her close ties with her father as daddy's girl. "Because my dad wanted a boy he always gave me boy's jigsaw puzzles and lego. I was proud because my young sister was only given dolls. But he pushed me to do more and more. I was brainwashed into being masculine and competent."

I commented how her father had pulled Megumi away from her mother by his possessiveness. She said that he was always loading her with contradictory demands and intruding into her way, even nowadays. I said to her, "It is as if your Dad knew the exact timing of when to intrude. It is as if he can not resist coming in at the moment your full attention goes to your baby. Well, he could have been somewhat jealous that he felt like intruding into your intimate relationships. I wonder what kind of infancy or childhood could he have had?"

Following this, Megumi produced a narrative of her father's wartime and postwar trauma as a war orphan. He was eleven years old when the War ended. His life turned upside down overnight. Previously, he was the son of a prestigious wealthy Japanese diplomat in China. The defeat of Japan turned Megumi's father into a child refugee. He lost his parents during the upheaval of the defeat and flight for life. He arrived in Japan as an orphan. He was taken care of by his relatives, who were equally suffering from the postwar nationwide famine. Each household soon wanted to get rid of this hungry voracious boy. "We don't want this boy!" they said, and he was pushed out from one house to the other. "I don't want this boy!" were the very words Megumi uttered in the first session. Humiliated and abandoned, the boy resolved to survive on his own under a bridge. Then one day a teacher picked him up and took him under his wing. With his support he struggled to proceed into high school and graduated at an evening university.

The ghost was the grandfather's unresolved wartime trauma. Megumi's first words "I don't want this boy" proved to be the key to the nightmare of her father's wartime and postwar trauma as an orphan returnee from China. Step-by-step Megumi remembered and sorted out parental conflicts to which she was exposed as a child. When she told me how she was struck by the exact timing of her father's interruption into Megumi and her mother's joint response to Ken's cry, she was perhaps retrieving her implicit memory of her father's intrusion into her intimate interaction with her mother when she was a small child. I commented that her father could still feel deprived and therefore jealous of Ken. Each statement Megumi made in the session seemed to carry her own and her father's survival theme. At the end of the session Megumi smiled as if her clouds had gone away.

The sixth session

Megumi came alone in casual jeans two weeks later for the sixth session. She spoke in Japanese to me for the first time. She said her life had become much easier and that she felt more and more comfortable with herself. She got on very well with her own mother and was finding Ken lovable. She appeared more relaxed, attractive and was more open too. "My father pushed me to get married and give birth to a boy. Yet he sounded derogatory when I gave birth to Ken. He said 'So you are a mere housewife and mother.'" I felt betrayed by him.

The seventh session

Megumi looked fine, enjoying life with Ken more. She confided how she was hurt by her father's derogatory comment when Ken was born. He had said "so now you are a mere . . . mother". She felt betrayed because she had produced his long-wished-for grandson. As a girl she had known how much he had wished for a son. I commented that on one level the grandfather wished to have a son and a good comrade. However, he could not tolerate a boy enjoying his mother's love. She was no longer intimidated, for she could now understand what underlay his words and could empathize with his unresolved trauma as a war orphan. Although he denigrated her again by comparing her with a well-known actress, who had given birth to a second baby, she was no longer affected by it. Now she was able to appreciate her mother's wisdom, who had stooped to conquer; as a psychological mother surrogate she had tried to contain the resentment of abandonment in her husband.

One month later, I met the whole family, now ready to go back to their country of residence. Megumi was no longer depressed and was off her medication. With John she reflected that coming to the session helped her to give names to her self-doubts and fears and this led them to understand themselves better. The past four months had provided, especially for Megumi, an opportunity to sort out her conflicts as an Asian woman.

Nearly three years later, I had an opportunity to hear from the child psychiatrist who had initially referred the family to me. He told me that the maternal grandmother had ventured to disclose to him that she had been a wartime sex slave to the Japanese military. This was a mind-boggling revelation, which explained to me why the grandmother endured such humiliation from her husband. Not only Megumi's father, but also her mother, had been a victim of the war. The grandmother knew that the time was ripe for her to redeem her plight, having retrieved a good bond with her daughter. Such a disclosure of wartime trauma would hardly happen in Japan even today.

Discussion

"I don't want this boy!" was a frightful statement Megumi made on our first encounter. It alarmed me with fear of her impending suicide or abuse. I started to wonder who this boy stood for and which level of baby she was referring to. Ken appeared to be a well-cared for baby. Megumi's ambition for a career life was initially thwarted by Ken, but some other impingements must have hindered her transition into a new motherhood. Observing Megumi's strong resentment towards her uncultivated mother and mother-in-law, I hypothesized that the birth of Ken evoked implicit memories of her own infancy with less than optimal maternal care.

Megumi resisted becoming a plain Asian mother. However, to my surprise, she immediately followed my advice to be looked after by her mother according to traditional Japanese postnatal care. I felt as if I gave her permission to be close to her own mother and to her baby, which had been forbidden by someone or something. She found life easier and baby care enjoyable, while she started to be in touch with her neediness and loneliness, which she could express more honestly and openly to her husband and mother. This renewed emotional interaction with them facilitated her transition into motherhood.

Megumi gradually realized that although she had been proud to be her dad's girl, she had in fact been suffering from a sense of neglect and deprivation because she could not be close to her mother. Her father despised her mother openly, which forbid Megumi to identify with her mother. Megumi's observation of the funny and strange punctuality of her father intruding into the mother-infant relationship, led to the revelation of his massive postwar childhood trauma. Megumi then began to see her mother in a new light: her mother was also a wise woman, who stooped to overcome the trauma that had impinged on her family.

Infant-parent psychotherapy became an arena for the re-enactment of the past trauma stemming from the grandparents' generation. Unconsciously Megumi was repeating the humiliating experience of returning to Japan defeated as her father had been. Unkempt and withdrawn because of her postnatal depression, she was less than an ordinary Japanese housewife and was the shame of her highly respected family of origin. She felt like a worthless orphan, unable to seek emotional support from her parents. How similar this was to her father's flight from China as a former diplomat's son turned into an orphan of the defeated empire!

In the second session, she remembered having been neglected when her younger sister was born and the baby she "did not want" stood for her baby sister to some extent. Then in the forth and fifth session, through remembering her constant performance in front of her father as a child, she started to realize that her father was forcing her to behave like a boy and kept her away from her mother. Megumi had been a receptacle of her father's neediness. He thwarted her intimate relationship twice, once when she was a baby and again when she was to become a mother.

When Megumi talked about her fear of Ken being damaged by John's illiterate parents, an irrational statement considering John's high profile as a scholar, she could have been unconsciously referring to the inferiority complex that her father suffered as an uneducated orphan. She despised her mother because she was hysterical and lowly. She admired her father because he treated her specially and like his first son. This skewed attachment reflected a conventional Japanese male domination and female subjugation. On the surface Megumi was raised as a modernized woman but, in fact, she was deeply affected by her father's conventional values of male chauvinism. Trapped by his possessiveness she could not form close ties with her mother or younger sister. To enjoy ordinary womanhood went against her father's wishes. She had to flee abroad in order to get married and have a baby.

In the fifth session she showed relief when I gave her a hint about why she could have said, "I don't want this boy!" She had been puzzled and guilty at her own words. She could then recognize that her father had possessed Megumi out of his infantile neediness. Her capacity to understand my thoughts convinced me that she was either resilient in predisposition or raised by a good enough mother. I conveyed to her my guess that her father might have had to defend himself from his fear of being excluded from the intimacy of his own family. He could have desperately taken Megumi away from her mother not to feel like an orphan again.

Following this fifth session, Megumi came to me on her own in plain jeans and talked in Japanese. She was then able to voice her grudge that it was her father who had shocked her into depression. Instead of triumphantly congratulating her for having given birth to a boy he denigrated her as a mere housewife and mother.

Trying to understand the level of the baby she was referring to in the first encounter helped the therapist to focus effectively on the mother's earlier experience as a baby. But how could Megumi's mother stand such a role of a humble despised wife? The enigma had lingered on long after Megumi's family returned to their country. I surmised that Japanese mothers and wives had accepted the cultural submission for centuries. This deep-rooted masochism, combined with postwar academic and economic factors, could have made a mother into a remote figure for a child (Watanabe 1998). When, however, I learned that Megumi's mother had had to endure life as a sex slave, it became clear to me why she put up with such a low profile in her own household.

In the aftermath of Japan's defeat in China, diplomats and their families were the first target of retaliation by the oppressed Chinese people (Chang 1992). In the throes of massive persecution, where death was impending and unavoidable, many mothers chose to die in a ditch and save their children's lives by harshly reprimanding them, saying, "Go away, I don't want you!" Paradoxically the more abusive parental words were, the quicker the children took to their feet and fought for their lives, striving for their survival. In this light Megumi's first statement, "I don't want this boy!" could also have carried her unconscious wish to liberate Ken from her depressive, self destructive world.

When Ken's grandfather was a boy, he managed, miraculously, to return alive to Japan, only to be rejected again and again. With the fall of the Japanese Empire in China he was nobody in Japan. He was bombarded with words such as, "We don't want this boy!" The words could have become ingrained into implicit memories of his core self, while he maintained a brave face like a samurai warrior and took refuge under a bridge. He was picked up by a kind teacher, who took him under his wings and helped him to "climb the ladder" from scratch and to establish himself as an elite banker. However, all these predicaments during the sensitive phase of adolescence could have left deep conflicts in him, which re-emerged in the course of his later life. As an infant, Megumi could have been caught up in the dead mother complex as depicted by Andre Green (Green 1986). During her early infancy and childhood her mother must have suffered difficulties in caring for her baby, which was constantly intruded upon by the needy father.

Throughout the four months of therapy I remained vigilant and concerned about Megumi. There was always a pervasive threat of impending disaster in the air. Although in each session Megumi's state of mind steadily improved, she lapsed now and then into despair and this alarmed me a lot. My own countertransference feelings were initially those of fear of defeat as a therapist and a dire wish to survive in our working relationship. They resonated well with Megumi's helplessness in the face of the unexpected collapse of her confidence and her desperate wish to survive. Also they resonated with the crisis of her father as a boy when he fled from China and struggled to survive.

Such a family story would never have come into the open had it not been for infant-parent psychotherapy. In Japan, where people tend to hide their feelings for fear of stigmatization, infant-parent psychotherapy provides a unique window into unresolved family trauma and an opportunity for repair and redemption. Simply by being there, a baby can become a catalyst for family reflection and repair. Winnicott's words ring true also in the Far East in a broader sense: There is no such thing as a baby. A baby is part of some one, the mother and the motherland with its unfathomable history (Winnicott 1965).

References

Buxbaum, E. (1983). Vulnerable mothers-vulnerable babies. In: J. Call, E. Galenson, & R. Tyson (Eds.), *Frontiers of Infant Psychiatry* (pp. 86–94). New York: Basic Books.

Chang, J. (1992). *Wild Swans: Three daughters of China*. London: Flamingo.

Cramer, B., & Stern, D. N. (1988). Evaluation of changes in mother-infant brief psychotherapy: a single case study. *Infant Mental Health Journal*, 9: 20–45.

Ehrenberg, D. B. (1992). *The Intimate Edge: Extending the Reach of Psychoanalytic Interaction*. New York: W. W. Norton.

Fraiberg, S. (1983). Treatment modalities. In: J. Call, E. Galenson, & R.Tyson (Eds.), *Frontiers of Infant Psychiatry* (pp. 56–73). New York: Basic Books.

Fraiberg, S., Adelson, E., & Shapiro, V. (1975). Ghosts in the nursery: a psychoanalytic approach to the problems of impaired infant-mother relationships. *Journal of the American Academy of Child Psychiatry*, 14/3: 387–421.

Green, A. (1986). *On Private Madness*. London: Hogarth Press.

Lebovici, S. (1988). Fantasmatic interaction and intergenerational transmission. *Infant Mental Health Journal*, 9: 10–19.

Malloch, S. (1999–2000). Mothers and infants and communicative musicality. *Musicae Scientiae Special Issue. Musical Narrative, and Origins of Human Communication*, pp. 29–54.

Panksepp, J. (1998). *Affective Neuroscience*. Oxford: Oxford University Press.

Santayana, G. (1905). *Reason in Common Sense: Volume One of "The Life of Reason"*: New York, Dover, 1980.

Schore, A. N. (1998). The experience-dependent maturation of an evaluative system in the cortex. In: K. H. Pribram, & J. King (Eds.), *Brain and Values:*

Is a Biological Science of Values Possible? (pp. 337–358). Mathway, NJ: Lawrence Erlbaum.

Trevarthen, C. (1983). Interpersonal abilities of infants as generators for transmission of language and culture. In: A. Oliverio, & M. Zapella (Eds.), *The Behaviour of Human Infants* (pp. 145–176). New York: Plenum Press.

Tronick, E. Z., & Weinberg, M. K. (1997). Depressed mothers and infants: failure to form dyadic states of consciousness. In: L. Murray, & P. J. Cooper (Eds.), *Postpartum Depression and Child Development* (pp. 54–81). New York: Guildford Press.

Watanabe, H. (1987). Establishing emotional mutuality not formed in infancy with Japanese families. *Infant Mental Health Journal*, 8: 398–408.

Watanabe, H. (1992). Difficulties in amae: a clinical perspective. *Infant Mental Health Journal*, 13: 26–33.

Watanabe, H. (1998). Paranoia and persecution in modern Japanese life. In: J. Berke, S. Pieridis, & A. Sabbadini (Eds.), *Even Paranoids Have Enemies* (pp. 189–202). London: Routledge.

Watanabe, H. (2002). The transgenerational transmission of abandonment. In: J. M. Maldonado-Duran (Ed.), *Infant and Toddler Mental Health: Models of Clinical Intervention with Infants and their Families* (pp. 187–206). New York: American Psychiatric Publications.

Winnicott, D. W. (1965). *The Maturational Processes and the Facilitating Environment*. London: Hogarth Press.

INDEX